Anne de Courcy is a well-known writer and journalist. In the 1970s she was Women's Editor on the London *Evening News* and in the 1980s she was a regular feature writer and columnist for the *Evening Standard*. In 1992 she joined the *Daily Mail* where she has done interviews, historical features and book reviews, as well as editing a page on readers' dilemmas. She has written nine books including *The English in Love* (1986), *1939: The Last Season* (1989), *Circe: The Life of Edith, Marchioness of Londonderry* (1992), *The Viceroy's Daughters* (2000) and a biography of Diana Mosley which will appear after the subject's lifetime. She lives in London.

By Anne de Courcy

The Viceroy's Daughters
Circe: The Life of Edith, Marchioness of Londonderry
1939: The Last Season
The English in Love

1939
The Last Season

ANNE DE COURCY

PHOENIX

A PHOENIX PAPERBACK

First published in Great Britain in 1989
by Thames and Hudson
This paperback edition published in 2003
by Phoenix,
an imprint of Orion Books Ltd,
Orion House, 5 Upper St Martin's Lane,
London WC2H 9EA

A CIP catalogue record for this
is available from the British Library.

ISBN 0 75381 672 5

Typeset at The Spartan Press Ltd
Lymington, Hants

Printed and bound in Great Britain by
Clays Ltd, St Ives plc

For Robert

ACKNOWLEDGEMENTS

Among the many people who have been kind enough to offer assistance or share their memories with me I would particularly like to thank Margaret Duchess of Argyll, Mr Idris Byfield, Lady Aline Cholmondeley, Sir Cyril Clark, Dame Ninette de Valois, the Duke of Devonshire, Dr Harold Edwardes, Lady Maureen Fellowes, Pamela Lady Harlech, Mr Peter Hampton, Mr David Hartnell-Beavis, the Rt Hon Denis Healey MP, Mr Neil Hughes-Onslow, Sir John Lambert, Miss Marjorie Leaf, Lady Anne Mackenzie, Dr Jean Toynbee, Mr Silvano Trompetto, Miss Betty Vacani, Mr Anthony Wallace FRCS, Miss Margaret Walmesley, Mr Harry Waugh, Mr Nat Witte and the Reverend Peter Wyld. I owe an especial debt of gratitude to Rosemary Verey for allowing me to look at the diaries of her late husband, David Verey. I am also very grateful to Kate Perry, the Archivist of Girton College; to the Royal Archives for assistance, and for their gracious permission for the republication of certain copyright material; and to the executors of the late Sir John Wheeler-Bennett; the staffs of the London Library and the Newspaper Library at Colindale; the National Trust, in particular the Curator of Polesden Lacey; the Naval Historical Branch, the Admiralty; the History of Advertising Trust; the University of Birmingham Library for permission to quote from the Neville Chamberlain papers and to Cartier and the Savoy for access to their archives.

Picture research: Alla Weaver

CONTENTS

INTRODUCTION: THE WAY IT WAS

What was Great Britain like in 1939? It had just under 47,000,000 inhabitants; or, as *Picture Post* put it, 'If we set down two people on a football pitch, we would have a picture of the density of our population.' The birth-rate, which had been steadily dropping all through the thirties, stood at 15.3 for every 1,000 people, and there were 1,081 women for every 1,000 men. The average bachelor was 27.72 years old when he married, his bride 25.58. For most, their union was lifelong: in 1938, a mere 6,250 marriages were dissolved by divorce, for which the commonest ground was adultery. A new scientific discovery was about to render the issue more clear-cut in some cases. It had just been realized that a child inherited the blood group of one of its parents, so that if neither husband nor wife had a blood group which matched the child's, the husband was not the father. In March 1939, the House of Lords was debating the Bill which would allow the courts to take account of blood tests in paternity cases.

Violent crime outside the confines of the home was uncommon, apart from terrorist acts by the IRA, who on 15 January had proclaimed a renewal of the campaign to force the British out of Ireland. A wave of bombings immediately followed. In the country, children could wander freely and, although certain areas of London were regarded as unsafe, in ordinary residential districts the inhabitants could walk the streets without fear.

Young men might knock helmets off policemen on Boat Race Night, but armed robbery was virtually unknown. Even when death resulted, motoring offences were often treated as unfortunate accidents rather than crimes. In much the same way as a king presiding at a tournament might console a medieval knight for accidentally killing his opponent, one judge told the motorist he sentenced to three months for manslaughter caused by dangerous driving: 'It is no reflection on you morally to go to prison.' Magistrates in Slough were unwilling to lay the burden of conviction upon the conscience of a woman motorist who had suffered a nervous breakdown when a summons was served on her. Her doctor testified that he could not bear to think of the effect that finding her guilty would have on her nervous system, and she got away with the payment of £2 8s 7d costs.

At the beginning of the year, the level of unemployment was high, with two million out of work. Twelve months earlier the National Unemployed Workers Union had organized a series of demonstrations to draw attention to the increasingly desperate plight of the jobless. A hundred of them were sent to order tea at the Ritz, a clever ploy which filled many columns of newsprint with indignant contrast between their lot and that of those who usually took their five o'clock refreshment in these pink and gold surroundings. In another protest, five days before Christmas 1938, two hundred unemployed men lay down among the Christmas shoppers in Oxford Street, while on New Year's Eve others carried a black coffin containing the message 'Unemployment – No Appeasement' into Trafalgar Square, before attempting to deliver it to the Prime Minister. As the months passed, Civil Defence and rearmament work reduced the number of unemployed. But life in industry could be very hard; in coal-mining, for example, the number of casualties was enormous. 'For every day of 1939 so far,' recorded *Picture Post* in February, 'three miners have been killed and over 400 injured underground.' And many of these men were uninsured.

New industries were bringing more hope. By now plastics were widely used – there were even Bakelite coffins – and light but strong metal alloys were being produced. Both of these had made possible a revolution in aircraft design. Although the first commercial air crossing of the Atlantic was made by a giant flying boat (Pan American Airways' *Yankee Clipper*), the slow and cumbersome seaplane was rapidly approaching obsolescence now that the largest airliners, whose weight had made a ground landing impossible, no longer had to land on water. Above all, a new generation of fighters was taking to the skies, the unbeatable Vickers Supermarine Spitfire and, almost as famous, the Hawker Hurricane, single-seater monoplanes, mounting four machine guns in each wing, which were replacing the old Gloster Gladiator biplane. Across the Atlantic, the Americans were just beginning the commercial production of nylon, invented the previous year and later used for wartime parachutes.

In 1939 the countryside was made up of small fields, as well as grass, woodland, scrub, heath and fallow. The price of land varied enormously. The rich black silt land of the Fens, which produced a crop of potatoes normally worth about £40 an acre, sold at £100 or more an acre, while marginal land might fetch as little as £1.50 an acre. The number of farm workers had dropped from 869,000 in 1921 to just over half a million, for although 45 million of Great Britain's total 56 million acres was agricultural land (almost one food-producing acre for each man, woman and child in the country), cheap imports of food had made farming so uneconomic that it had become increasingly run down. Wheat was grown only on the best land because the price of imported wheat was so low that it was not worth the farmer's while to spend money on fertilizing and cultivating thin soil; fully one-third of British farmland was either mountainous or moorland that would support only sheep or hardy mountain cattle; another three million acres was woodland – the Forestry Commission was planting conifers and pines to exploit the sandy Breckland in East Anglia.

Poor though the grazing was in many places, this did not worry Britain's vast rabbit population. The plague of the farmer, they were shot, trapped, snared, coursed, or driven by ferrets into nets stretched over the mouths of their burrows or to a waiting gun. At harvest time, a horse-drawn mechanical reaper and binder started cutting the field from outside round and round. As the corn dwindled to a shrinking central island of tawny, rustling fronds, there would be a sudden explosion of rabbits in all directions. Amid the frantic barking and yelping of the chasing dogs and a hail of missiles, many were shot or killed with sticks. But nothing seemed to have any effect on their numbers – or on the immense damage they did to crops.

The life of a small farmer was hard. A drought could cause real problems because many had no piped water supply. Although the National Electricity Grid had been set up by 1935, its heavy cables, draped from enormous and hideous pylons, reached few rural areas. Of England's 400,000-odd farms, under 35,000 were connected to the mains. The rest relied on their own generators, oil lamps or candles. Most of the heavy work on a farm was done by Britain's 668,000 farm horses. In the summer, the hay was cut, usually by a horse-drawn mechanical cutter, to be turned as it lay on the ground by a man with a fork until it was dry; then it was raked into loosely piled haycocks. Finally, it was pitchforked on to haycarts to be taken to the corner of a field or farm paddock where the haystack was to be built. Wages, fixes by local Wages Boards, varied from one county to another, according to what the land could pay, though the average minimum weekly wage for a man over twenty-one was 34s 7d.

In London, there were pea-soup fogs in the winter, gas lights in the streets, and errand boys whistling as they made deliveries by bicycle. At Billingsgate the porters wore special headgear called a bobbin-hat, made of heavy waterproof leather on a wooden frame. On these they carried boxes of fish at 2d a stone (about 6.4 kilos); a skilled man could earn up to £8 a week. Such a handsome salary probably enabled him to live in one of the new houses built over the last five to six years at the cost of a few hundred pounds – the thirties had seen not only ribbon development but also a vast explosion of suburban building. By May 1939, four million houses had been built since the Armistice of 1918.

Politically, the scene in 1939 was bleak. Although everyone still hoped desperately for peace, preparations for war had been well under way for some time – especially to counter the death expected to rain from the skies. It was believed by everyone from leading politicians to the man in the street that this would take two forms, each almost as horrible as the other. At 4.30 on the afternoon of 26 April 1937, the Condor Legion of the Luftwaffe had appeared over a small, undefended Spanish town called Guernica and systematically reduced it to a heap of rubble, blood and broken bodies. The power of the modern bomber to inflict wholesale slaughter and devastation had become an established article of belief and dread, reinforced by newsreel pictures of the Germans bombing other Spanish cities, and the destruction wrought by Japanese bombers on Shanghai. Thus the Air Staff estimate of British casualties in the coming war was immensely higher than proved to be the case. The experts reckoned that the German Air Force could drop 700 tons of bombs a day over a period of several weeks. As the official estimate was that each ton of bombs would cause 50 casualties – 17 dead and 33 seriously injured – it was expected that more than 83,000 would die in the first week of bombing. In fact, the total number of deaths in the UK from bombing during the whole war was 51,509.

In addition, it was believed that war would inevitably involve the immediate and widespread use of poison gas, which would saturate alike the streets of London and the remotest Yorkshire dale. Even cigarette cards carried instructions for avoiding contamination by mustard gas. Accordingly, when Sir John Anderson, Home Secretary and *ipso facto* chief of the ARP (Air Raid Precautions) services, announced the issue of gas masks, he stressed that they must be kept on the person or beside the bed at all times of day or night. Children under the age of two were the first to be issued with these protective masks.

In journalism, 1939 was above all the year of the newsletter. The *Broadsheet* (dealing with legal matters), *Father Desmond's Views*, the *Fleet Street Newsletter*, *King Hall Newsletter* (started by Commander Stephen King Hall the previous year and already up to a circulation of 50,000), and *In Plain English*, were all characterized by the implication of specialist or behind-the-scenes knowledge, and most of them took an optimistic approach to the events in Europe.

This view was shared by the heavens. By the end of the thirties all popular newspapers were publishing horoscopes – the most famous were those of R. H. Naylor, which occupied a whole page in Lord Beaverbrook's *Sunday Express* – and, as the name had not been patented, there were no fewer than nine versions of *Old Moore's Almanac*. With the honourable exception of Naylor, whose warning notes were sounded in direct if discreet contradiction to his proprietor's message ('There will be no war') on the mast-head, most of these prognostications announced that war would be averted. At Britain's first astrological conference, which took place at Harrogate in April 1939, it was confidently predicted that the dogs of war would remain leashed ('there may be alarm and difficulty, but nothing very serious is going to happen').

One of the few publications to take the opposite view was *Picture Post*. Launched the previous year, it was possibly the most innovative magazine of the century, with a revolutionary *photo-vérité* technique that brought not only facets of Britain but also of Hitler's Germany to sharp and vivid life with an unmatchable combination of words and pictures – as in this description of Berlin in the spring of 1939:

'Even in the most ordinary discussions you are reminded more and more of New York as it used to be when the grip of the Tammany machine was heavy on it. You could have spent weeks in New York in those days and never "run across" Tammany.

There were plenty of British visitors who came back thinking that the Tammany grip, the Tammany violence, the Tammany cruelty and corruption of every phase of civic life, were grossly exaggerated. But the New Yorker, when he chose, could tell a different story. He knew. And the Berliner knows, too. But he talks less. He looks on.

'Sometimes, as among the ardent Christians who see their religion torn to bits, and the walls plastered with the barbaric obscenities of Der Sturmer, or among the working-class people, with all their traditions of independent organisation, the Berliner not only looks on but works to end all this. But sometimes, like the toads in the Tiergarten, he just sits and looks.'

One

THE PROSPECT IN 1939

The year opened with a glimmer of hope. A few months earlier, Prime Minister Neville Chamberlain had signed the Munich Agreement (or, as *The Week* would have it, 'turned all four cheeks to Hitler') and in November, odds of thirty-two to one against the outbreak of war were laid at Lloyds. As January and February gave way to the early days of March, even the weather – brilliant, still, with hours of sunshine, warm as a day in May under the clear deep blue skies of early spring – conspired, if not to optimism, then at least to a raising of spirits. Was not unemployment dropping by four thousand a day (no need for the moment to think of the reason)? Did not one hundred thousand people – the highest number for several years – now have an annual income of over £2,000? Were not two million cars on the road? Was there not a plane to Paris every two hours for those who preferred to shop for their spring clothes in the Rue de la Paix rather than Bond Street? And – most reassuring of all to some – had not the Prime Minister himself announced on 10 March, 'The outlook in international affairs is tranquil'?

In Paris, the spring sunshine was greeted in the traditional way with new clothes. At the Auteuil races, smart women wore inch-wide striped silk suits with flowered hats. The Parisienne was able to don such frivolous attire with fewer worries about sudden showers than her London counterpart for the latest amenity, provided by the French post office and obtainable by dialling

Invalides 8800, was a twelve-hour weather forecast for the Paris region.

In London, the Prime Minister pleaded that the friendly sentiments expressed unofficially by leading Germans 'should be made the basis for a determined attempt at general understanding'. *The Times*, which had defended the Munich Agreement and fanatically supported Chamberlain, was still resolutely doing so. The Foreign Secretary, Lord Halifax, told Parliament, 'It is a mistake to see crisis in every event'. Although every known fact, every rumour, and most personal reports confirmed Hitler's aggressive intentions, the longing to believe that war could be avoided was so strong that every straw was snatched at. Where optimism was possible, it was emphasized. The *Daily Express* adopted its 'No War this year – or next' slogan, and ordinary life continued in an air of unreal normality.

Nowhere was this more apparent than in that esoteric social ritual known as the Season, those few brief summer weeks when all Society threw itself into a frenzy of carefully organized gaiety. Much of this was focused on the debutantes (nobody shortened the word to 'debs' in those days), more or less naive seventeen- and eighteen-year-olds suddenly flung into a round of gaieties frenetic and sophisticated by any standards. The cult of youth was unknown; 'She should be spanked!' was the spontaneous exclamation of a judge when told of a child of twelve who asked to have her hair permed. Making the sudden step across the gulf that separated being grown up, or 'out', from the simplicities of the schoolroom could be nervous work indeed.

What sort of world were the debutantes of 1939 launched into? It was an age of convention and conventions. Table manners were dinned into children, who were expected to finish what was on their plate and remain silent when their elders were speaking, though there were certain subjects these elders were careful to avoid. These were usually signalled by the phrase 'Pas devant les enfants!' Or 'Pas devant les domestiques!', for neither children nor servants were expected to understand French.

Bills were paid in guineas as well as in pounds, half-crowns, florins and shillings. Table tennis was called ping-pong and badminton known as battledore and shuttlecock. The cheapest fare from Victoria to Paris was £3; and one could live comfortably on £5 a week.

The social rules, complicated though they were, did at least provide a set of unwavering guidelines. None was stricter than that governing sexual behaviour. Everyone knew that it was 'wrong' for a girl to go to bed with a man before marriage. Nice Girls Didn't – and if, once they were well into their twenties, they finally Decided To, they kept this fact firmly to themselves for fear of outraging society. This moral absolute was implicit in every stage or screen love story, in every romantic novel and every nuance of social behaviour. Even the presents a Nice Girl could accept from a man had to be those which she could with propriety allow him to remove from her person; thus gloves, handkerchiefs, scarves or jewellery were all right, but underwear was not. A woman's virtue, and thus her reputation, were precious possessions. In 1939, an unsuccessful High Court action for slander was brought by a married couple against a female friend (represented by Mr Norman Birkett, KC), who had allegedly said at a cocktail party that their son had been conceived before they were married. Other women sued for breach of promise – one girl got £1,000 out of a Cambridge Blue when he backed out of their engagement.

Snobbery was not so much a common fault as a wholesale acceptance of the idea that society was divided into classes, which might meet, mingle, respect, like and even love each other, but never blend. The public schools provided an education still heavily biased towards the classics; they produced an élite whose members were at best men of honour and integrity, and at worst, inadequates who sheltered behind the social cachet given by a good school. The public school spirit, with its insistence on a code of conduct based on honour and its emphasis on 'character', and character-building games, was considered a pearl beyond price. Sexual freedom, though regarded with more indulgence in the male than the female, was still frowned on, and the man who had a string of affairs was known pejoratively as a womanizer and – worse still – a cad. This ethos produced a hero-figure much nearer to Richard Hannay or Bulldog Drummond than to James Bond.

As one critic of the system remarked in March 1939, 'It is still true that although the public schoolboy is marvellous at ruling several square miles of African swamp, he has a great deal to live down before he achieves his full value in the day-to-day world of modern England.' Another verdict was even more succinct: 'Acceptable at a dance, invaluable in a shipwreck but no earthly good as an ordinary citizen on an ordinary occasion.' Nevertheless, England continued to be ruled by men who had been at the same handful of schools, the same two universities, and who belonged to the same clubs.

Everyday life among the comfortably off was considerably more leisured than it would ever be again. Tea was a regular and important meal, with all the paraphernalia of silver teapot, silver-plated kettle on spirit lamp, slop bowls, lump sugar, finely cut bread and butter, scones, cucumber sandwiches, several kinds of cake from rich dark gingerbread or fruit cake to fluffy sponges, and, on festive summer occasions, strawberries and cream. The tea party was recognized as a social occasion as much as an invitation to luncheon or dinner. Special cafés, called tea shops, catered specifically for this meal. Some, like Gunter's – famous for its brown bread ices – were fashionable rendezvous, and an invitation to tea at one of them was a useful preliminary staging post in a flirtation, while the walnut cake found at the Fuller's chain of teashops was a treat for schoolboys and weary shoppers alike. Still others provided a cheap alternative to restaurants for those less well off. In the country, tea provided a welcome punctuation during a tennis party, and even young officers – daily becoming more numerous – ate tea with each other in default of better company.

Society lived well. The rich drove Daimlers, Rolls-Royces and the now forgotten Lanchester (its selling point: 'At 50 m.p.h. you can knit comfortably'). A normal evening out in London could start with dinner, followed by the theatre ('going to the play' as it was still often called) or cinema, and winding up with supper and dancing at one of the many night clubs or bottle parties dotted around the West End. It was possible to eat very well for six or seven shillings a head.

Most hotels and restaurants were clustered round Piccadilly and Park Lane, with a few around the Strand. For a meal that was cheaper and less formal, the adventurous made their way to Soho, where artists such as Walter Sickert and Duncan Grant lived. Here, the Gargoyle Club, where H. G. Wells lunched regularly, had a membership of 1,400. Typical of the small proportion of foreign restaurants in the capital were the Hungarian Csarda and the Italian Café Bleu, while the Eagle Club in Old Compton Street was a favourite haunt of coloured people. At the York Minster, which drew a clientele of artists, prizefighters, writers and bookies, M. Victor Berlemont, the only French publican in London, became famous for the absinthe he filtered through sugar into decorative glasses.

Evening dress was invariably worn at grand hotels such as Claridges, the Berkeley, Grosvenor House, the Dorchester, and the Savoy with its dance floor that could be raised or lowered. It was the same at the restaurants like Ciro's, Oddenino's, Manetta's, Hatchett's, and Quaglino's, where one night seven assorted kings and princes were among those dining, and at the Café de Paris, famous for its cabarets. All of them did their best to intrigue and attract customers with special celebrations and galas on every possible occasion. On St Andrew's Night, for example, the Savoy's menu included haggis, which was brought in to the ceremonious accompaniment of bagpipes. New Year's Eve at the Hungaria saw 'the old Hungarian custom' of carrying round a live baby pig, which guests were invited to hold while they wished for good luck in the coming year; at the Café de Paris there were more bagpipes; and at Quaglino's, decorated with mimosas and daffodils, trumpeters dressed in Ancient Roman costume played a fanfare at the stroke of midnight.

In these surroundings, meals were of course more expensive than they were in Soho, though Claridges served a special theatre dinner for 10s 6d and a four-course luncheon for 6s 6d, with a choice of five *plats du jour* including cold lobster and roast beef. A large carafe of wine cost 4s. At the Berkeley, where both the Berkeley Dance Band and John Salisbury's Orchestra were in attendance until 2.00 a.m., the à la carte menu included caviare at 7s a portion, sole and turbot for 4s, pigeon at 6s, veal and quail at 5s, puddings at an average 3s 6d and savouries for half a crown. The Savoy's theatre dinner, served from 6.30 p.m., offered *plats du jour* that began at only 3s, amongst them mushroom omelette and red mullet.

Cheap air freight had not yet brought the joys of the international, all-year-round menu, so meals consisted mainly of what was fresh and in season, from Norfolk duckling and Scotch salmon to early vegetables from the Scilly Isles. Certain foods, of course, were imported: grapes from South Africa, Cox's orange pippins from New Zealand when the home-grown variety was out of season, new potatoes from Tenerife or Algeria – anything, in fact, that could stand a comparatively long voyage.

Another difference was the length of the menu: a couple dining at the Savoy, for instance, would – after a glass of champagne or a cocktail at the popular American Bar – enjoy four or five courses. Starting with soup, or possibly oysters if in season, they would proceed through fish, meat, a sweet course and perhaps a savoury, with various wines to accompany the meal and often a glass of port to follow. For those arriving after the theatre to dance, most restaurants also served a lighter *menu de souper*.

At the Berkeley, Philip Ferraro, the restaurant's director for seventeen years, suggested a dinner to lure tycoons into making big deals: caviare or oysters to start with, then fillets of sole fried in butter with soft roes, followed by loin of beef with red wine sauce, new potatoes, green peas and salad and a soufflé of cheese and mushrooms. 'With appropriate wines, that menu will soften the heart of the hardest-boiled businessman and put him into an excellent frame of mind for negotiations,' said Mr Ferraro. For romance, he suggested blue trout with new potatoes and melted butter, followed by breast of Surrey chicken with cream and mushroom sauce, head of asparagus and salad, and iced orange sorbet.

Though there were numerous courses, the portions were small. The fish course might be one small fillet of sole, the meat a couple of dainty noisettes rather than two large chops. At a dinner party or restaurant, fewer than four or five courses was unusual. 'The best dinner I ever ate had only three courses – caviare, roast partridge, and peach flambé,' wrote one contemporary cookery expert, Ailma Vallance, 'so do not imagine that a party dinner *must* include both fish and meat.' Less wine was drunk, but it was of a much higher quality: the age of cheap table wine, or 'plonk', imported in large quantities, had not yet arrived.

Band leaders such as Debroy Somers, Jack Hylton, Harry Roy, Jack Payne and Roy Fox, were paid huge salaries and had tremendous personal followings. Their records sold in hundreds of thousands, and the movements of their star musicians from one band to another were invariably reported.

Perhaps the best-known was the American-born Carroll Gibbons, leader of the Savoy Orpheans, who had studied at the Boston Conservatoire and toured the US as a concert pianist before he was sixteen. Originally engaged in 1926 to play in England under Debroy Somers, he returned to America, but was invited back in 1931 to reform the Orpheans, who had been disbanded. His 'Hello everybuddy!' quickly became, like his white piano, a trademark. Under his leadership, the Orpheans achieved a popularity which reached far beyond the circle of those who danced to the nightly strains of current hits like 'Deep

Purple' or 'I Get Along Without You Very Well'. Their broadcasts, opened by the signature tune 'On The Air' (written for them by Gibbons), achieved audiences of two million. William Walton wrote a programme of music specially for them and they often played at concerts – one such, with the Boston Symphony Orchestra, took place at Queens Hall in February 1939. Two other band leaders in the same league as Gibbons were Ambrose, whose signature tune was 'When Day Is Done', and Henry Hall, whose performances always finished with 'Here's To The Next Time'.

For Latin-American music there was Geraldo. His real name was Gerald Bright, and he was the London-born son of a master tailor. He had begun his career by playing piano in an Old Kent Road cinema, but had left to travel to South America to learn about Latin-American music. When he returned to England, his speciality – in contrast to his signature tune of 'Sweet and Lovely' – became the intricate rhythms of rumba, tango and samba.

At Hatchett's in Piccadilly, there was the band of Arthur Young (whose wife, Karen Verne, was filming with Rex Harrison that summer); its violinist was Stephane Grappelli, its guitarist the famous Django Reinhardt. The Embassy, famous as a favourite of the Prince of Wales, had lost much of its popularity since the Abdication, but was still preferred by many of the slightly older crowd. The Old Florida was dark inside, and thus a haven for debutantes and their boyfriends escaping from a dance for an hour or two on their own. The Four Hundred, then fairly new but already renowned, was to become the smartest and most fashionable nightclub in London during the War. 'It was wonderful, with marvellous food,' recalls one *habitué* of those days, 'so if you got very hungry after staying up all night playing records or acting plays at someone's house you'd all say "We'll go to the Four Hundred." They didn't have a menu but just asked what you wanted – eggs and bacon, grouse in season, champagne – anything. One of their specialities was a Chinese meal, which was unusual then.'

Outside, on the east side of Leicester Square, there were always three or four hansom cabs waiting, in which ardent young men sufficiently in funds would accompany girls home in the small hours. During the long hot nights of late August, just before the war started, these romantic but expensive carriages were in almost constant use. Once at the front door, a man would ask the girl for her latchkey, and politely open her door for her.

Bottle parties, devised some seven years earlier as a way of circumventing the law against serving drinks after hours, were beginning to decline as a result of a London County Council crackdown. At one time, fifty-two of these could be found in five West End streets alone. The theory behind them was simple: the organizers claimed the bottle parties were private parties, to which each guest contributed a share of the expenses. By May 1939, their numbers were cut by half and at the best-known ones, the Femina in Regent Street, the Old Florida, the Coconut Grove, the Blue Lagoon and the Havana (for some reason bottle parties seemed to evoke the Caribbean), the cabaret girls were given notice and prices dropped to the level of the Embassy Club. What their customers thought is not recorded.

Men's clubs, on the other hand, were flourishing. They were the focus of fierce loyalty from their members and, not infrequently, the recipients of bequests of pictures, tapestries and sizable sums of money. Here, service was silent, tolerant, discreet and impeccable; newspapers were ironed to remove surplus printers' ink, and coins were boiled to clean off the dirt. For some members, their club meant a way of life, and it was certainly the place in which most of their daylight hours were spent. These men were not necessarily bachelors. The well-off married man who did not choose to work would leave his home and its bustling servants soon after breakfast for the deep peace and undemanding company of whichever club (many men belonged to several) he was in the mood for that day. Men who worked in the City often dropped in to their club after work for a drink or a rubber of bridge before going home to dinner.

There were clubs for those of all political persuasions, for every type of gentleman and for almost every interest he could be thought to possess. Perhaps the grandest was White's (annual subscription fifteen guineas, entrance fee twenty guineas) which was Conservative, landowning and aristocratic. Liberals in the old Whig tradition, such as the Duke of Devonshire and Lord Spencer, belonged to Brooks's, and foxhunting men to Boodles, where the Masters of Foxhounds' Association held its annual meeting to decide the boundaries between hunts. Other smart clubs were the Marlborough, founded by Edward VII for himself and his coterie of friends, Arthur's, at 69 St James's Street, the Bachelors', and Buck's Club. The last had been founded in 1919 by Captain Herbert Buckmaster of the Blues as a place where he and brother officers could meet; it organized an annual 'Buck's weekend' at Le Touquet, and the champagne and orange juice drink called Buck's Fizz was invented by the first barman there. Pratt's, owned by the Duke of Devonshire, was a well-known dining club, whereas the Beefsteak which was much patronized by the aristocracy and where all the waiters were addressed as 'Charles', was mainly a luncheon club, it had a communal table at which members struck up a conversation with whoever happened to be sitting next to them.

Conservative MPs automatically belonged to the Carlton, and Liberal MPs to the National Liberal Club and perhaps to the Reform. The Junior Carlton was active politically, a venue for speeches, lectures and fund-raising for the Conservative Party. The Travellers' Club (to which no one could belong unless he had been five hundred miles or more from London) was known as 'the Foreign Office canteen'. Regular officers could belong to the United Service Club (most senior officers belonged to it, and it was known as the Senior), to the Army and Navy, the Naval and Military, and Guards Club, the Cavalry Club and the RAF Club. Bishops, the headmasters, senior civil servants and dons belonged to the Athenaeum. Ballot Day at the Athenaeum, when new members were elected, was a well-known date in the

Clubland calendar. At the Turf Club, whose sporting members raced and hunted, the lavatories were distinguished by silver chamber pots. Actors, writers, lawyers and publishers belonged to the Savage, the Savile or the Garrick ('better that ten unobjectionable men should be excluded than one terrible bore admitted'). Diplomats were found in the St James's Club, which was known for its high gaming stakes.

For the artists and writers who lived in Chelsea, there was the Chelsea Arts Club – or drinking at the Pheasantry in the King's Road (Charles I's old hunting lodge). One popular pub was the Six Bells, on whose bowling green the Chelsea Pensioners played a weekly game of bowls.

Life in this bohemian 'village' was cheap, with a three-course meal at a restaurant like The Blue Cockatoo costing only half a crown. Rooms, too, were cheap; although most of the cottages in Chelsea and nearby Fulham were occupied by the charwomen who went to clean the large houses in Eaton Square, the creeping process of gentrification had already begun, and the more artistic, unconventional or hard-up members of the upper classes were busily penetrating the nearer reaches of Chelsea. Thus a small ground-floor flat in First Street, for instance, with the modern comforts of central heating and constant hot water, was let at 37s 6d a week, proportionately more expensive than the much larger unfurnished house in SW1 for rent at £160 per annum. Near Battersea Park, large unfurnished flats went for only £90 a year inclusive, and in equally unfashionable Fulham a flat in one of the new mansion blocks, with constant hot water, liveried porters, and views over gardens and a tennis court, cost even less at 30s a week. In Park Lane, however, three rooms with kitchen and bathroom could not be had for less than a weekly £2 10s.

Most girls lived at home until they got married. Young actresses lived in residential clubs like Persse House in Gordon Street, Bloomsbury, where the sixty or so all-female inmates could manage, with a certain amount of frugality, on as little as

21s 6d a week. Very few men could or would cook, and the better-off bachelor often chose a service flat where he need do nothing for himself except clean his own teeth. When he rang the bell in the morning, breakfast was brought up; by the time he returned from his day's work, the bed had been made and the flat cleaned. If the flat was in a block, there would be a restaurant where tenants could dine; beneath Arlington House (not too popular because its thin walls at that time allowed tenants to hear each other moving about) was an excellent restaurant called the Monte Carlo, which later became the Caprice. Service flats were also found in profusion in the small houses in Half Moon Street, Clarges Street or Shepherd Market, usually rented by young men whose social backgrounds were impeccable even if their bank balances did not match.

There was plenty of entertainment for all. Theatres were enjoying an excellent season, with packed audiences and sparkling plays. As the first Courts took place (the receptions held at Buckingham Palace at which debutantes were presented to the King and Queen), Noel Coward's *Design For Living*, with Diana Wynyard, Rex Harrison and Anton Walbrook, was playing at the Haymarket, Hermione Gingold was starring in the *Gate Revue*, and at the Duchess, Sybil Thorndike was acting opposite Emlyn Williams in his play *The Corn Is Green*. Terence Rattigan's *French Without Tears* was on at the Piccadilly, and Marie Tempest and John Gielgud were playing in Dodie Smith's *Dear Octopus*. Frances Day, backed by '12 of America's loveliest girls', was performing in George Hale's nightly Gala Cabaret at the Café de Paris, and on 23 March Ivor Novello's *The Dancing Years*, which was to run for most of the War, opened at Drury Lane.

Sir Thomas Beecham was busy organizing a seven-week international opera season at Covent Garden, to which he planned to ask the Prague Opera and the Italian tenor Beniamino Gigli. In the summer every open space in London seemed to be alive with music. In Hyde Park, there were two performances every day of the week, including Sundays, from May to September; one was at lunchtime, the other timed so that office workers returning home could enjoy it. Over a hundred bands oompahed their way through a medley of light music in forty-one different parks throughout the capital; the most popular tune was the Overture to *William Tell*, for which there were up to thirty requests a day, followed by selections from Gilbert and Sullivan.

But for the majority, the great, and often the only, entertainment was the cinema – Merle Oberon and Laurence Olivier in *Wuthering Heights*, Ralph Richardson in *The Four Feathers*, Irene Dunne and Charles Boyer in *Love Affair*, Jean Gabin and Simone Simon in *La Bête Humaine*. On 10 March the Curzon Cinema celebrated its fifth anniversary with a showing of the Yvonne Printemps film *Trois Valses*, attended by a chic audience in evening dress. Newsreel theatres were also popular.

On Saturdays, most cinemas provided special morning or early afternoon showings of films suitable for the already vast and still growing audience of children. Already there was heated debate about whether behaviour, particularly in the young, was affected by what was seen on screen. 'That the cinema influences the child's habit of speech nobody can seriously doubt, who has heard a six-year-old patient reply "Okay Chief" to a request to put out his tongue,' said the *Lancet*.

The leading gossip columnist of the day was Valentine Castlerosse, a corpulent Irish viscount notorious for the wild extravagance of his lifestyle and for his wit, who had been employed by Lord Beaverbrook on the *Sunday Express* for the last thirteen years. When in the spring of 1939 Lord Castlerosse fell ill (typically during a luncheon at Claridges), the consternation and the interest of his readers were so great that Lord Beaverbrook asked his son Max Aitken to write a full-page article giving an account of the great man's illness and convalescence. This in itself was noteworthy. At first the stricken Viscount, propped up by twenty pillows and attended by Lord Horder, Sir Charles Wilson (later Lord Moran, Winston Churchill's personal doctor), nurses and his own secretary and chauffeur, lay in bed at Claridges, where he had insisted on remaining. Here, surrounded by flowers which overflowed down the corridor, he received fifty or sixty telephone calls a morning, occasionally correcting names or titles mispronounced by the overworked operators. He also insisted on practising his golf swings in front of the open window, drank too much champagne, ate too freely, and entertained too many visitors.

When Lord Beaverbrook (who was footing the bill) ordered him to be moved to the London Clinic, Castlerosse bent all his energies towards subverting the clinic's stricter regime. He was extraordinarily successful. Waiters still scurried round from Claridges bearing large and delicious meals. Despite the strict instructions of both Lord Beaverbrook and the doctors, Castlerosse's friends, mainly pretty and fashionable women, were still allowed to visit him as he languished at the clinic. When one of them, the elegant Mrs Euan Wallace, called to enquire how he was progressing, she found out how he had managed to achieve this unceasing flow of exquisite companions. Told she could see him for ten minutes, she expressed surprise that the ban on visitors had been lifted so soon, to receive the reply: 'It is still in force, but Lord Castlerosse told us this morning that if any ladies called they were to be shown at once to his room as they would be faith healers sent on Lord Beaverbrook's instructions.'

Two

THE SITUATION OF WOMEN

The position of women in 1939 was ostensibly one of freedom. The battles of the suffragettes were more than two decades behind them, much of the nation's workforce was female, and married couples were now thought of as partners.

Yet in many ways, woman's role as wife and mother had seldom been more sharply defined. Although the vote had been won, most wives still voted according to their husband's dictates, and the 'women's vote' as a political force was unknown. Women worked, but they had jobs rather than careers and usually gave up working when they married; and they held subordinate positions which reflected society's view that what women did in office or factory was peripheral to their 'real' work, that of looking after a husband and bringing up the next generation.

In Germany, all pretence that a woman should aspire to be anything other than the mother of future Aryan soldiers had long been abandoned. When Hitler's 'ideal woman', Frau Gertrud Scholtz-Klink, chief of all the Nazi women's organizations and mother of four, landed at Croydon Aerodrome the day before the first Court, her freckled face with its unplucked eyebrows was bare of make-up, her fair hair twisted in Gretchen-like plaits round her head. She wore a severe black suit with white shirt and tartan tie. 'These are the clothes Herr Hitler believes Nazi women should wear,' she explained, before leaving for London to speak that night at a dinner of the Anglo-German Fellowship.

Here she sat next to the beautiful Lady David Douglas Hamilton, better known as Prunella Stack, head of the League of Health and Beauty. (The League, a 160,000-strong all-women organization, had been founded in 1930 by Prunella Stack's mother, the suffragette Mrs Bagot Stack. When Mrs Stack died suddenly in 1935, the twenty-four-old Prunella took it over. In a romantic match that thrilled the nation, she had married Lord David, the younger brother of the Duke of Hamilton, in 1938.) It was to Britain's Perfect Girl, as Lady David was known, that Frau Scholtz-Klink explained why she had earned the title of Perfect Nazi Woman: in addition to her gift of fecundity, she did not smoke, drink – or talk.

Often, the ban on the working wife was a condition of employment rather than a matter of social pressure. Women workers were required to leave the Civil Service, for example, on marriage. When Miss Violet Hodge, a clerk, was told she would have to leave her job when she married, her appeal against this decision was supported by seven thousand other Whitehall girls. But the existing powers prevailed, and Miss Hodge decided sadly that she could not afford to tie the knot with her fiancé of nine years' standing. 'We are still engaged but we both realize it would be unwise to marry on his salary. I want to go on working *and* be married.'

In the teaching profession, the great majority of local authorities made difficulties about marriage for female teachers. 'Miss' was literally Miss almost always. As Mr Cedric Lane-Roberts, a distinguished gynaecologist said (in a Ministry of Labour report): 'Of the 900,000 married women who go out to work, 300,000 pretend to be single, because often the truth would lose them their jobs.'

True, progress had been made in this area in other branches of the public service. Of the 19,000 members of the Metropolitan Police Force, one hundred were women, and it was hoped shortly to double their numbers. The female police constable of 1939 had to be a healthy young woman between twenty-four and thirty-five, at least 5 ft 4 in tall; her navy serge uniform was worn in winter with high-legged boots (then a rarity), which took a good five minutes to lace. Her duties were confined to those which could be undertaken without physical danger – such as the reporting of accidents and the finding of lost girls. In all other respects the primary consideration appears to have been the moral danger her presence caused her male colleagues. Instead of a helmet, she wore a sensible felt hat with its brim turned down all round, under which all curls had to be tucked severely out of sight. And although she shared her training with the male recruits to the Force, she was not allowed to mix with them at lectures.

Many trades and professions were actively antagonistic not just to the married woman worker, but also the idea of all female labour. Partly, of course, the roots of this attitude could be traced back to the bitter miseries of the recent past. The Depression of the late twenties, followed by the mass unemployment of the early thirties, had conspired to force women back into the home, so that what little work there was could be shared among their menfolk. At the very beginning, of 1939 there were 1,841,372 registered unemployed – a ten per cent increase on 1938 – and many more who had not registered. Only as the demands of rearmament and the war industries mopped up all available labour would this figure gradually fall.

Not until 8 May 1939 was the first woman professor seen at Cambridge (Miss Dorothy Annie Elizabeth Garrod, MA, D.Sc. Oxon, elected to the Disney Chair of Archaeology) and she, naturally, was single. There were only 970 female trades union members, and keeping them out became almost a full-time occupation for some men. Fairfield, the anti-feminist association of the Civil Service, was formed that March to try to ban the entry of *all* women or, in its own words, to 'guard against the invasion of women into the Civil Service to the detriment of men workers'. Three thousand men joined Fairfield in its first four months, a response so enthusiastic that two other men's societies

– the National Men's Defence League and the Modern Men's Movement – suggested that all three should merge into a single, and thus more powerful, body. They planned a march down Whitehall in the autumn and attempted to persuade their ex-service members to return the medals gained in the 1914–18 war as a protest against women being given jobs in Government employment while many ex-servicemen still remained unemployed.

Their uncompromising attitude was not tempered by the fact that many women did the kind of job no man would tackle, from charring and childcare to lacemaking and shoe testing – in the north of England, there were girls who year after year walked twelve miles a day, wearing a pedometer, and returned to the factory in the evening to hand in the new model they had been road-testing, reporting any faults of wear or comfort before it went into production.

The same ambivalent approach ran through the whole question of female health. On the one hand, women were regarded as emotional creatures, whose problems could largely be put down to 'nerves', and who, in extreme cases, were not always responsible for their actions; on the other, medical opinion had it that eighty-five per cent of women passed through the change of life without any interruption of their daily routine. For those who did have difficulties, one suggested aid was bromide. 'The disabilities from which women suffer have usually been regarded as natural and very little effort has been made to find cures for them,' wrote the medical journalist John Langdon-Davies. 'Not so long ago, indeed, a robust healthy young woman was regarded as something not quite nice.'

Nowhere was this more apparent than in the field of procreation. Menstruation was a subject so taboo that it could never be mentioned in mixed company. Women sidled into chemists' shops to ask in a muttered whisper for sanitary towels – and would sidle out again if there were no female assistants to serve them or if a male customer was standing close enough perchance to overhear what they were asking for. Any idea that this dread word would one day be seen in the pages of respectable family newspapers would have sent a paroxysm of shock rippling round the nation. Treated half as an illness, half as an atavistic curse, the monthly period sheltered behind a series of euphemisms that did nothing to alleviate the real distress felt by many women. Boys grew to manhood knowing little or northing of the internal workings of the female reproductive system – though perhaps wondering vaguely why their sisters seemed to suffer so frequently from 'headaches' or 'chills' which prevented them from bathing, hunting and even playing tennis.

Infertility was regarded as an entirely female problem. In the same way, the difficulties and disgrace of bearing an illegitimate child were a woman's responsibility. Although in some country districts pregnancy was accepted as a sign that the bride was fertile – in many parts of Scotland, for instance, no crofter in his senses would have dreamed of marrying his betrothed until she had produced at least one baby – the child of an unknown father suffered the stigma of illegitimacy all its life. So horrified were most families at the thought of a grandchild's illegitimacy that the child was sometimes passed off as the offspring of its own grandmother and brought up in the family as its mother's small brother or sister.

Childbirth itself often took place at home. For the rich, this was largely through choice, for the sake of comfort, convenience and the undivided attention of one's own doctor. The poor had little choice; but in practice, home was often the safest place for both. Puerperal fever was still a common threat: in 1938 it had killed 555 women after childbirth, with more succumbing after abortion or an obstetric complication; and even hospitals as famous for their gynaecological expertise as Queen Charlotte's were not immune. Though M & B (one of the sulphonomide drugs developed a few years earlier and known by the initials of the manufacturer, May and Baker) had dramatically cut down the incidence of 'childbirth fever', there was always the chance of cross-infection by other virulent organisms. However poor the conditions in the slum dwellings of the time, mothers who were delivered at home had at least developed an immunity to the family 'bugs'.

For upper-class women, pressure to conform to the traditional female role was not so overt. Ostensibly, they had plenty of freedom – to ride and swim, pilot aircraft, gamble, travel, write, paint, decorate, entertain. And indeed, they even had those traditional masculine symbols of independence, their own clubs.

Possibly the most famous of these was the Alexandra Club, in Grosvenor Street. This, the first real women's club in Britain, had been founded in Queen Victoria's reign by a group of titled women living in the country, to enable them to make occasional visits to London, even when unaccompanied by their husbands – staying alone in a hotel, with its connotation of nameless improprieties, would of course have been unthinkable. Despite the fact that only those who had been presented at Court were considered for election, the Ladies' Club, as it was originally known, was at first considered rather dissipated. However, it quickly became so fashionable that special leaded lights had to be installed in the dining-room windows to prevent battles for the 'best' tables – those at which the lunchers could be viewed in all their glory from the street. Such was its exclusiveness that one day, when the Princess of Wales was lunching there, the Prince of Wales was refused entrance by the doorman. The future King Edward VII laughed and said that any club as respectable as this was entitled to bear his wife's name, upon which it was immediately rechristened. A reputation for spotlessness could go no higher; but alas, the Alexandra Club was to close down for good a few weeks before the outbreak of World War II.

Far more successful that last summer was the twenty-year-old Forum, of which the Chairman was Princess Marie Louise. It had 2,300 members, most of whom kept their hats on within the Club premises; it was managed solely by women, and it had a large library, bridge tables in use all day and special groups for everything from aviation to needlework. It was also more generous towards the opposite sex than most male clubs, allowing men into all its reception rooms instead of only the occasional guest dining-room. 'Modern' was how its members described it – and themselves.

Even so, the female stereotype was reinforced by social as well as economic factors. It was women's job to attract and they were never allowed to forget it. 'Never look a man straight in the eye,' counselled beauty expert M. Dono Edmond, former adviser to the late Queen Marie of Rumania. 'It is not alluring.' Such an uncompromising gaze, he explained, makes its object feel inferior. 'He feels you are trying to probe his mind.' What a woman was likely to find there was not particularly reassuring. So deeply rooted was the idea of the female, if not as the possession of, then at least as adjunct to, some male, that it surfaced oddly in unexpected corners of the public consciousness. The Chairman of the Brentford Bench, addressing the husband of a twenty-year-old woman caught stealing clothes from the house where they lodged, told him sternly to 'exercise that control a husband should exercise over his wife', before binding her over for a year.

Another woman and her sixteen-year-old daughter from the slums of Bethnal Green were accused at Old Street Police Station of the theft of a pair of shoes, a handbag and two pieces of cloth (goods with a total value 19s 11d). When the mother pleaded guilty, she received a ferociously patriarchal telling-off from the Bench. 'You ought not to have married! You ought not to have had children!' She would never steal again, she said. 'Do not speak to me – I will not hear a word! You have behaved in a perfectly shocking way towards your husband,' thundered the magistrate, adding without conscious irony, 'and you have made this child of yours, who has been given every chance of a distinguished career, into a thief!' In the end, he discharged her, explaining his leniency with the words: 'I am going to take a course which is perhaps unfair to the public entirely out of consideration for your husband.' His attitude was not exceptional: in the House of Commons the Conservative Member for Forfar suggested changing the law so that women who deserted their husband, home or children could be prosecuted.

At the same time, however, it was just beginning to be recognized that in one aspect of life, the hand on the tiller was the woman's. Then, as now, women made most of the buying decisions. Those who made and sold the goods, and above all those who advertised them, were forced to find out how to appeal to these potential customers, if possible without upsetting the status quo. As a first step, The Housewife was invented – a concept which succeeded brilliantly. Soon it was recognized by everyone, including the housewife herself, that total responsibility for the welfare of her husband and children rested on her shoulders; her acceptance of this burden enabled advertisers to manipulate her through every emotion from altruism to guilt (it is noteworthy that many advertisements of the day begin, 'Can you afford *not* to buy X for your family?').

Above a certain social level, of course, women ceased to think of themselves as housewives. Yet the well-born, well-off female's dependence on the male was at least as great as that of her counterpart in what were then unashamedly known as the working classes. Few members of the upper classes brought up their daughters to earn their own living, let alone take up a serious career. Whereas boys were sent to public school, their sisters – especially when the family lived in the country – shared a governess with the daughter of a similar neighbouring family; often this tutor was French, which meant a sound education was promised in at least one subject. Other girls went to boarding schools where the 'tone' was good though the educational standard varied (it was always well below that of the equivalent boys' schools, however). This was followed by what many parents believed was a much more important preparation for their future: finishing school, or a spell in France, Italy or Germany.

Of those girls who did become dedicated doctors, teachers, or workers in some scientific field, most sprang from families that were professional or had a strong academic tradition. For marriage – to the right sort of man, needless to say – was both goal and expected destination. And to achieve the best, in terms of both love and money, a wide acquaintance and careful preparation were necessary. These, fortunately, could be achieved through that established ritual known as the Season. In short, for a young woman of the upper classes, adult life began with a curtsey.

Three

THE FIRST COURT

For debutantes, the Season of 1939 started early. With a state visit of the King and Queen to Canada and the US planned for May, the first three Courts, usually held in that month, took place instead on 9, 15, and 16 March.

By now, the Courts once again took place in the evening, which, for many of the mothers and aunts, was a welcome return to the old tradition. One of the innovations of the previous reign had been Edward VIII's introduction of afternoon Garden Parties instead of the customary evening Courts. These Garden Parties, held in July 1936, with attendance restricted to debutantes and their sponsors, had proved a dismal flop, thanks to the one factor that had to be left purely to chance – the weather. Although the majestic red and gold canopy under which the King sat enhanced his golden hair and boyish good looks, his subjects did not look their best. On the afternoon of the first of those Parties it rained heavily, presentation finery was soaked, and those who could took refuge in the refreshment tents, which quickly became overcrowded and unbearably hot. To everyone's relief, on their accession King George and Queen Elizabeth restored the evening Courts.

From early February, mothers of debutantes were establishing power bases in the shape of rented houses or flats as near the heart of the action – Mayfair and Belgravia – as their purses would allow. The essential feature was a drawing-room large enough to serve as a ballroom for a night. A little later on, those rich or grand enough to have their own London houses would be opening them up.

The age at which debutantes were presented varied slightly, according to certain rules as immutable as the laws of the Medes and Persians. A lady who wished to present someone at Court must herself have been presented, and there had to be a three-year gap before she could make another presentation. It was also customary for a woman to be presented for a second time on marriage. Ladies of foreign nationality (unless they happened to have married a British subject) and British women married to foreign nationals could be presented only through the diplomatic representative of the country concerned. For the mother of a solitary daughter there was no problem, but when two were close in age, this often meant a certain amount of juggling with dates, times and family connections.

Sisters with only two years between them were often presented together, hence the phenomenon that some girls were officially 'grown up' at an earlier age than others. Alternatively, an aunt, cousin or friend who happened to be presenting her own daughter, was often pressed into service. As for the daughters of women outside the charmed circle, some impoverished peeresses (of whom the best-known was probably Lady St John of Bletsoe) made a handsome living by sponsoring the children of the socially ambitious who possessed neither the required social qualifications nor the necessary circle of friends.

Almost always, presentation for a debutante was preceded by one vital lesson: learning how to curtsey at the Vacani School of Dancing. This august establishment had been founded before the Great War by the Vacani Girls – a young widow and her sister – both brilliant dancers; later they were joined by one of the widowed sister's three children, who was known as Miss Betty. It was she, with her aunt Marguerite, who taught both Princess Elizabeth and Princess Margaret Rose the skills of the waltz, the foxtrot, the polka and of course the curtsey, in their schoolroom at 145 Piccadilly.

The Vacani studio classroom was conveniently situated in the Brompton Road beside Harrods (and its car park). Here, debutantes and young married women would practise both the small bob, with straight back and slightly bent knee (for the informal curtsey at a party where royalty was present), and more importantly, the essential movements of the deep Court curtsey.

The first step towards the required degree of fluency and grace could have come from the repertoire of the *corps de ballet*. Holding the *barre* along the wall of the studio with her right hand, every member of the Court class would put her right foot along the wall, place the left foot behind, and practise rising and sinking down, in one smooth straightbacked movement.

Once this basic skill was mastered, conditions were made more realistic. A curtain kept in the studio was pinned on the girls' shoulders to give them practice in managing the train each of them would wear; some feathers and a piece of net gave them the feeling of the three ostrich feathers and veil that would adorn their heads; and a bunch of artificial flowers served as the regulation bouquet.

Then, with Miss Betty sitting in a chair to represent the King, her assistant would announce, 'To be presented, Miss Mary Burch'. Gliding forward, the future debutante, eyes fixed firmly on the petite figure in the chair, would sink down, with her weight on her right foot, her left foot behind it. 'Incline the head only at the deepest point of the curtsey and smile as you rise,' Miss Betty would instruct. Rising, still with her weight on the right leg, the pupil was told: 'Give a little kick to get your dress out of the way of your foot – still looking at the King, please – then take three steps to the right and curtsey to the Queen. You can smile at the Queen all the time – she always smiles back.'

After a day notable for ten hours' undisturbed sunshine, the night of 9 March was clear though cool. In Buckingham Palace, the work of preparing the State Apartments had begun at 8.00 a.m. By 11.15 a.m., the flowers chosen by the Queen and ordered by the Ministry of Works had arrived; by early evening, it looked as if weeks of work had gone into the preparations.

Attendance was due at 8.00 p.m. All evening, Daimlers, Bentleys and Rolls-Royces inched forward down the Mall. Inside sat debutantes and their mothers, wrapped in fur coats, discreetly hugging hot water bottles under lap rugs, reading or even knitting, while watchers on the pavements stared through the windows. Once in the Inner Court, where a further hour's wait could be expected, some ate picnic meals or drank cups of soup or coffee, while a gold-braided official watched to see that no one contravened the strict no smoking rule – several girls who were lighting cigarettes were quickly spotted and reproved – until the moment of arrival finally came.

Inside the palace, all was brilliance, ceremony and dazzle. Yeomen of the Guard lined the red-carpeted stairs, powdered footmen received wraps or discreetly indicated the route. Once in the White Drawing Room, debutantes waited on rows of gold chairs, mentally practising their curtseys, while Viennese waltzes, Irish airs, and light opera music floated out from the Guards Band in the Throne Room.

That year, the fashion was for full-skirted dresses with off-the-shoulder bodices. These had the fortunate bonus of showing off the family jewels to advantage; and most of the smartest debutantes wore this crinoline style. The royal ladies were pale but dazzling. The Queen glittered in a dress of white slipper satin, its wide skirt banded with gold lace; sparkling gold paillettes emblazoned the front, a gold lamé train embroidered to match hung from her shoulders, and a diamond tiara, necklace and bracelets flashed from her head, neck and wrists. Hardly less splendid was Princess Alice, Countess of Athlone (first cousin of the late King, and sister-in-law of Queen Mary), in grey lace embroidered with diamanté, and a silver train. She was adorned with diamonds and held a large ostrich feather fan. The Duchess of Kent, in contrast to the prevailing mode, shimmered like a slender silver column. Also with the royal party on their dais at the end of the room were the Duchess of Northumberland, Mistress of the Robes, in a dress of gold sequins with a golden train, and the Emir Feisal of Iraq in Arab dress. Other men wore uniforms and decorations. The Gentlemen of the Household were dressed in the knee-breeches, silk stockings and buckled shoes of full Court dress. Ambassadors, members of the Corps Diplomatique and official guests shone in the glittering and decorative uniforms of their respective countries, ablaze with medals, orders and jewels. Those not entitled to a uniform of some kind wore black velvet Court dress, against which orders gleamed. All this splendour was displayed again at the Court Ball which followed.

The mothers of the debutantes dressed in vivid colours, whereas their daughters usually wore white, or at least a pastel shade. Lady Bowater, the Lady Mayoress of London, for example, wore blue velvet embroidered with silver to present her two granddaughters: one in a white and silver crinoline, the other in a gold and cream brocade dress. The design for this dress had been inspired by a portrait of Mrs Samuel Wilson which hung in the Mansion House; she had been Lady Mayoress of London exactly a hundred years earlier and her husband had set up a trust to give a diamond ring to every Lord Mayor of London elected, as he himself had been, from the Castle Baynard ward of the City. Sir Frank Bowater was the most recent.

Whatever the difference in their dress, all the women wore gloves of fine white kid reaching to the upper arm, so tight it was almost impossible to pull them on. Once this had finally been accomplished, a line of tiny pearl buttons stretching for several inches from the palm upwards had to be done up, a process that needed a special buttonhook, patience, and a certain amount of physical strength. After a while, the warmth of the hand stretched the glove, making it possible to undo the buttons by hand and peel it back, to hang limply like a discarded second skin, while its wearer got down to the serious business of eating supper or an ice.

Though dresses were sometimes bought 'off the peg' from the couture departments of big stores such as Jays, Marshall and Snelgrove, Harvey Nichols and Harrods, most were specially made. Many dressmakers specialized in this lucrative field of dressing those who wished both to look their best for their sovereign and to emerge with honour from the scrutinizing gaze of another four or five hundred of their own sex. These 'Court dressmakers', as their discreet signs announced, could all be found in or around Mayfair; among the famous names of the day were Madame Claire, Jacqmar, and Worth in Grosvenor Street; Handley-Seymour, and Camilla, in New Bond Street; Paquin in Dover Street; the young Norman Hartnell in Bruton Street; and Reville, where Queen Mary bought many of her clothes, in Hanover Square. In all, around two thousand dresses were completed in their workrooms that week in March, some only hours before they were worn.

Trains, often the veil of Alençon or other old lace worn by the debutante's mother at her wedding, were attached at the shoulders and trailed a regulation eighteen inches along the floor; they were carried over the left arm when walking, with the bouquet (or, in the case of the older women, an ostrich-feather fan) in the right hand. Bouquets were delivered as late as possible, sometimes only moments before leaving the house, so that they should remain as fresh as possible; not surprisingly, this was a frequent cause of last-minute panic. At that first Court of 1939, many of the debutantes carried small and simple spring posies; those with large bouquets seemed to find some difficulty in managing them.

The debutante head-dress of three white ostrich feathers and a veil – generally a yard of lace or tulle – was fastened high at the back of the head and slightly to the left. The necessary clips and pinnings were usually hidden with a glittering headband or similar decoration. That year, dramatic waves at the back of the head were the latest in Court coiffure – a style sometimes adopted by the Duchess of Gloucester.

Despite the number of guests, things moved surprisingly quickly. Presentations might last barely an hour. First came the diplomatic and official presentations, during which the King stood while the Queen remained seated. Then the King sat down and the debutante presentations began.

Here also a strict order of precedence was observed. In the following day's *Times*, those presenting debutantes were listed in sequence from duchesses through marchionesses, countesses, and viscountesses to ladies (with no visible distinction between the wives of barons, baronets and knights), honourables and mesdames. As each sponsor was announced by the Lord Chamberlain, she rose, moved forward into the Throne Room, made her curtsey, then disappeared into an anteroom on the far side. Then came the moment for which the debutante had been waiting – and despite the hours of practice most had put in, it was still a nerve-racking experience. 'Every detail of your appearance is scrutinized by an official,' recorded one, describing those first few terrifying moments of presentation. Only when he was satisfied did this dignitary – a Court usher – take the train looped over the girl's left arm and arrange it carefully on the floor behind her.

Next, the Card of Command was handed to the Lord Chamberlain and the name on it announced in the Throne Room. The handing over of these pink cards, anxiously clutched by each debutante as she waited, was no mere formality: one unfortunate young woman (Lady David Douglas Hamilton, being presented 'on marriage'), who found she had mislaid hers when the moment came for her to start for the Throne Room, had to stand aside, giving way to others, while one of the Lord Chamberlain's staff made out a new Card of Command for her.

Now the debutante entered the Throne Room – the great red, gold and white ballroom, lit by six large rose crystal chandeliers, in which Courts were always held (when the number of guests was too great for the State Dining Room, the larger State banquets were also held here). As she walked towards the royal couple seated on their golden chairs, our debutante would glance momentarily and, she hoped, unobtrusively downwards at the red carpet beneath her feet until she found what she sought: a small gold crown embroidered on the spot where she was to pause in front of the King and curtsey. Holding her bouquet low in front of her, her left arm straight, she sank down, inclining her head only at the lowest point of the curtsey. Smiling as she rose, she made three gliding steps to the right and curtseyed to the ever-smiling Queen. After another discreet kick to ensure her skirt was free, the debutante moved smoothly, without turning her back on the King and Queen, to a door on the far side of the Throne Room, where an usher would loop her train over her left arm again.

Next door, in the Blue Drawing Room, its walls lined with more Yeomen of the Guard and more powdered footmen, she rejoined her sponsor and those already presented until the ceremony was over. The King took the Queen's hand, and they then appeared through the door from the Throne Room to walk side by side the length of the gallery.

Once the royal couple had passed, she would proceed through the Picture Gallery, down more red-carpeted stairs, again with Yeomen lining the walls, to where a champagne supper was served by liveried footmen, on porcelain decorated with gold crowns, as gold plate gleamed from illuminated wall alcoves, until finally a voice on the loudspeaker cut through the talk and laughter to announce the car.

What did it all cost? One 1939 debutante gave her breakdown of expenses as follows: feathers 30s, gloves 21s, shoes 30s, evening bag 10s 6d, train (she bought her own material and had it made up) £5, dress 15 gns, car with footman from 7.00 p.m. until midnight 3 gns, tips 1 gn, flowers 25s, hair styled for feathers 7s 6d ('I had a lacquer finish sprayed on and it stayed immaculate all evening!'). Photographs accounted for another 5 gns. It was customary to be photographed in all one's finery; after a Court, the well-known Court photographers stayed open until 11.30 p.m.

to accommodate the debutantes who dropped in for a portrait sitting on their way to a post-presentation party. The grand total was £36 8s. 'Not such a large amount,' reflected the 1939 debutante (summing it up for the *Evening Standard*), 'for the privilege of calling on the King and Queen.'

With luck, our debutante would not be taken straight home. All over London, presentation parties were taking place at the grand hotels, where debutantes were unhooking their trains to leave them, along with veil, feathers and posies, in cloakrooms, or looping them up over their arms while they danced with fathers, brothers or friends. The men were dressed in uniform, or in evening or Highland dress (if at a Scottish party). After the first Court there were five such celebrations and three twenty-first birthday parties at Grosvenor House alone, and at the Savoy, Miss Margaret Dalgleish's cyclamen pink satin stood out amid the sea of white dresses. Among the latter, a white tulle ballerina dress with Victorian corsage bordered by camellias and outlined by lace was much admired.

Once commanded to a Court, little could keep women away. Even a death in their immediate circle, or their own illness, proved no deterrent. Lady George Scott (the artist Molly Bishop, whose pastels of society beauties appeared regularly in the *Tatler*) postponed an appendectomy in order to be presented; and at the second Court of 1939, a number of women were in mourning, their black dresses of chiffon, lace and tulle as elegant as the Court dressmakers could make them. The Queen was again in white, the bodice of her picture-dress of white tulle thickly embroidered with gold paillettes, and its skirt of three layers of tulle powdered with gold sequin embroidery. Over this she wore a *manteau de cour* of white tulle bordered with deep frills and sprinkled with gold embroidery; her jewellery was of diamonds and rubies.

Miss Rosamund Fellowes, youngest daughter of the enormously rich Mrs Reginald ('Daisy') Fellowes, famous hostess and a perennial fixture on the 'best-dressed' list, was presented at this

1 For those who preferred to shop in the Rue de la Paix, a de Havilland DH91 Albatross Class airliner flew to Paris every two hours (photo Edwin Smith)

2 A Mayfair wedding. The thick London 'pea-soup' fog casts a gloom over this January afternoon

3   The Dining Room at White's

4   Couples dine and dance to the music of Roy Fox and his band at the Monseigneur Restaurant

5 Merle Oberon and Laurence Olivier in *Wuthering Heights*

6 Anton Walbrook, Diana Wynyard and Rex Harrison in Noel Coward's *Design for Living*

7 The Throne Room at Buckingham Palace. George VI and Queen
Elizabeth hold Court. The girls waiting to be presented are seated on the
right

8   An evening dress by Paquin

9   Lady George Scott, the
former Miss Molly Bishop,
presented on her marriage to
Lord George Scott at the third
Court by the Dowager Duchess of
Buccleuch

10   Court dresses were
sometimes bought 'off the peg'

11   Queen Elizabeth in her white picture-dress, which she wore at the
second Court (photo Cecil Beaton)

12 The new and sudden threat to Europe. *Punch*, 22 March

13 Negotiations with Russia were to prove difficult and extremely long drawn out

14 Loelia, Duchess of
Westminster, painted by Glyn
Philpot

15 Doing the Lambeth Walk

second Court. For Mrs Fellowes, the Court was not an altogether happy occasion. In order to decide which pieces from her £4,000,000 collection of jewels to wear, most of them had been brought to one of her various homes, a villa near Paris; and £36,000-worth was stolen by audacious thieves while she herself was in the house. The missing pieces included a particularly lovely five-strand pearl necklace, and a pair of amazing bracelets so wide they were almost like cuffs, studded with diamonds and fringed with cabochon emeralds which fell over her hands.

At this Court, too, a correct but ingenious way of circumventing the strict presentation rules was demonstrated by Lady Schuster who, having been presented by Lady Ritson, a few minutes later herself presented her own daughter, Miss Ann Schuster.

The next day, 16 March, a socially unprecedented event occurred. For the first time, the usual full-page report on the previous night's Court was missing from *The Times*. Instead, there was an account of the invasion of Czechoslovakia. For while the cars of the debutantes and their mothers were massing along the Mall and in the forecourt of Buckingham Palace, Hitler had been marching on Prague. With the Czechs booing his troops, he entered their capital at 7.15 p.m.; half an hour later – just before the Court began at 8.00 p.m. – he was installed in the ancient castle of Hradschin, the gold and black Nazi flag was unfurled, and an immediate curfew ordered. He was there a mere twenty-four hours, but reputedly walked to the windows of this ancient castle at least fifty times to admire one of the finest views in Europe. 'I had no idea,' he said repeatedly, 'that Prague could be so beautiful.' The Munich Agreement was dead.

Four

THE IDES OF MARCH

Overnight, with the occupation of Prague, everything had changed, from the face of Europe to attitudes at Printing House Square. On 16 March, *The Times*, in a complete reversal of its former editorial stance that war could and must be avoided by negotiation, stated that Hitler obviously had no intention of honouring the Munich Agreement. A few hundred yards away, foreign residents jammed the Aliens Registration Office in Bow Street in a belated attempt to register themselves as British.

In the House of Commons that evening, Geoffrey Shakespeare, Parliamentary Secretary to the Admiralty, announced while presenting the naval estimates that a convoy system for merchant shipping was ready to be put into operation, but added over-optimistically, 'as regards the submarine menace, there are reasons which have convinced me it will not be as strong as it was in the last war'.

This comment did not pass without scathing criticism from Winston Churchill, who was astonished to find that no destroyers – the 'greyhounds of the sea', whose speed and manoeuvrability made them the most effective counter to a submarine menacing a convoy – were under construction. As he said prophetically: 'Nothing could be more obvious and necessary' than the need for more destroyers. Shakespeare countered with the ringing declaration: 'Britain's navy is so strong today that we believe it can confidently accept a direct challenge in battle by any combination of foes.' However, the shortage of destroyers almost lost Great Britain the war: in the summer of 1940, Churchill had to persuade the United States to lend the Royal Navy fifty obsolete reconditioned American destroyers.

Churchill and his supporters advocated conscription, but the Government felt the time was not yet ripe. Persuasion was another matter: the largest advertisement in England was put up on the centre span of Waterloo Bridge. Painted on a piece of sailcloth 143 ft long and 9 ft deep was the question, 'National Service – have you offered yours?' But the most significant words of all came from Neville Chamberlain. With all hope brought back from Munich now in shreds, two days after the entry of German troops into Prague he made a major speech rebuking Hitler in the bitterest terms heard from a prime minister in many years. He spoke from Birmingham, home and citadel of the Chamberlain family, a fact which may have given his words an added edge. 'Is the seizure of Czechoslovakia the beginning of an attempt to dominate the world by force?' he asked, warning the German leader that, if this were so, 'the people of Britain will never surrender the liberty which has been theirs for hundreds of years.'

Indeed, they responded by volunteering in thousands for some form of National Service. In Germany, according to the *Daily Mail*'s Berlin correspondent, G. Ward Price, Chamberlain's speech made a profound impression on those Germans able to listen to the reports of it broadcast by the BBC. Since German propagandists had, for their own purposes, consistently empha-sized the British Prime Minister's attitude of understanding and goodwill towards Germany compared with the warlike attitude of some of Chamberlain's countrymen, its effect was doubly telling.

Chamberlain's speech also contained the seeds of a complete revision of foreign policy. The first and most important step towards this was the formal invitation issued by the British Government to Soviet Russia to consider joining in a pact with Britain, France and any other powers prepared to resist German aggression. As the months dragged on, the possibility of this alliance was to become the last frail thread by which peace hung.

The German press, after rejecting the British and French Notes of Protest at Germany's occupation of Czechoslovakia, retorted that the Anglo-German Naval Agreement would undoubtedly be repudiated if 'Britain continues to maintain the absolute unreasonableness, the political and historical ignorance, the moral megalomania and the manifest power-political hostility of her present attitude'. A few days later, Hitler moved again, demanding the immediate return to the Reich of Memel (the Baltic port taken from Germany after the 1914–18 war and then under Lithuanian rule). As German troops marched across East Prussia, Memel's Jewish community fled.

The Spanish Civil War was then entering its final phase. Earlier in the month, Dr Juan Negrin had left his country for Toulouse, to be followed by nearly all the Spanish Cabinet; eleven Spanish warships sailed to Bizerta, the French naval base near Tunis, where they were promptly interned; and Franco declared a full blockade of the coast of Republican Spain, giving his fleet orders to sink any ship coming within a three-mile limit. In Madrid, the few remaining cattle attempted to graze on weeds pushing up through the roads as the inhabitants foraged for food and firewood. While lorries filled with escaping women and children poured out of the capital, the tanks rumbled nearer.

The first detachments of Franco's troops entered during the last weekend in March. 'Within a few hours our flag will float from the highest point in the capital,' said General Franco. 'Our army is conquering all resistance!' There was none; not a shot was fired as Madrid surrendered, ending a siege that had begun on 6 November 1936, twenty-eight months and one week earlier. With the golden banners of Nationalist Spain hanging from every rooftop in the capital, the Nationalist station at Burgos was able to broadcast on Tuesday 28 March that the Spanish Civil War had ended. The cause for which Englishmen as well as Spaniards had given their lives, and which had engaged a whole generation of intellectuals in a love affair with communism, was lost.

Five

THE RITUALS OF COMING OUT

Even before the first of the Courts, the coming-out dances had begun. The first, given by the mothers of two debutantes, Miss Elizabeth Hely-Hutchinson and Miss Victoria Douglas, who were to be presented the following night, was fairly typical: it was held at 16 Cadogan Square and two hundred guests danced in the first-floor drawing-room, converted into a ballroom for the night and decorated with spring flowers.

But before the Misses Hely-Hutchinson and Douglas donned their respective blue and white satins, planning as involved as that of any military campaign had taken place. There were mothers' and debutantes' tea parties (the best ones had the added attraction of a fortune-teller), and lunches at which the girls 'got to know' one another and the mothers traded the names of young men suitable to ask to their dances. For while convention decreed that girls or their chaperones must be known to the hostess of that night's dance (usually the mother of another debutante) no such formality was necessary in the case of their dancing partners. Hence the importance of the List.

Every future hostess had her own address book full of the names of 'suitable' (that is, socially, though not necessarily morally or financially, impeccable) bachelors, which she swapped with her best friends and added to, if she heard – or indeed overheard – another name. After a few weeks a definitive version of this pool of dancing partners and escorts would have emerged.

When a man was on the List, and thus vouched for as matri-
monially eligible, he was automatically asked to all the dances,
whether or not he was known to the hostess. When he married,
he was equally automatically crossed off.

But never were there quite enough of these elusive creatures.
'Can you possibly bring a man?' was the leitmotif floating through
most debutantes' days; and mothers would telephone each other
frantically when an evening's dinner party was uneven. For dance
hostesses invariably conferred with their friends beforehand
when giving dinner parties, specifying which girls to invite, but
leaving the question of men open; theoretically, each girl had to
bring a man. 'There always seemed to be two men short,' recalls a
debutante of 1939. 'My mother was always ringing up her friends
and saying, "I want a man for tonight – *any* man."'

At the dance itself, the shortage was often even worse. Men
who worked were frequently not prepared to waste good sleeping
time on a dance they thought boring. After dining – and for most
young men, at the beginning of their careers and often impecunious, a free and delicious dinner was a considerable
inducement – they would go on with their party to the dance,
rapidly assess the situation and, if it looked unpromising, quietly
slip away. The hungrier ones waited until after supper – lobster,
salmon, strawberries, ices – served on hired china in the dining-
room. Champagne, which few of the girls drank, was available
throughout the evening. Later, around 3.00 a.m., there was
breakfast of coffee, scrambled eggs and bacon.

For the girls, almost as bad as the fear of not finding a partner
was the fear of not finding something to talk to him about.
Making conversation, both at the dance and, worst of all, at the
dinner party beforehand, was always considered the girl's responsibility; and the idea that someone who had until then led a
sheltered and strictly regimented life, with only family, school or
schoolroom friends and pets for company, could suddenly sparkle
away when confronted with an older and often blasé stranger
of the opposite sex, was one of the commonest social delusions of

the time. 'Two good subjects if you are stuck for conversation are ghosts and the royal family,' was the advice of Loelia Ponsonby (later Duchess of Westminster).

A debutante whose dance was one of the many held in Cadogan Square that spring, remembers that 'it was drilled into you that you *must* talk – it didn't matter what about, as long as you *talked*. The hostess would look down the table and if you weren't talking to one of the young men on either side of you it would be a black mark. As we usually didn't know our partners – though it got better as the Season went on – one was in a complete conversational vacuum. I don't think the young men were ever told about making conversation. Certainly, I've always found that after Guardees *anyone* was easy to talk to.'

Scoring a conversational success with one of these anonymous faces above the regulation white tie, with no ready-made topics except the band and the state of the dance floor, was difficult enough; it was worse if a girl became thought of as 'clever'. 'I acquired the unsavoury reputation of being "intelligent",' said Lady Mary Clive, one of the 'clever Pakenhams', in her book *Brought Up and Brought Out*. 'No harder word was used. No harder word was needed.' And a girl who came out in the 1939 Season recalls 'Laura Grenfell having a wild success as a debutante and a mutual governess we had saying to me accusingly, "You see, Laura is intelligent enough to hide her intelligence." She was able to make these slightly brainless young men chatter away, whereas I was nervous and bored at the same time.'

Smoking helped to bridge the conversational gap. 'In the debutante world, not smoking was considered the sign of the dull country mouse,' observed Mary Clive. Cigarettes in long holders were considered particularly chic, and Turkish cigarettes smarter than Virginian. If they were the gold-tipped oval Black Russian brand or some other exotic colour, so much the better. Most men smoked cigarettes, as a glance at pre-war photographs will confirm. (Pipes were reserved for the masculine atmosphere of club or study, or the open air. In 1939, their connotations were not so much of thoughtfulness and wisdom but of the outdoor, sporting life; in the world of advertising, their image was of a rugged virility barely restrained through an iron self-discipline.)

Another feature of these dances was their suffocating heat, as two hundred people and a five-piece band crammed into a first-floor drawing-room converted into a ballroom for the night. 'In my mother's generation the young men always wore gloves,' recalls another 1939 debutante, 'and when I felt all those sweaty hands on my bare back I remember wishing they still did.' Some houses had gardens or terraces to stroll in; otherwise on hot nights dancers often had no option but to take the air on the pavement outside or in a garden square.

Garden dances, given during the Season by the famous hostesses for their friends and contemporaries, and occasionally for some lucky debutante, took place in Belgravia and Mayfair; on some nights, there were parties all round Grosvenor Square. Lady Londonderry entertained royalty and politicians in London-derry House, while the tremendously rich American Laura Corrigan rented Dudley House in Park Lane for two months at the height of the Season, paying the then phenomenal sum of £5,000. For Mrs Corrigan, one of the chief attractions of Dudley House (built a hundred years earlier by the eccentric Lord Dudley, who became Foreign Secretary and of whom it was said, 'He promised much, did little, and died mad') was its fine ballroom. Later in the summer, at the height of the Season, she gave a ball there for the Duke and Duchess of Kent.

Dance tunes were romantic American favourites, most of which seemed to contain some reference to the hours of darkness: 'Deep Purple', 'Night And Day', 'Stardust', 'Blue Moon', 'So Deep Is The Night', 'Shine On Harvest Moon', 'Cheek To Cheek', and 'Lullaby Of Broadway', although the homegrown 'Lambeth Walk', 'The Chestnut Tree', 'Boomps A Daisy', 'A Nightingale Sang In Berkeley Square' and the 'Palais Glide' were also popular. Sometimes American hit tunes were played, such as the one that Mary Martin was singing on

Broadway, 'My Heart Belongs To Daddy'. Every dance ended with a galop (usually 'John Peel' for debutantes whose families lived in the country), followed by 'Auld Lang Syne'.

Where a ballroom was big enough, reels were generally part of the programme. There were reels at Lady Craigmyle's dance for her daughter at Claridges (although nobody came in a kilt), enough Scottish guests to make up several sets and certainly plenty of space in the ballroom, which had decorations of apple blossom, tulips and rhododendrons around the great wall mirrors. There were also, of course, the various Scottish balls, in particular the Caledonian. 'One of the leading Scottish debutantes, Lady Jean Graham, daughter of the Duke and Duchess of Montrose, will not be taking part in the reels at the Caledonian,' reported the *Evening Standard*; 'she has just left England for Scotland.'

Lady Jean, fair, good-looking, and at 6ft 2in the tallest debutante of the year, was one of the girls who quickly became noticed. Miss Sonia Dennison, Lady Sarah Spencer-Churchill (whose dance at Blenheim later in the summer was the grandest of the Season), the beautiful Miss Ursula Wyndham-Quin, Barbara Dewar (for her dance in Sussex her mother had their enormous garden lit up with torches and fairy lights), Miss Flavia Meade, who was studying languages at London University, and Miss Elizabeth Hely-Hutchinson, whose interest in politics led her to listen to debates in the House of Commons, were others. One of the best-known, inevitably, was Mrs Neville Chamberlain's niece, Miss Valerie Cole, a pretty girl with dark curly hair and blue eyes, who lived with her aunt and uncle during her debutante season and was presented at Court on 16 March by Mrs Chamberlain. 'The new debutantes are exceptionally pretty,' wrote David Verey in his nightly diary after the Hely-Hutchinson dance. Verey, a young architect making the most of the Season, was like many other eligible young men also undergoing military training at the same time; in his case, on the Supplementary Reserve of the Royal Fusiliers.

King Leopold of the Belgians, a widower, was a fantasy figure to many. 'We were all madly in love with him,' recalls one debutante. 'He was so good-looking – his mother's looks, blond and rather teutonic – tall and upright, with fair curly hair. In his high-necked tunic, with plenty of gold braid on the shoulders, he looked dazzling.'

A certain amount of paperwork figured in the debutantes' world. From the beginning of the Season, the mantelpiece would be thick with invitations, each of which had to be formally answered. If several fell on the same night, most girls accepted them all, then dance-hopped or decided with their friends which to go to. At the dance, small programmes with pencils attached were handed out to everyone, and prospective partners' names written beside the number of each dance. It was an unwritten rule that each man danced at least once with each of the girls in the dinner party to which he had been asked, so that theoretically even the shyest or plainest girl was sure of at least half a dozen dances. But alas, this rule was not always observed, and if there were not a fair sprinkling of initials in the programme, hours might have to be spent in the ladies' cloakroom (for each dance lasted about twenty minutes) to avoid the shame of being seen without a partner. Popular girls arrived with their programmes already full, their admirers having reserved dances by telephone earlier in the day. This entailed still more work with the pencil: the numbers of these dances were written with the corresponding names in small 'dance books' kept in the evening bag and transferred to the programme on arrival. Finally, the following morning, thank-you notes had to be written to both dance and dinner-party hostesses. Sometimes, if a girl had been to several dances on the same night, up to four or five of these 'bread and butter' letters had to be laboriously composed.

But probably the greatest difference between pre- and post-war debutante dances was the chaperone (then spelt without the final 'e'). This duenna was a fixture by the well-brought-up young woman's side at almost every social event during her debutante year, after which the girl's own principles were trusted to provide the same moral corset. Chaperones were usually mothers, sometimes close relatives or friends who happened to be bringing out daughters of their own; though fathers who enjoyed dancing or those who, like Mr George Howard (owner of Castle Howard), were widowers, occasionally took on this chore.

Such exceptions were highly popular with the mothers and aunts otherwise condemned to sit around the edge of the ballroom floor until three or four in the morning, talking to their neighbours on each side or nodding off under the family tiara. And as one social correspondent reported a week later: 'Chaperons at dances for debutantes usually have to look after themselves at supper-time, but at Mrs Leslie Melville's dance for her daughter Miss Helen Leslie Melville there were almost as many fathers as mothers among the guests and every chaperon had a supper partner.' It was also pleasant for a mother who herself might be no older than thirty-nine or forty to have a partner to dance with to the tunes that set her feet tapping night after night.

Not that chaperones were able to prevent behaviour they all deplored in their charges, such as the common habit of disappearing in the middle of one dance to visit another. 'You simply weren't supposed to go off alone with a man in a taxi,' recalls one debutante of those days. Wickeder girls did something even worse: sneaking off with a beau to a night club. 'If found out, one's mother would reproach one severely: "I've taken all this trouble, spent all this money and all you do is slip off to night clubs,"' was the general theme. 'But we were incredibly innocent. I never let anyone kiss me because I knew you only kissed people you were in love with and wanted to marry.'

Sometimes mothers would go home early, unable to keep up the 4.00 a.m. bedtime five nights a week that was required of the chaperone of a popular debutante. This meant making an arrangement with another chaperone to bring her charge home – never, never could this task be entrusted to any male other than brother, cousin or father. And even though, after a girl had been 'out' for a year or so, the ban on unrelated male escorts was relaxed, all mothers tried to ensure that only young men who were 'suitable' (that is, trustworthy) brought their daughters home.

The system worked slightly differently for dances given in the country, where girls would stay in house parties. As no young girl of debutante status was supposed to travel about the country or stay in a strange house alone – although her hostess, as a married woman, was automatically of chaperone status – she was supposed to take a maid with her. Sometimes this was her mother's lady's maid, sometimes someone much more formidable: the girl's own old nanny, who would not hesitate to chide, argue or flatly refuse to allow a course of conduct of which she disapproved. Even when absent, her aura could be peculiarly potent. After one such visit, reported Lesley Lewis, in her book *The Private Life of a Country House*, 'I felt outraged when my aunt's lady's maid, on saying goodbye to me, said, "And tell Nanny I think you have improved wonderfully."'

Six

OFFICIAL ENTERTAINING

On 1 March, M. Maisky, Soviet ambassador to the Court of St James for the past seven years, had launched the Little Season (the early parties, balls or dances before the Season proper began with the Royal Academy Private View) with a reception. It was an extremely grand affair, and the 450-strong guest list augured well for the hoped-for Anglo-French alliance with the USSR. For the first time, a British prime minister was a guest at the Soviet embassy. Mrs Chamberlain had 'flu, but Miss Valerie Cole accompanied the premier. The guests included MPs of all parties and members of the Cabinet, though the foreign secretary, Lord Halifax, was another stricken with 'flu. The Diplomatic Corps was there in force, including the popular Danish ambassador Count Reventlow; so were the literary lions H. G. Wells and J. B. Priestley (whose new play, *Johnson over Jordan*, had opened the previous week), and the distinguished physicians Lord Dawson of Penn and Lord Horder. One notable absentee was the German ambassador, who had returned to Berlin the week before and there fallen ill with the prevailing 'flu – this time the virus was possibly of the diplomatic strain.

The food and entertainment were lavish. There were three buffets, with 20 lb of best Beluga caviare (even then costing £3 a lb), turkey, lobster mayonnaise, smoked calf's tongue, mousse of sole and, more prosaically, roast legs of Surrey chicken, along with copious supplies of vodka and Russian champagne, claret cup, champagne cup and mulled wine. Guests danced foxtrots and waltzes to the decorous strains of a quintet, but towards midnight a wild Russian dance was performed with explosive energy by two Cossack dancers, just after which R. A. Butler appeared, having been delayed by an important debate in the House. (Although Under-Secretary, Butler was, unusually, the chief Foreign Office spokesman in the House of Commons, as the foreign secretary himself was in the House of Lords.)

The following night there was a gala performance by the Comédie-Française at the Savoy Theatre, attended by the King and Queen. It was an evening of special poignancy: everyone there knew that once again their two countries might shortly be standing together against a common foe. Afterwards, Lord and Lady Bessborough gave a reception at the Savoy Hotel; here, the Queen, her famous complexion radiant against a jacket of her favourite white fox fur, her smile as dazzling as her diamonds, met the Comédie-Française's star actress, Madeleine Renaud. Afterwards, Mlle Renaud sighed rapturously: 'Your Queen is *so* charming.' At midnight, in an atmosphere charged with emotion, the 650 people present rose to their feet and stood to attention as they sang that most stirring and passionate of national anthems, the Marseillaise.

On 7 March, the King held a levee at which public servants and officers of the armed services were presented. It was to be the last before the outbreak of war, and was notable for the number of those among the King's attendants whose names would shortly become famous. The principal air ADC in attend-ance was Air Chief Marshal Sir Hugh Dowding (who, with the thirties passion for nicknames, was always known as 'Stuffy' Dowding); a year later, as commander-in-chief of Fighter Com-mand, he fought the decisive Battle of Britain. The field officer in Brigade Waiting was Lieutenant-Colonel F. A. M. 'Boy' Brown-ing, husband of the novelist Daphne du Maurier. He was later to command the Airborne Corps in the Arnhem operation. The naval representative was Rear Admiral Bruce Fraser, later Third

Sea Lord, who as commander-in-chief of the Home Fleet sank the *Scharnhorst* – the last German capital ship to be sunk by gunfire.

On Tuesday 21 March, the president of France and Mme Lebrun arrived on a state visit. Halfway across the Channel they were met by British destroyers and escorted to Dover, where warships of the Second Cruiser Squadron fired a salute, and there was a fly-past by six squadrons from Bomber Command. The French party was met at Dover by the Duke of Gloucester, and at Victoria station by the King and Queen.

That evening, the King and Queen gave a State banquet for their French visitors. Its main feature was a display of the royal gold plate, so dazzling it almost rivalled the combined wattage of the guests' diamonds. Large gold centrepieces were ranged along the horseshoe dining-table with smaller gold plates for the guests; more gold pieces were displayed on four large stands covered with red baize. Menus, on gold-edged cards, were headed with the royal cypher – the monogram GRE, beneath a crown; the plates on which the food was served were white with a gold border and gold crown in the centre. As the State Dining Room was not large enough for the number of guests, the banquet was held in the Throne Room. The King and Queen sat at the head of the table in gilt armchairs upholstered with red damask, their guests sat on other, smaller red-upholstered gilt chairs. The thrones on the crimson dais, with the royal arms above them, were floodlit. During the dinner there was light music provided by the Scots Guards; afterwards, marches, strathspeys and reels were played by the Scots Guards and the Black Watch.

The eight-course menu, from the Consommé Quenelles aux Trois Couleurs and the Filet de Truite Saumonée George VI, through the Mignonettes d'Agneau Royale and the Salade Elysée to the Corbeille Lorraine, delicately reflected the themes of royalty and Anglo-French friendship. The wines accompanying it were drunk from the magnificent Windsor service of Garter glass, each piece engraved with the Rose of England and the badge and motto of this ancient Order. In honour of the discriminating palates of their French guests, the wines were the finest in the Palace cellar, from the 1865 sherry that accompanied the soup to a Perrier Jouet 1919, Château Haut Brion 1904 and an especially choice Château Yquem with the pudding – an ice christened Bombe l'Entente Cordiale. The only less tactful note, perhaps, was that the date of the brandy – 1815 – celebrated England's greatest victory over France.

It was by all accounts a dazzling evening. The Queen, in gold and silver, and the homely Mme Lebrun, clad for the occasion in silver lamé, were both adorned with splendid, coruscating jewels. Diamonds and rubies sparkled from the hooped skirts of aquamarine satin worn by Mrs Joseph Kennedy, wife of the American ambassador. The Duchess of Kent caused a minor fashion sensation by wearing sandals, instead of the customary dyed-to-match satin shoes. (She had also been pictured recently in peeptoe shoes, said to have been invented by a Mr Poitier from New York who, in a drinking-match, downed a shoeful of beer the fastest by cutting off the toe of his impromptu tankard.)

The Duchess was, in any case, famous as the epitome of chic and glamour. Slender, elegant, intelligent and beautiful, she had amber eyes, a low, rather guttural, heavily accented voice and great sweetness of manner. Her influence on contemporary fashion cannot be exaggerated: everything she wore was copied, from her favourite Marina blue (a greenish turquoise to which she gave her name) to the pillbox hats she introduced. When she asked her dressmaker to design summer frocks made not of the usual silk but of cotton (unheard of then) because of the Lancashire cotton mill depression, cotton frocks became the fashion. Her preference was for plain, simple, classic clothes, their perfect tailoring never achieved in fewer than four or five fittings instead of the usual two or three. As the daughter of an impoverished, exiled family, she had in girlhood often made her own clothes and always bought 'off the peg', trimming, dyeing and reshaping the previous year's purchases until the French couturier Patou, recognizing her style and chic, let her have his models at a discount. She still bought many of her clothes in Paris – but, in deference to her adopted country, from the English house of Molyneux.

Together, the Kents were a breathtaking couple. The Duke, Prince George, tallest and best-looking of the royal brothers, was slim and athletic; he loved shooting, hunting, jazz and dancing. His attractiveness was enhanced by a faintly dissolute aura; stories were told of 'wild' parties, and it was well known that as a young man he had climbed Big Ben, using the scaffolding then in place outside the House of Commons. He was a qualified pilot, loved fast cars, and was musical and artistic – the only one of the brothers to have inherited his mother's good taste, and her love of collecting. His passion for jewelled boxes, Chippendale furniture, Sèvres and Spode china, was such that the already limited Kent finances were severely strained. His flair did not stop at objects: it was the Duke who decorated their country home, Coppins, and remade its garden, the Duke who planned the menus and decorated the table for dinner parties at 3 Belgrave Square, their London house (which they rented from Lady Juliet Duff furnished, but with the proviso that they could redecorate inside as they wished). Both Duke and Duchess were wonderful dancers although both, curiously, had suffered problems with their feet. An operation on a left foot that turned outward at birth had left the Duchess with a slight limp and a discrepancy of shoe sizes between her right and left foot; the Duke had had both little toes amputated (they were 'hammer' toes).

For once, though, the sartorial interest of the evening lay not in the Duchess of Kent's clothes but in the sheer tonnage of precious stones which adorned the noble guests. Much of this was displayed in the tiaras which married women wore at most grand evening occasions and always when royalty was present. These flashed arrows of light under candelabra and chandeliers at banquets and balls, gleamed star-like from stalls or boxes at the opera, glittered from the heads of chaperones at the smarter debutante dances, and were seen in profusion at the parties given by the great hostesses.

In many ways, tiaras were as much tribal insignia and cultural totems as jewelled ornament, accurately reflecting the status, ancestry and social pecking-order of their wearers. Some were magnificent, crown-like affairs, so heavy that they imposed a regal deportment on the wearer; others were known for their beautiful and perfectly matched brilliants. Some noble families had several tiaras, the reigning duchess or viscountess wearing the one that reflected most exactly the importance of the occasion; others, more impecunious, borrowed from relations or sometimes from the family jeweller, who lent them partly as a discreet advertisement for his wares, partly in hopes of a future sale. Important family ones, made for another head and borrowed by a married daughter or sister for an evening, sometimes fitted so badly they caused a 'tiara headache'.

On this occasion, several famous tiaras were on view; the Countess of Airlie's diamond and pearl tiara, and the tiara of huge diamonds that blazed from the head of Lady Spencer in contrast to her simple blue princess-line dress. By common consent, though, the most impressive diamonds were those of Lady Londonderry, icon-like in the famous Londonderry crown tiara, with long earrings to match and an immense diamond ornament on her impressive corsage.

To the regret of most of the guests, the evening ended at the early hour of 10.30. Not everyone, however, had enjoyed it; for the Prime Minister, it was the climax of the stressful days immediately following the invasion of Czechoslovakia. 'No sooner did I arrive,' he told his sister Ida, 'than Hore-Belisha came up and whispered, "We have just confirmed that the Germans have mobilized 20 divisions on the Western Frontier. This is like the Brussels Ball." I had already heard a vivid account of the interview between the Lithuanian minister and Ribben-trop when the latter demanded the immediate surrender by peaceful agreement of Memel, and intimated that if it were not forthcoming the German army would march in and would not stop at Memel. You can imagine that with these things in my mind it was more than usually difficult to keep a smiling face.' Nevertheless, he recorded with satisfaction, one of the Frenchmen present had complimented him upon his 'bonne mine', appearing comforted by the fact that he was always 'calme et souriant'.

Once home, though, it was a different story. 'That night I swallowed a tablet of Sonoril which enabled me to sleep soundly from 12.30 to 7. I couldn't afford a broken night just then but I have been able to do without any artificial aid to sleep ever since, and that is remarkable because I was much worried over the possibility of a surprise air attack. It didn't seem to me in the least probable but with this fanatic you can't exclude entirely the conception he might well say "This is life or death to my people. I am justified in breaking the unwritten or written rules if I can go for a knockout blow before the other fellow has had time to prepare."'

The following night, on Wednesday 22 March, the Lebruns reciprocated with a banquet at the French embassy. The menu, more exotic than that of their royal hosts, included Loire salmon and foie gras glazed with port served just before the pudding. The wine list, though shorter than that at the Buckingham Palace Dinner, was equally delicious: a Meursault 1929, a Lafite-Rothschild 1923, a Romanée St Vivant 1923, a Château Yquem 1928 and a Champagne Pommery brut 1929. The first tune played by the small French orchestra accompanying the banquet was the delicately complimentary 'Si j'étais Roi'.

Afterwards, at ten o'clock, it was the turn of the King and Queen again; they entertained the Lebruns at a Gala performance at the Royal Opera House. The royal party sat in the exquisite royal box, decorated by Rex Whistler and Mary Newall. The King and Queen, the President and Mme Lebrun, Queen Mary and the Dukes and Duchesses of Gloucester and Kent were at the front of the box, with what amounted to a small crowd behind them – twenty people, who included other members of the royal family, courtiers and the French President's suite. To the left was the government box. Chips Channon, the rich American-born Conservative MP and socialite, noted in his diary that night, 'Mrs Chamberlain looked like a Gunter's cake in pale pink with a pink boa'.

Most of the royal ladies wore the Royal Victorian Order, with the exception of the Queen and Queen Mary – seated one on each side of the French President – both of whom wore the ribbon of the Grand Cross of the Légion d'Honneur across the bodices of their sparkling white and gold dresses. The performance began with the Marseillaise, and the President responded to this gesture by clapping vigorously after the national anthem, which followed immediately. Then, amid the rustling of silks and the dying whispers of conversation, the audience settled down to watch acts One and Three of *The Sleeping Princess*, conducted by Constant Lambert and danced by the Vic-Wells company, followed by the orchestra's performance of Debussy's *Iberia*, conducted by Sir Thomas Beecham.

Again, diamonds blazed so brightly that sometimes the footlights seemed unnecessary. Queen Mary's three-inch-high, crown-shaped tiara made a piquant contrast to Mme Lebrun's small diamond head-dress, lent by a jeweller in the Rue de la Paix and the simplest, as one keen-eyed observer noticed, in the entire house. But her clothes, borrowed from Worth, had for once overcome her own natural lack of style. A BBC commentator drew inadvertent attention to this fact by exclaiming in friendly but faintly astonished fashion, 'She does not look a bit out of place!' Mme Lebrun's homeliness made it easy to understand the popular belief that the president called her Pom-Pom in private.

While Lady Halifax kept up the British tradition of superb jewellery with her beautiful pearls and diamonds, worn with an elegant white dress, a certain lack of *tenue* could be observed in the box reserved for diplomats. Although Mme Maisky was correct if not dazzling in long white dress, ostrich-feather cape and with two pink roses in her hair, her husband's attire made him instantly noticeable in that stylized and formal gathering. Alone among the audience, the Soviet ambassador wore neither Court dress nor white tie and tails, but an ordinary dark suit.

Seven

RECEPTION AT THE INDIA OFFICE

The French state visit concluded with the most elegant and successful party of all – dinner and a *divertissement* afterwards, held at the Foreign Office in Whitehall. The evening began at 8.15, when Lord and Lady Halifax entertained the King and Queen and the President and Mme Lebrun to dinner. There were seven courses, beginning with caviare and Colchester oysters; but what made it truly notable were the wines. Eight in all (exclusive of liqueurs), they began with sherry, followed by a Grand Chablis Valmur 1929, Château Palmer Margaux 1875, a Krug 1928, Chambertin Clos de Bèze Vieux Cépages 1915, a 1920 Château Yquem, and an 1897 Allnutt port, 1820 brandy and liqueurs. They dined to the strains of music by Gounod, Delibes, Offenbach and Massenet, played by the band of the Royal Air Force.

The walls were hung with old and beautiful tapestries, and the magnificent plate on the dinner-table was greatly admired. Much of it belonged to Sir Philip Sassoon, who also lent thirty superb Louis XVI chairs from the dining-room of his Park Lane house for the occasion. Even the waiters had a new and gorgeous livery, for which Lord Halifax was partly responsible: impressed by Parisian style during the state visit to Paris the previous year, he had immediately on his return given orders that the footmen who worked for the Government Hospitality Fund should have a more becoming uniform. Sir Philip Sassoon and Major Eric Crankshaw together designed the striking livery, seen for the first time that night: a scarlet waistcoat, bright blue coat with gold trimmings and dark blue plush breeches, worn with the usual white stockings.

Much of the evening's success was, in fact, due to Sir Philip, the man officially responsible for the while *mise-en-scène*, and from whose gardens at Lympne had come the profusion of imaginatively deployed and magnificent flowers, trees and shrubs which embellished the entrance, staircase, reception rooms and courtyard. Conservative MP for Hythe and a former Under-Secretary of State for Air, he had been appointed the first Commissioner of Works by Chamberlain two years previously. There could have been no better choice. He was a man of impeccable taste coupled with artistic knowledge and flair (his advice had been invaluable to Mrs Chamberlain when she was refurbishing 10 Downing Street, particularly in the choice of pictures). He had a particular gift for creating beautiful gardens – as Commissioner, he inaugurated the planting of drifts of spring bulbs to grow, as if naturally, in the grass beneath the trees in the London parks.

One of the great social figures of the age, Sassoon was in many ways the last flowering of Edwardian opulence and style. Almost more to the point, he was immensely rich. The Sassoons, a grand Jewish family, came originally from Baghdad and had settled in Bombay for several generations, where they had amassed their fortune; his mother, a Rothschild, was a woman of charm and culture who had influenced him greatly. He was now aged fifty, and had never married, declaring in his youth that he would not do so unless he could find a woman as beautiful as his sister Sybil. He talked, according to Chips Channon, in a clipped, sibilant accent often imitated, rolling his r's rather like a French-man (he also had French blood), which gave an irresistibly funny edge to his highly idiosyncratic use of the English language. He had two houses of great grandeur in the country but most of his time was spent in his equally splendid London house at 25 Park

Lane (later to become the Playboy Club), with its marble hall, its superb pictures, its mirrored blue and gold ballroom decorated by the artist José-Maria Sert.

Here his sister, the Marchioness of Cholmondeley, acted as his hostess until the demands of marriage and her young children – who often stayed with their benevolent uncle – made this more difficult and her role was taken over by their cousin Hannah, Mrs David Gubbay. He was a generous host and a giver of wonderful dinner parties where the food was cooked by one of the most brilliant chefs in the country. He was an intimate friend of the Royal Family, and in a way even his death two months later was in part brought about by three of the main preoccupations of his life, loyalty to his sovereign, the claims of friendship and social obligation. The King had summoned him to Windsor to discuss some point concerning the entertainments there for the French visitors; while he stood about in the icy corridors of the Castle and later in its courtyard, on what was a freezing cold day, the bad cold he was suffering from turned into an infection from which he never recovered.

But on the evening of the Foreign Office party he was enjoying a well-deserved triumph. The entertainment afterwards was held in the India Office, and as the glittering and bejewelled crowd arrived, the glamour of the setting he had devised drew murmurs of appreciation. The stage and its decor had been designed by the foremost architect of the period, the President of the Royal Academy, Sir Edwin Lutyens. The production, heralded by fanfares from the trumpeters of the Life Guards, was by Sir Seymour Hicks (a Chevalier of the Légion d'Honneur), and there was music from the band of the Grenadier Guards. The Prologue and Epilogue, both written by the Poet Laureate, John Masefield, were spoken by Edith Evans and there were performances by some of the most notable young actors of the day.

Lord Zetland, the Secretary of State for India, was dining at the Foreign Office, so the guests were received by his son, Lord Ronaldshay, and Lady Ronaldshay (in palest chartreuse-green satin and the customary tiara). All the royal ladies wore white, with the Queen in her favourite wide skirts, Queen Mary in a silvery dress trimmed with sparkling embroidery, the Duchess of Gloucester in plain white, and the Duchess of Kent with a white fox cape over her narrow white dress. Mme Lebrun wore silver lace with, again, a white fox cape. Tiaras, of course, were out in force: the Duchesses of Devonshire and Buccleuch sported 'two of the largest ever seen', and Lady Londonderry wore the famous Londonderry diamonds.

As the guests arrived, their first sight was of Life Guardsmen, motionless and glittering in scarlet and silver, lining the walls of the staircase and reception rooms. Ranged between them stood tubs of flowering Japanese cherries and magnolias. Everywhere there were flowers: drifts of coral, pink and golden azaleas framed the balconies, pillars hidden by climbing roses, and in the courtyard, now transformed into a theatre, great banks of heavily scented white Madonna lilies separated stage from auditorium. Scarlet velvet hung on the walls behind the gilt chairs on which the audience sat.

The entertainment began with a performance of the balcony scene from *Romeo and Juliet* given by John Gielgud and Peggy Ashcroft. Sacha Guitry and Seymour Hicks acted out a sketch they had written about their attempts to speak each other's language; its flow was hindered by Guitry's insistence on the inclusion of his young protégée Geneviève Sereville, whose acting was more wooden than comic. After this, the applause was polite rather than rapturous, but Cicely Courtneidge's depiction of a young woman inconveniently seized with hiccups after too strong a cocktail 'fairly sent the royal family into convulsions', as the Prime Minister later wrote to his sister. He also noticed the extravagant behaviour of one of the French guests. 'A constant source of joy during the whole visit was the conduct of one of the suite, M. le Général de Division [Major General] Braconnier, the French president's military secretary.

'On a somewhat foolish face with puffy cheeks he wore an

enormous pair of mustachios with a Napoleon III beard to match. I suppose he would be in the late 50s but he was a desperate ladies' man and never missed an opportunity. The Duchess of Norfolk complained to me that as she was trying to make a dignified entry into the Royal Box he seized her hand and kissed it rapturously. The Duchess of Buccleuch, who is one of our great beauties in society, was led by him into a corner of the Secretary of State's room in the India Office where she informed me "He would keep kissing my shoulder", and even Valerie was immediately the subject of compliments till Mme Braconnier came up and tapping her on the arm said warningly, "C'est mon mari." I told the Queen this story and she complained afterwards that I had given her a fit of the giggles which lasted all evening.'

Eight

DINNER WITH THE CHAMBERLAINS

Six days after the India Office reception, the King and Queen dined with the Chamberlains. It was only the third time in the century that the Sovereign had dined at 10 Downing Street: the first time was when King George V and Queen Mary came to dinner with the Asquiths in 1911, and the second when George VI and Queen Elizabeth had previously been entertained two years earlier by Mr and Mrs Baldwin.

The royal couple arrived punctually at 8.25 p.m., the door was opened by a footman in the dark Downing Street livery and a moment later they were shaking hands with the Chamberlains in the daffodil filled hall before signing the visitors' book.

Along the cream-walled, red-carpeted corridor they went, past the Cabinet Room and up the famous staircase hung from top to bottom with portraits of previous prime ministers, Mrs Chamberlain as hostess leading with the Queen, and the Prime Minister following with the King, and up to the first-floor State Drawing Room decorated in shades of white by Mrs Chamberlain, its freshness enhanced by the bowls of her favourite spring flowers – vases of mixed tulips in pinks, amber, yellow and white, daffodils, polyanthus, anemones.

The twenty-four guests stood waiting in a half-circle ('Come early,' Mrs Chamberlain had begged her great friend and con fidante Caroline Lady Bridgeman, 'just after 8.15, so I can tell you the plan of campaign'); presentations were made, and immediately these were finished (no sherry was drunk), dinner was announced by the butler shortly after 8.30. As the company processed through the other two Downing Street drawing-rooms, the doors of the oak-panelled dining-room were flung open and the Prime Minister led the Queen in to dinner, followed by the King and Mrs Chamberlain and, in strict order of precedence, the other guests.

In anticipation of this dignified and elegant moment, there had been considerable behind-the-scenes activity. First, there were informal approaches to Buckingham Palace to ensure that an invitation to dinner would be welcome and, if so, to fix a date. The official invitation was accepted by Sir Alexander Hardinge, who wrote, on Buckingham Palace paper:

'I have conveyed to the King and Queen the kind invitation from the Prime Minister and Mrs Chamberlain to dine with them at 10 Downing Street on Wednesday March 29th and I am desired to say that Their Majesties accept with the greatest pleasure. Their Majesties are most grateful to Mr and Mrs Chamberlain for asking them and they will be very interested to see the renovations at Number 10.'

Following the custom of the day, Mrs Chamberlain then wrote to the Queen.

'Madam

'We are delighted to hear that Your Majesties will honour us by dining with us here on Wednesday March 29th. It will give pleasure to us to show you the changes that have been made in the old house. We believe they have brought it back nearly to what it was when the picture was painted which my husband saw in the King's Room at the Palace.

'We shall submit a list of guests for Your Majesties' approval and we propose, if agreeable to you, to limit the numbers to about 24. we are looking forward to the occasion with the keenest anticipation [in the original letter, the word "appreciation" is crossed out]. I am, Madam, Your Majesty's most humble and obedient subject

'Anne Chamberlain.'

The response was a letter of acceptance from the Queen's lady in waiting, Lady Katharine Seymour, followed by a list of prospective guests from Downing Street to be submitted to Sir Alexander Hardinge ('at the same time, would you ask him to ascertain whether the King wishes knee breeches to be worn'), along with a request for the names of those who would be in waiting on the royal couple so that they might also be sent invitations, and for confirmation that 8.30 was a suitable time for dinner.

The King, it transpired, did not wish knee breeches to be worn ('knee breeches are only worn when the host wears the Garter', an Order the Prime Minister did not possess) and found 8.30 an extremely convenient time. Lady Hambleden was to be the lady-in-waiting while the King would not be bringing a lord-in-waiting but an equerry, Commander Campbell. 'His Majesty also entirely approves of the list of guests.' They too received first formal invitations, then a letter from Mrs Chamberlain to the wife; in turn, each formal reply on behalf of the couple was followed by a personal letter from the wife to Mrs Chamberlain. Those invited included friends at the highest political level, known to be greatly liked by the King and Queen, and members of the Chamberlain family.

Among the distinguished political figures were Lord Maugham, the Lord Chancellor (brother of the novelist W. Somerset Maugham); Lord Halifax, the Foreign Secretary and a former viceroy of India, a High Churchman and keen foxhunting man; and the Marquess of Lothian, former Private Secretary to Lloyd George, Christian Scientist and ambassador-designate to the US – so highly regarded did he become in this post that when he died in 1940 of peritonitis (brought on by his refusal to have himself medically treated) he was given an American state funeral.

Other guests included Sir Samuel Hoare, noted penal reformer (he was a great-nephew of Elizabeth Fry) and arch appeaser, who was to be sent as ambassador to Spain the following year to keep Spain neutral and thus save Gibraltar; his wife, Lady Maud

Hoare; the government Chief Whip, David Margesson; and Sir John Simon and Lady Simon. (Sir John had been Attorney General in Asquith's Liberal Cabinet in 1913 and had succeeded the Prime Minister as Chancellor of the Exchequer. He was a man of notable unpopularity – it was said he spent his whole political life trying to find someone who would call him John.)

The Londonderrys, also invited, were a couple who combined politics and social grandeur. The seventh Marquess, whose book giving an account of his meetings with Hitler had come out the previous year, had been Secretary of State for Air in the mid-thirties and visited Germany as the guest of Goering in both 1936 and 1937. He had invited Goering to stay at Londonderry House for the Coronation but fortunately Goering had refused. His wife Edith was the most famous political hostess of her day. Statuesque, fascinating, with a tattoo of a snake winding up her leg from the ankle, 'Circe' Londonderry was the friend and intimate of leading politicians; her bewitchment of the Labour Prime Minister Ramsay MacDonald, whose confidante and great friend she became, played a part in his repudiation by his party. The brilliant entertainments at Londonderry House were a noted feature of the Season; every year (up to the outbreak of war) Lady Londonderry held an eve-of-session reception for the Conservative Party.

Also present were the Duke and Duchess of Devonshire, intimates of the royal family and great friends of the late King George V and Queen Mary, to whom they had frequently lent houses. The Chamberlain family was represented by their daughter Mrs Stephen Lloyd and her husband, and by Valerie Cole.

Additional guests were Lord and Lady Swinton, Caroline Viscountess Bridgeman, and Admiral of the Fleet Lord Chatfield and Lady Chatfield. Immensely distinguished, Lord Chatfield was the only one who could have been said to represent 'the face of Mars' at that gathering: he had been appointed Minister for

Co-ordination of Defence two months earlier. (He had also served as Beatty's flag captain in the Battle Cruiser HMS *Lion* at Jutland. When first the *Indefatigable* and then, half an hour later, the *Queen Mary* had blown up, it was to Chatfield that Beatty turned as they stood together on the bridge with the remark: 'There seems to be something wrong with our bloody ships today.')

Representing the arts was the portrait painter Oswald Birley, for whom Mrs Chamberlain had just sat. A New Zealander, Birley's well-cut clothes, neat military moustache and genial manner gave him more the air of a soldier than of the artist and music lover that he was. He and his dark Irish wife, also invited, shared an interest in Indian philosophy and had visited India seven times already. For him, the invitation to dinner held an additional bonus: he was able to study the King, the subject of his next portrait, at close quarters.

The King and Queen (the King, according to Chips Channon, 'good, dull, dutiful, goodnatured', the Queen 'well-bred, kind, gentle, flirtatious in an entirely proper way'), sat opposite each other at the centre of the table, with Mrs Chamberlain and the Prime Minister at their respective right hands. Although the order of precedence of the various distinguished guests was unequivocal, the seating plan had not been achieved without a certain amount of anguished consultation.

When the list of precedence (the Lord Chancellor, the Duke of Devonshire, Lord Lothian, Lord Londonderry, Lord Halifax, Lord Swinton, Admiral of the Fleet Lord Chatfield, Sir John Simon, Sir Samuel Hoare, Captain Margesson, Captain Birley and Mr Lloyd) was sent along with the table plan to the Palace, it needed an accompanying letter to explain: 'Since the Prime Minister and Mrs Chamberlain have to be where they are, it necessitates the numbers being uneven on either side, and I am writing to let you know therefore that to get the precedence going into the dining room right, Lady Simon will be taken in by Lord Chatfield even though he is not sitting next to her. I know you will see how this works although it is rather complicated at first sight.'

Food, drink, the chairs the guests were to sit on, the King and Queen's preferences (neither of them drank soup, the Queen was fond of meat and the King of vegetables), and the question of who they would like to talk to after dinner all had to be settled in advance.

Mrs Chamberlain had to borrow chairs, silver, china and glass from Government Hospitality. Samples of silver and china – including a dessert service and coffee cups – were sent round two days before the party, in the careful hands of the Government Butler, Mr Watson. Mrs Chamberlain was particularly anxious to have the same red-cushioned, gilt chairs used by the Baldwins at their royal dinner party; more correspondence established that these were hired from Kingston Miller and Company, who fortunately still had them.

Government Hospitality was equal to its responsibility. The room, with its rich red curtains, Persian carpet, pale parchment-shaded chandeliers and portraits of Nelson, the Duke of Wellington, Gladstone, Charles James Fox and Lord Salisbury, made an impressive background. Now the long dining-table was adorned down its length with silver candelabra, and cream-coloured lace mats were used instead of a tablecloth, with finger bowls in front of each place. In a silver-gilt epergne were massed yellow freesias, deep apricot and orange clivia and copper and orange autumn roses. There were four services of waiters; after dinner the King and Queen were each served their own special pot of coffee.

The food, however, was strictly a domestic matter, and the entire dinner was prepared by Mrs Chamberlain's cook, one of the twelve Downing Street servants. This was made much easier by one of the alterations Mrs Chamberlain had effected: modernizing the kitchens, which now served fifty people at a time (she had also installed new electric fires and open grates in the reception rooms). In deference to royal tastes, the menu was comparatively simple: Consommé Madrilène, filets de sole Bercy, selle d'agneau bouquetière with pommes Parisienne were followed by Poussin à la Polonaise, salade de laitue, asperges vertes, Parfait contesse Marie aux fraises Grand Marnier with crème Chantilly.

After dinner, when it was time to move, Mrs Chamberlain caught the Queen's eye, and the ladies then settled in the drawing-room, where coffee was served to them. When the King came up later with the gentlemen, he was installed in a separate drawing-room. Consulted on this point beforehand, Mrs Chamberlain's friend Lady Granard, who had also had the King and Queen to dinner, thought that both should be in the same room, but the Chamberlains felt there should be no possibility of the two conversational circles overlapping, 'and we found this best'.

The names of those brought up to talk to Their Majesties had been carefully arranged, albeit a mere two days before ('In order to avoid delay after dinner I wonder whether you would be so kind as to tell me who Her Majesty would like me to bring up after dinner?' 'The Queen suggests starting to talk with Moucher Devonshire and Lady Londonderry, followed by as many of the others as there is time for.') In the event, Mrs Chamberlain made twenty-two presentations to the Queen, and the Prime Minister made six or seven to the King 'including several men'.

According to Mrs Chamberlain's accounts, the total cost of the evening (excluding the cost of wine) was £77 7s 9d. Hire of the table linen was £11 6s 3d, flowers cost £15 15s 3d, printing (menus, place-cards, etc.) £7 12s 9d, food £38 18s (of which the green-grocer accounted for £20 13s 6d, the fishmonger for £7 15s 9d and the butcher for only £3 18s). Wages for extra staff were a mere £3 15s 6d. The royal couple stayed until 11.40 p.m., thanking the Chamberlains enthusiastically afterwards through Sir Alexander. A letter on the Queen's behalf to Mrs Chamberlain was to follow later.

Alas, the Prime Minister's memory of the evening was not so

happy. In a long letter to his sister Hilda four days later, written from Chequers, he described first his mental state of those last few March days ('this last week has been no child's play for me'); next, the evening in question:

'My worst day was Wednesday. The King and Queen were due to dine with us at 8.30 and about six o'clock I was in the middle of an interview when Halifax rang up to say he had a man with him who had just come back from Berlin with important news and he thought it was greatly necessary he should bring him along at once with Cadogan. The man turned out to be a journalist with intimate contacts with certain Germans and the news that Hitler had everything ready for a swoop on Poland which he planned to split up between annexations and protectorates. This would be followed by the annexation of Lithuania and the other states would be easy prey.'

After this, announced his visitor, his German contacts saw 'the possibility of a Russo-German alliance' as the next step, and finally 'the British Empire, the ultimate goal, would fall helplessly into German hands'. Ribbentrop, it was said, was helping the Fuehrer to strike while the British were still undecided as to whether to make an alliance with Poland and Rumania.

The young man had told him a good many more things, wrote the Prime Minister, 'not all so terrifying but some of them seemed to me so fantastic as to doubt his reliability . . . but it so happens that at the same time we got the same tale from quite another source of this weekend swoop, and the thought that we might wake up on Sunday or Monday morning to find Poland surrendered to an ultimatum was certainly alarming. For once I decided to say nothing about all this to Annie until next morning but you can imagine how much I enjoyed our dinner party with this awful thing weighing on my stomach. Still, the dinner was a great success.'

Nine

THE PRIME MINISTER

Neville Chamberlain was not a typical politician, let alone a typical prime minister – except, perhaps, in his possession of that priceless political asset, the ability to do with much less sleep than the ordinary mortal. When Parliament was sitting, Chamberlain's average night's sleep was five and a half hours, and 'though sometimes when I wake I feel a little tired and headachy, the moment I get up my head seems to clear and I feel quite fresh and able to cope with whatever comes along'. His health seemed excellent, apart from the gout which – rather unfairly, as he was most abstemious – crippled him from time to time.

As the son of Joseph Chamberlain and half-brother of Austen Chamberlain, his family history and tradition made his entry into public service of some kind virtually inevitable: nevertheless, Neville Chamberlain was forty-nine before he took his seat in the House of Commons (although he had an enormous reputation in local politics). The Chamberlains were well off. The family owned a prosperous manufacturing business in Birmingham and, just before Neville Chamberlain became Prime Minister in 1937, the salary of that office was raised to £10,000 a year.

Before the Chamberlains moved into Number 10, they put in hand a massive structural and decorative overhaul that took a year to complete. Mrs Chamberlain had disliked the idea of moving into a house in which the private living accommodation, including the main bedrooms, was cheek by jowl with official rooms and offices on the first floor. So she determined to turn the second floor, then the servants' quarters, into apartments for the Prime Minister's family (as it has remained ever since). The main part of the work entailed building a new staircase to the second floor, previously only reached by a servants' staircase at the back, and enlarging windows, raising ceilings, straightening the walls in the new second-floor family bedrooms and installing bathrooms.

When the work was finished, the Prime Minister's bedroom was in the north-western corner of the house, overlooking both St James's Park and Horse Guards Parade. Mrs Chamberlain's room was opposite, with a large new bathroom next door. Another of the new bedrooms was occupied by Valerie Cole. Seven small attic rooms on the floor above remained as staff quarters. These alterations freed the two large bedrooms on the first floor that had been occupied by previous prime ministers and their wives. The inner one became Neville Chamberlain's study and the large room on the north-west corner (immediately below his new bedroom on the second floor) was turned into an extra drawing-room. This greatly increased the space available for entertaining by forming a sequence of three large reception rooms.

Just as much thought, care and time were lavished on the decoration of the house. The large State Drawing Room was painted white and new furniture installed, much of it eighteenth-century; here were also kept the Chamberlains' blue and gold Coronation chairs. The middle drawing-room was done up in pink, one of Mrs Chamberlain's favourite colours – others were apricot, *eau-de-nil*, greenish turquoise and yellows. The Pillared Drawing Room (the former bedroom) was decorated in yellow, and the main staircase walls painted a Bloomsbury 'greenery-yallery'. A suite of red-upholstered furniture which had formerly belonged to Clive of India gave the Red Drawing Room its name, and the large old kitchen in the basement was modernized and equipped with a service lift to bring food up to the passage outside the State Dining Room. Another innovation of Mrs

Chamberlain's was the display of superb pictures now hanging on the walls – a large Turner landscape, several Dutch interiors, a Claude Lorrain. Many of these, on loan from the National Gallery, were already in Number 10, stored in the cellars. From start to finish, the whole process took almost a year, and cost £25,000. Until it was completed, the couple remained at 11 Downing Street, which had been their official home when Chamberlain was Chancellor of the Exchequer.

Mrs Chamberlain was a handsome, erect, well-built woman. She wore her greying hair in a *soigné* French plait and her beautiful complexion was embellished with only a little discreet make-up from Cyclax. She dressed well, though not extravagantly, in her preferred colours of navy blue, light blue and olive green. She adored flowers, and Number 10 was always filled with them, brought either from Chequers or from the family house in Birmingham. An excellent and painstaking hostess, she entertained frequently, usually giving luncheon parties since the sitting of Parliament in the evening precluded dinners. Her Irish ancestry gave her her charm and her strong sense of humour (her brother was the famous practical joker Horace de Vere Cole). A trifle unpunctual – though never when accompanying her husband – she was almost more than a trifle vague. She had a habit of losing spectacles all over London, leaving them in official cars, at Harrods, and in the houses of friends, from which, with a varying rate of success, they would be retrieved.

By 1939 the Chamberlain children, a son and daughter, were grown up and living away from home. The Chamberlains were a most devoted couple and the only fly in the amber of their marital happiness was Annie's 'nerves'. References to her depressive attacks appear again and again in her husband's correspondence. But whatever Mrs Chamberlain's nervous or emotional state, she remained a tower of strength to her husband. 'Annie is wonderfully good in a crisis,' he wrote touchingly. 'You might suppose that with her temperament she would become hysterical but on the contrary the blacker the outlook the calmer she grows and, where many women would be an additional burden, she helps me because she can stand anything I tell her.'

His own tastes were simple and his personal style quiet and unobtrusive. He dressed invariably in wing collar and striped trousers, and although his clothes were slightly old-fashioned for the time, they had a certain elegance – in April he was picked out by the *Daily Mail* as the best-dressed man at the Private View of the Royal Academy's Summer Exhibition.

He was meticulous and efficient, and throughout every crisis that year his desk was, as always, cleared of every scrap of paper by lunchtime. He hated wasting time, and punctuality, if possible to the second, was a fetish; often a train had to be held for two or three minutes because the Prime Minister's ideal of arriving just as it was due to pull out had been minimally misjudged.

He was not particularly prepossessing in appearance. Tall, lean, dark-eyed, gaunt-faced and sallow, with a high, thin voice that did not lend itself to oratory, he had none of the warmth, ease of manner, expansive personality or ready wit that help to make a public figure popular. It was impossible to produce a nickname from his name, nor did he have any instantly recognizable physical traits save, perhaps, a harassed expression. He did not smoke a pipe nor, as Anthony Eden did, always wear the same distinctive hat, although the cartoonists made the most of his ever-present umbrella. (In New York, one enterprising manufacturer went even further, making a lapel pin for women in the shape of this famous brolly. It was advertised, in April 1939, using the words 'Wear a Chamberlain on your chest this spring' and, according to US commentators, signified a swing of sympathy towards the British Prime Minister after Hitler's entry into Prague in March.)

Chamberlain was shy, intensely reserved, and painfully sensitive to any imputation that he felt was unfair or unjustified ('Attlee made a most vicious personal attack on me today . . . quoting Gilbert Murray's letter commenting on my "habit of radiating satisfaction at the calamities of the innocent".') He had so stern, dry and depressed an approach that Conrad Russell (nephew of Bertrand Russell), in a letter to Lady Diana Cooper, referred to him throughout as the Old Coroner. Yet he was regarded as a saviour by those who believed, as he did, that the longer war was postponed, even at the cost of presenting an appearance of weakness, the less likely it was to take place. 'Praise be to God and to Mr Chamberlain,' wrote Godfrey Winn at the time of Munich. 'I find no sacrilege in coupling these two names.'

Chamberlain was possessed of immense inner resources. The anvil on which his character had been forged was the seven years he had spent in the Bahamas where, rather like one of the heroes in the Conrad stories he so much enjoyed, he had from the age of twenty-one single-handedly attempted to develop a sisal plantation bought by his father on the island of Andros. Here he learned self-reliance, and the ability to commune with nature and with himself, which developed and expanded his already formidable clarity of mind. It was a life of extreme hardship and social isolation; by the time the venture finally failed and he returned to England, he was twenty-eight, and the pattern of intense reserve coupled with the habit of relying only on his own judgment had become fixed. Even his pleasures were solitary ones. While he was musical and well read, with a taste catholic enough to embrace both Shakespeare and adventure stories – such as those of the elder Dumas – his interests were above all those of the country gentleman.

Though he did not hunt, he enjoyed shooting – he was once described as 'a good average political shot' – and was a brilliant fisherman: he would take a house in Scotland in August, and often stayed with fishing friends such as Sir Francis Lindley, the former ambassador to Japan, at Alresford in Hampshire, where he spent Whitsun 1939, and with Lord Forbes in Scotland.

It was when staying at Castle Forbes for the Easter break in April 1939, that he was recalled, to his intense disappointment, by the news of the Italian invasion of Albania on Good Friday.

On 9 April, he wrote his sister Ida a letter revealing several of his major preoccupations of the time: the state of the country, his sporting interests and his feeling of personal isolation overlaid by a faint sense of grievance:

'Of course it was hopeless to try and stop at Castle Forbes and the only question was when and how to return. I had an aeroplane standing by but that would have taken three and a half hours and I decided that I would spend the daylight on the river and return by the night train. This had the advantage that Annie could come back with me for though she was beginning to think that if I flew she would like to fly too I felt that that would be more than my nerves could stand. So I fished yesterday afternoon in my London clothes and got two pulls but I got no satisfaction out of it. I couldn't concentrate on fishing and I was conscious of fishing carelessly and badly.'

It had been another completely wasted holiday, he concluded gloomily. 'Though my physical condition is luckily wonderfully good I must admit that the mental strain is very great when it is so prolonged and I am disappointed at having to come back before I could get any benefit from the change.'

It did not make things any easier, he added, to be badgered at a meeting of Parliament by the Opposition 'and Winston, who is the worst of the lot, telephoning almost every hour of the day. I suppose he has prepared a terrific oration which he wants to let off.'

Always happiest out of doors, he was a keen and know-ledgeable gardener. He planted freely at Chequers and enlisted expert aid ('I've got a man from Kew here at work on the trees and hope to be allowed to keep him until he has dealt with most of those near the house'). Of Chequers itself, which he adored, he commented: 'I get an extraordinary amount of pleasure and satisfaction out of my outdoor amusements here, specially in connection with trees. I have now completed my album of tree photographs.' These were of the tulip trees he had planted near the Lodge, groups of red oaks near the house, some hawthorns, black walnuts and a maidenhair fern.

He wrote occasional articles on natural history or botanical subjects and collected butterflies and moths (an interest which could have almost been called familial: one West Indian butterfly, Terias Chamberlainii, is named after a cousin). But above all he was a passionate ornithologist. When Chancellor, he had even found time to write an article in the *Daily Telegraph* on the curiously imitative habits of the London blackbird.

'One of the pleasantest features of No 11 Downing Street is its outlook on the old L-shaped garden that lies between it and the Horse Guards Parade, with its ancient shaded wall, its marvellous turf and its venerable ilex and hawthorn . . .' He goes on to describe how the first sound that came in through his bedroom window in the morning was the song of a thrush: 'Hey! Ho! Hey! Ho! He sang so joyously and vigorously that his exuberance became spiriting and infectious and I got in the habit of listening for him in the daytime as well as the early morning.'

When he was Prime Minister, Chamberlain would take morning walks in St James's Park, always with his wife and his two detectives. These walks became a well-known feature of the London scene and a regular fixture in his day, whatever the political tensions. If an unfamiliar migrant was spotted, a letter would be despatched to *The Times* and the details noted down privately. 'I got an interesting bird record in St James's Park last Friday when I saw a heron flying up the lake with the gulls. I can't remember seeing one there before.'

When R. A. Butler, also recalled to London over the Albanian crisis, came to Number 10 for instructions, he was shown into the small study, where he found the Prime Minister feeding the birds on a small table hanging outside the window. Butler began to talk of the threat to the Balkans, but Chamberlain dismissed it along with Butler himself, telling him, 'Don't be silly. Go home to bed', and went on feeding the birds.

'At least,' wrote Butler afterwards, 'he did not tell me, as he had once advised Anthony Eden, to take an aspirin.'

Ten

NEARER TO WAR

On 1 April, in a speech made in Wilhelmshaven at the launching of the battleship *Tirpitz*, Hitler declared, 'The German Reich is not going to put up with a policy of intimidation or even of encirclement.' In Britain, the debate was raging over the growing demand for some form of military conscription. The three-month experimental period for recruiting men and women for national defence had ended at midnight that night with 700,000 new ARP volunteers.

But fire-watching and first aid were not, of course, the same thing as military service. Huge advertisements asking for volunteers for the RAFVR, the RNVR, and the Territorial Army ('In the Territorial Army, the sergeant is your friend') now began to appear regularly. The Prime Minister was firmly against conscription, contending that its introduction would appear to show that Britain accepted that war was inevitable. Winston Churchill, among many others, was convinced of its necessity. The Oxford Union, reversing the famous 'King and Country' vote of a few years earlier, voted by 432 to 232 that 'This House in view of this country's new commitments and of the gravity of the general situation in Europe welcomes conscription.' In Cambridge, sixty per cent of the three thousand undergraduates voting in a poll (in May) were in favour of conscription, and nearly half of those who voted against it were not opposed to military service. (When the Union debated the motion 'That this House is glad it was born when it was' a week later, there were thirty-one noes and only thirteen ayes.)

Those with memories of the 1914–18 war, however, were all too well aware of the inequities of any voluntary system. Duff Cooper, who advocated conscription because he believed that leaving it solely to the patriotic to defend their country was unfair, wrote in the *Evening Standard*: 'While still hoping for the best, we must prepare for the worst. Nor need we fear that the worst will prove too terrible . . . We have frightened one another long enough with tales of London lying in ruins and the end of civilisation. Our defences are in order, our plans are made, our resources are immense and our hearts are stout. Stern trials await us, but we shall face them with the fortitude with which our fathers faced them in the past, believing, as they did, that it is better to die as free men than live as slaves.'

Stirring as these words were, the reality was different and depressing. Only the Royal Navy was ready for war. The new weapons and aircraft for the army and the Royal Air Force were only just beginning to come through, and the manpower of Germany and Italy was greater than that of Britain and France. Perhaps it was these dispiriting facts that led Liddell Hart, military correspondent of *The Times* and close friend and unofficial adviser to the Secretary of State for War, Leslie Hore-Belisha, to declare that the advantage in any modern war 'was accentuated by the difference of aim between an aggressor and those he attacks. For him to succeed he has to conquer, but for them to succeed they have only to convince him that he cannot conquer, and that continued effort will bring more loss than gain. They are thus able to wage a far less exhausting kind of war. They would be wise to do so, instead of being misled by such catchphrases as "attack is the best form of defence", which is only true when the conditions fit it.' In modern war, he concluded, it is hard to find the right conditions for attack.

But at 5.30 a.m. on Good Friday, 7 April, the duty clerk at the

Foreign Office was awakened by the news that Italy had invaded Albania.

Mussolini had for long been regarded as, if not exactly A Good Thing, a benevolent dictator who at least made the trains run on time. In February, Chamberlain had found him 'straightforward and considerate in his behaviour to us . . . moreover he has a sense of humour which is quite attractive'. And had not that mirror of society, *Queen* magazine, written only recently: 'Mussolini first came into the daily consciousness of a great many people in this country by a gesture of simple humanity . . . he made Capri a sanctuary for birds'? From that moment his name was uttered affectionately by thousands who had never before given him a thought, said the magazine. 'He came to us a living force, liberating to our isle a myriad sweet-voiced messengers who but for him had struggled in trappers' nets and ended their winged destiny on toast in French restaurants.' This piece of sentimental twaddle did not, however, prevent *Queen* from featuring a hat decorated with what looked like an entire sweet-voiced messenger on the cover of its July issue.

The invasion and occupation of Albania were considered particularly outrageous. They were acts of naked aggression by a large country against a small one, and Mussolini's government in Rome, the central city of the Catholic faith, had chosen the most significant date in the Christian calendar for this iniquity. The bird-lover's troops occupied the Albanian capital, Tirana, and installed an Italian government; King Zog and his half-American wife Queen Geraldine only just escaped, fleeing with their two-day-old baby son to Greece. An English woman who heard the news on Good Friday said at once, 'This means war', and next morning her husband found her lying dead with her head in the gas oven. (The coroner criticized the alarmist tone of the news bulletin.)

The House of Commons was recalled, and met the following Thursday at 2.45 p.m.; the Prime Minister caught the night train back to London from Aberdeenshire on Easter Saturday; and the

Cabinet met on the morning of Easter Monday. Although 'disappointed' by Italy's behaviour, the Prime Minister said he did not see it as sufficient reason for bringing the Anglo-Italian Agreement to an end. Winston Churchill, chief Tory critic of the Prime Minister (after a firm speech by Chamberlain two weeks earlier, Churchill had supported him with the words: 'I find myself in the most complete agreement with the Prime Minister. I hope it will not do him any harm if I say so') asked why, at the crucial moment, the fleet had been scattered.

'If it had been in the Adriatic, and the Government had given a hint, the invasion might never have happened,' he said. One of the five great capital ships of the Mediterranean Fleet was in Gibraltar, another in the Eastern Mediterranean and the other three, said Churchill, were 'lolling about outside widely-spaced Italian ports'. He added that our destroyers were divided along the European and African shores while our cruisers were crowded into the harbour in Malta. Churchill wound up with a call for conscription – and another, more private, plea. On 15 April, Chamberlain was writing:

'. . . I heard from D. Margesson after the debate that Winston had asked him to dinner and, saying that this was no time for mincing words, informed him bluntly of his strong desire to join the Govt. In reply to enquiries he assured David of his confidence that he could work amicably under the PM who had many admirable qualities, some of which he did not possess himself. On the other hand, he too had great qualities and could do much to help the PM bear his intolerable burden, likely as it was to get worse as time went on. He would like the Admiralty but would be quite satisfied to succeed Runciman as Lord President. He thought Eden should be taken in too but observed that he could give much more help than Eden.'

Not surprisingly, the Prime Minister told Margesson, his Chief Whip, that he would let this suggestion 'simmer' a bit. 'It caught me at a moment when I was certainly feeling the need of help, but I wanted to do nothing too quickly. The question is whether Winston, who would certainly help on the Treasury Bench in the Commons, would help or hinder in Cabinet or in counsel. Last Saturday, for instance, he was at the telephone all day. Would he hear me out resisting rash suggestions of this kind?'

The US President, Franklin D. Roosevelt, had sent a message to both dictators urging them to give an assurance that for ten years at least they would not attack the independent nations of Europe and the Middle East ('hundreds of millions live in constant fear of a new war,' he wrote); if they would give such a promise, he would call a conference to discuss armaments reduction and the opening up of international trade. At the same time, he was hastily moving America's Atlantic Fleet to the support of its Pacific Fleet for, with the British Fleet now concentrated in home waters, the Japanese were becoming increasingly aggressive. The first reaction of the German press to the Roosevelt message was predictably hostile. 'A complete misrepresentation of the facts', 'a shameful war agitation', 'an impudent interference', thundered the German papers. On the same day, *The Times* carried a speech by Sir Arnold Wilson, MP, a noted appeaser.

'Behind Herr Hitler stands a united, virile and powerful nation which has given us all a lesson in the virtues and advantages of discipline and self-sacrifice. We and our Allies could keep the peace only if we follow the example of the totalitarian States in certain respects . . . we should base our attitude to recent Italian action in Albania on our own interests in the Mediterranean and the Baltic and not on sympathy with the old regime in Albania . . . [we] only expose ourselves to ridicule by posing as an authority on European morals', and so on. (It is only fair to record that Wilson was so shattered when war did break out that, although he was nearly fifty, he joined the RAF and became an air gunner in Bomber Command. He was eventually killed on a mission bombing the country he had once so much admired.)

Despite the threats and abuse from the German press which

were now daily directed at England, and the uncompromising statements of Hitler, the illusion that it was all some kind of ghastly dream or misunderstanding still persisted. A letter-writer to *The Times* described how he had met an old German friend, a liberal aristocrat with a withering contempt for the Nazis, who had expressed his countrymen's views of the international situation: 'There will be no war for the simple reason that we Germans will get everything we want without firing a shot. We all realize that you English haven't the faintest intention of fighting – only of rearming.' The writer objected: 'Surely you don't imagine we're rearming for fun? Don't you think it is some evidence of our intention to call a halt to aggression?' 'None whatever,' replied the German. 'You cannot humbug a military nation like us. If you had really meant to fight you would have brought in conscription long ago. Your rearmament is pure bluff. If it isn't, then it's just stupidity, for all the arms in the world are useless without the men to use them.'

He was not alone in his belief that war would not happen. On 23 April, the Prime Minister wrote to his sister Ida from Number 10: 'I have heard reports from Berlin both from Walter Buccleuch and Ronnie Brocket, who have been over there and had talks with many Germans including Ribbentrop. They say they were received in the most friendly fashion, that everyone was cheerful and calm, and expressed the greatest astonishment that there should be so much tension and anxiety elsewhere. They denied that they had broken the Munich Agreement, Hitler still considered himself bound by the declaration he signed with me, but he did not consider the Czech case was one that concerned the "common interests of our two countries". He was going to make a pacific speech on the 28th but I gathered would mock at Roosevelt as being completely out of touch with realities and with the really pacific nature of the German government. And finally, they were delighted that we were sending Henderson back and they would send Dirkson back too. So we are all under a complete misunderstanding. Hitler "really is a good young man" and we have all misunderstood him!! How are we to interpret all this?'

Reverting to a constant preoccupation – what to do with Winston – he added: 'The new Ministry of Supply was certainly not the post for him. Whether he should be taken into the Government is another question, but although his friends are very cross that he hasn't been invited on this occasion, the majority of my supporters are immensely relieved. The fact is that the nearer we get to war, the more his chances improve and vice versa. If there is any possibility of easing the tension and getting back to normal relations with the dictators I wouldn't risk it by what would certainly be regarded by them as a challenge, and I don't accept the view of the *Evening Standard* that if I don't take him in I shall get into serious trouble. Perhaps Hitler has realized he has now touched the limit and has decided to put the best face on it, but we won't take any chances. Look out for news on Wednesday.'

For Wednesday brought the news that the Prime Minister had finally made up his mind to bring in conscription, albeit of a limited kind. On 26 April, he announced in the House of Commons that young men of twenty and twenty-one – there were believed to be about 200,000 of them – were to be called up immediately for three months of intensive military training. Later, those from twenty-two to twenty-five would also be called up.

Reaction was immediate. In the ensuing debate, the Leader of the Opposition, Clement Attlee, rose to protest. Was the PM aware that this decision would break the solemn pledge given to the country and reaffirmed only four weeks ago that compulsory military service would never be introduced in peacetime? He concluded that such reneging on a promise could only increase mistrust in the Prime Minister.

Chamberlain replied that when people had time to consider 'the circumstances in which we are now living' they would agree that introducing conscription at this moment could not possibly

16 The Gala Performance at the Royal Opera House, Covent Garden. *From left to right:* the Duke and Duchess of Gloucester, Queen Mary, the French President, Queen Elizabeth, King George VI, Mme Lebrun, the Duke and Duchess of Kent

17 The artist Rex Whistler, who decorated the Royal Box for the Gala night (photo Howard Coster)

18 Robert Helpmann and Margot Fonteyn dancing *The Sleeping Princess* at the Gala Performance

19   Sir Philip Sassoon (photo Howard Coster)

20   Chamberlain with his Parliamentary Private Secretary Alec Douglas-Home
outside No. 10 Downing Street, 3 September – the day war broke out

SALUTE – to adventure

When the wings of the Royal Air Force sweep overhead—you have no need to look enviously upwards, The Royal Air Force has a place for men like you—men who want adventure and a life they can believe in. An engagement as a Short Service Pilot or Observer—for four or six years. Here is the chance you've been waiting for. Here is *your* opportunity to satisfy your ambitions. You'll be well paid. You'll find every facility for sport. You'll be among the grandest company you could wish for. You, too, will be flying in the world's finest aeroplanes. *Write to-day for full details to Air Ministry Information Bureau, Kingsway, W.C.2.*

JOIN THE **RAF**

IMPORTANT
Men in the provinces who cannot give full-time service to the R.A.F. can still become Pilots ; if they join the Royal Air Force Volunteer Reserve they will be trained to fly in their spare time. Write for full details to the Air Officer Commanding Reserve Command, Royal Air Force Volunteer Reserve, The Hyde, Hendon, N.W.9.

21   Advertisements campaigning for volunteers for the armed forces now began to appear regularly

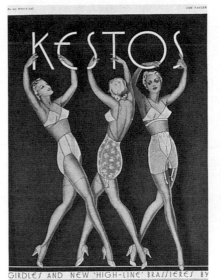

22   Girdles covered the wearer from waist to upper thigh

23   Hairstyles framed the face with curls or waves

24   Out in the country, sporting a good tweed suit

25   More women were now beginning to wear trousers, although they were still looked upon as rather daring

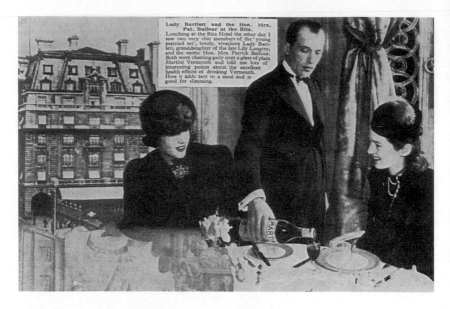

Lady Bartlett and the Hon. Mrs. Pat. Balfour at the Ritz.
Lunching at the Ritz Hotel the other day I saw two very chic members of the 'young married set', lovely, vivacious Lady Bartlett, granddaughter of the late Lily Langtry, and the exotic Hon. Mrs. Patrick Balfour. Both were chatting gaily over a glass of plain Martini Vermouth and told me lots of interesting points about the excellent health effects of drinking Vermouth. How it adds zest to a meal and is good for slimming.

26 Lady Bartlett and the Hon. Mrs Pat Balfour, lunching at the Ritz

27 Mrs Charles Sweeny, a famous beauty of the day

28   Princess Elizabeth, pictured a week before her thirteenth birthday, with corgi Dookie

29 Junior Kennedys: *from left to right*, Joseph Jr., Patricia, Robert and Kathleen

30 The great staircase of Londonderry House

be called a 'peacetime' measure ('A quibble!' retorted Attlee); the German newspapers described it as 'Chamberlain's laughable threat' and made every effort to explain to the German public that it had been introduced in the teeth not only of the Opposition but also of the British people.

The Italians, who had been constantly repeating that the great weakness behind all British diplomacy was Britain's inability to count on an army up to continental standards in numbers and training, called it 'a vain attempt under French pressure to intimidate Germany'. A few days later, Hitler, as he had threatened at Wilhelmshaven, repudiated the Anglo-German Naval Pact which had limited German naval tonnage to thirty-five per cent of the aggregate tonnage of the naval forces of the British Empire.

Hitler had celebrated his fiftieth birthday on 20 April. George VI, on the advice of his Prime Minister, sent the Fuehrer congratulations. Among the eagles and the swastikas of the festivities, Dr Goebbels declared: 'There is no one on the globe who can remain indifferent to the name of Hitler. For some this name means hope, faith and future, for others it is the object of distorted hate, base lies and cowardly calumny. The great German Reich has now been brought to pass in the broadest sense, and the Fuehrer has brought peace to central Europe.'

Eleven

THE RIGHT WAY TO DRESS

One of the requirements of social life was the 'right' clothes, for men no less than for women. There was only one place in the world for the well-dressed man to attire himself: London was the world capital for tailoring, as it was for all other male accoutrements, from bespoke boots and bowler hats to black silk umbrellas with cane handles from Briggs. In Savile Row, a three-piece suit cost from twelve guineas or so to the twenty-three or twenty-four guineas charged by H. Huntsman and Sons, arguably London's best tailors. Douglas Fairbanks Senior would order forty suits a time from his London tailor.

In the country it was the day of the good tweed suit, again for both sexes. 'A good tweed suit will take you *anywhere*,' mothers would tell their daughters in satisfied tones (no doubt caused in part by a subliminal recognition of its anaphrodisiac qualities). It was worn with Aertex shirts, jerseys or blouses, wool or silk stockings according to the occasion, and highly polished brogues or, for racing, Newmarket boots. Both men and women often protected their shoes with galoshes.

The summer equivalent, for such outings as cricket-watching or tea parties, was, for women, the cotton dress (dresses, incidentally, were usually known as frocks), worn with little white gloves and stockings. Silk stockings were so ruinously expensive at six to eight shillings a pair, that all over London there were specialists who mended them invisibly by hooking up the dropped stitches of ladders: women who could be found sitting in corners of department stores, behind the scenes at a draper's, or in tiny booths with counters giving directly on to the street. War or no war, their departure was only a matter of time: the nylon stocking was on its way. 'A Du Pont employee has gone to work at the World's Fair for the past six weeks wearing the same pair of stockings and so far there have been no runs. At the end of the year the public may be allowed to buy them as cheaply as good silk stockings,' reported the *Sunday Express* in June; adding that this new stocking fabric might eventually ruin Japan's raw silk trade, which formed sixty-six per cent of its total exports to the United States.

Meanwhile, it was not possible to save by going without stockings on hot days. In London, to go barelegged was unthinkable – a woman in the Civil Service, for instance, who had turned up for work stockingless, would have been sent home for being improperly dressed, and the same rule held good in many other organizations. When skirts were long, twenty-odd years earlier, it had been possible to economize by buying 'half-silks' or 'quarter-silks' – stockings which were made of silk only to halfway up the calf or to two inches above the ankle, and thereafter of much cheaper lisle. But alas, 1939 was once more a Year of the Leg – the spring hemlines were seventeen inches above the ground.

What were unrealistically known as girdles covered the wearer from waist to upper thigh, while small, boned corselettes, the forerunner of the waspie, were just coming in to make the most of the new, waisted, spring clothes. However, a little relief was at hand: 'The newest device is an elasticated stocking top which saves wearing a girdle on hot days,' reported *Picture Post*.

Brassières, by contrast, were often cooler then than they are now, as they were made of natural fibres, usually cotton, the most luxurious ones mere wisps of silk or crêpe de chine. Most fastened with two long straps which, starting at each side, crossed over at the back beneath the shoulder blades and curved round the body to clip or button just under the opposite breast.

At bedtime, pyjamas were worn as often as night-dresses. Traditionally lace-trimmed and made of silk or crêpe de chine, night-dresses were on the whole for those who could afford someone to wash these delicate confections, or for the newly married, who wanted to enchant. Some rich women even had their sheets made of silk: one such woman recalls sleeping between pale pink crêpe de chine sheets embroidered with white satin appliqué. Young girls wore pyjamas – at boarding school, these were often of the ubiquitous Aertex – switching to night-dresses when they bought their trousseaux.

For men, an underwear breakthrough was at hand, with the triumphal arrival of jockey shorts, or as they were known in England, Y-fronts. Although they had been developed in 1933 by de Marly of Paris from the athletic jockstrap and quickly taken up in the US, these new pants did not arrive in England until 1938 and were only just beginning to catch on. 'The first really new idea in underwear for some time,' wrote the Editor of *Varsity* enthusiastically for his undergraduate readership. 'The pants are made with ultra-short legs and are a new style that gives maximum comfort, convenience and support,' he continued approvingly. 'Men need support every bit as much as women need the support of a brassière. Doctors have recommended jockey shorts because of their masculine support which takes the strain off important muscles. At the same time, bulges and shadows are eliminated so your outer garments hang better and look smarter. The new Y front has a convenient angled opening so that it cannot gape, while the Lastex belt keeps the garment in place. In the words of one American ad, it is "the underwear that ends squirming for ever".'

For both sexes, probably the most essential outdoor garment of all was the hat. Even in 1942, well on in the War, Beaverbrook was advising the young Tom Driberg that if he wished to stand for Parliament he should wear a hat: 'The British people will never vote for a man who goes hatless.' Smart women often wore hats indoors too, at private luncheon parties, perhaps for cocktails or the theatre, and always when lunching in a restaurant; and a hatless woman in church was unthinkable.

A few women challenged this unspoken diktat. A Miss Marguerite Martineau of Salisbury described in print the courage needed to lunch hatless in the West End; Lady Louis Mountbatten watched a polo match bareheaded (though she did wear a gold hair clip); and the *Daily Mail* considered it worthy of report when a woman magistrate took her hat off to sit on the Bench 'and won the admiration of all her sex'.

Not everyone connected with the Bench agreed that the wearing of a hat was irrelevant to the matter in hand. At the beginning of May, a woman witness was brought to court so hurriedly she did not have time to snatch up her hat. The solicitor who was calling her apologized on her behalf, but the Clerk said, 'She is entitled to be dressed as she likes so long as she is not disrespectful to the Court.' She felt so uncomfortable, however, that she would not enter the witness-box until she had borrowed a hat. Other Courts were not so liberal in outlook. In the same week a girl who had appeared hatless in a Fulham Court was told by the Chairman of the Bench to go and get herself properly clothed. And at Watford, not content with the solicitor's apology for his clients' hatlessness, the Chairman of the Bench said to the two women concerned: 'This case will be put back until you find something to cover your heads with.' Eventually they returned wearing handkerchiefs, and the case was allowed to proceed.

That spring, there was a fashion for tiny 'dolls' hats', worn perched high on the head, tipped slightly forward and to one side. They were generally embroidered with beads or feathers or, like Lady Illingworth's, made of silver fox fur. The silver trim on one such mini-pillbox was worked to represent the bonnet of a Daimler, 'though clients who own Rolls-Royces can also be accommodated,' said the milliner concerned. Otherwise, many were platter-shaped and speared with feathers, although black felt pillboxes to top chignons were coming in.

Hair was worn in tight curls or waves, usually framing the face, and the heavy fringe or bang of the twenties had disappeared. If long, it was put in chignons, or twisted in plaits round the ear as 'earphones', but never loose and flowing. Styling was a matter of intense moment; and around half the female population had a perm of some description. 'The most photographed girl in the world, Miss Helen "Front Cover" Bennet has arrived in London,' reported the *Daily Mail*. 'She can do her honey blonde hair in 40 different styles and was the first to wear it in a pageboy in the States.' Men wore their hair in the traditional short-back-and-sides; moustaches were popular with soldiers and, in civilian life, if a moustache was worn, it was generally given a military cut. Beards were seldom seen, except occasionally on naval men. A sailor with a beard decorated Players' cigarette packets.

Make-up by now was an essential article of elegance. No woman with pretensions to chic would have gone out without at least lipstick and powder on her face. Women spent between £26 million and £27 million a year on cosmetics and skin-care creams, and wax baths, sunray lamps, diathermy, massage and mud face-masks were treats for those with enough money and time, and part of the back-up routine for girls earning their living as models.

Most models were between eighteen and twenty-two, with a working life of about six years. Although there were several hundred photographic models in London, fewer than a hundred were in regular work. The earnings of the lucky ones were about £9 or £10 a week, with a few stars achieving as much as £30. The measurements of models and glamour girls (as showgirls were then described) were never mentioned publicly and were, presumably, a matter between the girls themselves and the confessional of agency or casting office. Glamour girls, many of whom had been models and who were now earning around £5 a week, arrived behatted and elegant at auditions, each carrying her small suitcase or attaché case. Inside it were high-heeled shoes and a swimsuit, cut a little higher on the thigh than the average (women's swimsuits tended to end in an inch or two of leg), in which they paraded up and down the stage showing off their figures, walks and smiles. They did not dance. Chorus girls, on the other hand, did. The most famous were C. B. Cochran's Young Ladies, all twenty-four chosen for their perfect legs, dazzling smiles and ability to keep in step. Something of the Edwardian tradition still clung to them; notes, flowers, chocolates and invitations arrived with pleasing regularity at the stage door of any musical show.

Another sartorial rule of the day concerned mourning, donned after the death of a near relative. In Court circles this was adhered to rigidly; many of Queen Victoria's legion of grandchildren were now at the end of their lives, and at some periods the Court seemed to be perpetually in mourning. First came black, for full mourning, then a period of half-mourning during which grey, violet or white could be worn; when the King and Queen had visited Paris two years earlier, a wardrobe of all-white was devised for the Queen, whose mother had recently died. Apart from mourning, black was not considered a suitable colour for young women, and consequently it acquired an image of sophistication and *soigné* glamour. 'We used to long for someone to die so we could wear black dresses,' recalls one debutante.

For women, trousers were making headway, though still considered rather dashing. To be forbidden to wear them (as Newnham undergraduates were, at their end-of-term examination) was newsworthy; to wear them would make even more news. At one of the cricketing weekends regularly held at Hyde Hall, the home of Sir Walter Lawrence, women won the annual match between the male and female Elevens for the first time. As the *Evening Standard* reported: 'The male XI, apart from two who were naturally left-handed, batted and even fielded left-handed but they won in previous years despite this handicap. But this year hard hitting by Miss Lawrence's sister and an ex-Roedean player took the girls to victory . . . Nearly the whole female team wore trousers!'

Mrs Robert Laycock, the sister of the Prince of Wales's former mistress Freda Dudley Ward, caused a stir when she played golf wearing shorts; and when Miss Gracie Fields went home to Capri in the summer of 1939 after recovering from an illness, the fact that she was wearing trousers was unusual enough to make the headlines. All the same, Dr Willett Cunningham, who had made a twenty-year study of women's fashions of the last two hundred years, prophesied that 'in the next generation girls will go to the office in trousers'. The *Daily Mail* reporter, clearly aware of how his readers would be reacting to this outrageous statement, reminded them: 'Remember, you are listening to a man who knows his subject.'

Most smart women had their clothes made, and dressmakers frequently came to the house for fittings, often in the evening for the convenience of their clients. In the smart world, unwritten rules governed what clothes were worn at what time of day. In Paris, tailor-made suits (*le tailleur*) were only for the morning; in England a coat and dress would take you through the day.

Jewellery was equally formalized. Twin diamond clips – or sometimes diamonds with rubies or sapphires – that linked to form a brooch still reigned supreme; 'fruit salad' brooches, with rubies, emeralds, diamonds and sapphires making up baskets of flowers, were also popular. Jewels were set as well on powder boxes, compacts, and cigarette cases. A handsome string of cultured pearls could be had for around £35. The most fashionable rings were diamond, or diamond and sapphire, both set in platinum (all the royal jewels were set in platinum, eighteen carat white gold or, sometimes, silver gilt). Rubies and emeralds were set in gold. Jewellery invariably figured in the lists of presents printed by *The Times* after a smart wedding along with the shagreen cigarette boxes, Cona coffee-making machines, hunting saddles, silver card cases, fitted luncheon baskets and leather blotters. The Duchess of Northumberland's wedding present to her daughter was a triple row of pearls with diamond and pearl clasp, a single row with black pearl fastening, and a summer ermine coat.

Luncheons at smart restaurants were dressy affairs involving furs, jewellery and smart hats. 'You couldn't be overdressed for a big luncheon party,' recalls Margaret, Duchess of Argyll. In the houses of the well off, changing for dinner was *de rigueur*; this invariably meant evening dress whether or not there were guests – a long evening-dress, probably one of her older ones, for a woman, worn with a shawl round the shoulders if the house was cold, and dinner-jacket or smoking-jacket for a man. Even dance hall hostesses observed this convention, wearing the usual long evening-dress and gold or silver slippers. Men in the Brigade of Guards or Household Cavalry were not supposed to take a girl out to dinner or to the theatre without wearing a white tie.

At the couture houses, a rigid and formal hierarchy prevailed. At Worth, for example, juniors, paid ten shillings a week, were not allowed to wear either cardigans or flat shoes, nor were they allowed to use the front stairs. Each vendeuse had 'her' clients, jealously guarded, for the creations hand-sewn in the salon's workrooms. These were of silk, crêpe, taffeta, marocain, brocade or satin. (Synthetics were still in their infancy; Terylene, invented in 1941 at the Calico Printers' Association works in Lancashire, was immediately declared a secret by the wartime Ministry of Supply.)

Debutantes, who needed as large a wardrobe as they could manage, did sometimes buy 'off the peg', taking advantage of the silk afternoon-dresses that shops such as Peter Jones sold for a mere 19s 6d, cheap even by the standards of the day. Soon these were to have a rival: when C & A opened in March 1939 at Marble Arch, its opening sale of over seven thousand garments offered dresses for under £1, a 'dressy frock or two-piece' for 19s 11d, gored skirts for 4s 11d and hats for 18s 9d.

But most of those who took part in the Season paid much more for their clothes. The average ball dress cost perhaps between £12 and £14 with a top price of £20 for the most expensive. Even the most sumptuous wedding-dresses, often involving weeks of sewing and embroidering, could still be had for less than £50. So cheap was labour that even underclothes were still sometimes hand-made – though most women would have looked with interest at an advertisement for 'all silk crêpe de chine slips reduced from 25s to £1, with panties to match at 8s 11d', along with a headline proclaiming 'Bargains in teagowns and furs!' Few debutantes wanted a teagown but all of them looked longingly at furs, more or less out of bounds until they were either married or older; one of the commonest wedding presents of the day from wealthier parents to their daughter was fur, in the shape of coat, stole or wrap. More often than not, this would be silver fox.

For if any fur could be said to represent a decade, silver fox stood for the thirties. Smart women wore it as a small cape over a crêpe or marocain afternoon-dress, swathed dripping from their shoulders as stole or tie anywhere from Ascot to a luncheon party, made up into hats and as huge collars and cuffs for cloth coats. Fox – white, silver or dyed in pinks and blues – was the Queen's favourite fur.

There were signs, however, that this monopoly was about to be broken. Silver fox in particular, once the epitome of style and *luxe*, was losing its exclusive image. Worse still, it was gaining quite a different one. A few years earlier, the ranching of silver fox had begun and by 1938 it was so widespread that a million of these skins were produced by the breeders of Canada, the US and Scandinavia. The result was that this indispensable glamour accessory was now within the financial reach of prostitutes, who by 1939 would march up and down Regent Street in their silver fox jackets. When last night's takings and old money sported the same pelt, it was time to move on – especially when both, as often happened, patronized the same showroom.

Regular customers now turned to a fur still high in price and comparatively rare. The age of mink had begun. Again, ranching was to lower prices but not until many years later, and 'mink' still meant to most people wild mink, expensive, scarcer and much paler than the rich dark brown of the skins just beginning to arrive from the first mink ranches. More expensive still was the rare chinchilla; to make a cape like the one Princess Arthur of Connaught wore took as many as forty skins.

With no scruples in that pre-war climate about the right of the original owner to retain its fur coat, the very rich would have a whole wardrobe of furs – a mink or a sable, a leopard or ocelot coat for sporting events such as race meetings, a beaver coat for exercising the dogs in the country, and several fur ties or stoles, at least one of which would be silver fox. Other popular furs were ermine – either white or dyed in different colours – Canadian squirrel, nutria, skunk, civet cat, opossum, Persian lamb, fitch. Most were made up into coats or stoles, although jackets, bulky and square-shouldered, in unfamiliar skins like wolf, raccoon, wolverine and lynx were predicted by the experts for the coming autumn. All of them, however, thanks to the less sophisticated curing techniques that produced heavier, stiffer pelts, shared two characteristics. Their lack of suppleness meant that not much tailoring was possible; the prevailing style had straight up-and-down lines, a shawl collar and turnback cuffs. And they were extraordinarily heavy. But with little or no central heating, no heaters in cars and no thermal underwear, fur was one of the few real defences against the cold.

Twelve

AS THE SUMMER STARTS

As April drew to a close, life, to all intents and purposes, was still normal. In America, the curious craze for that year was in full swing. After flagpole-squatting and marathon dancing had run their course, it was the year of the repulsive pursuit of goldfish-swallowing; the record was won by a Boston boy who swallowed twenty-nine of the unfortunate fish, all alive, using milk as a chaser. In Paris, a 'naughty' fashion was seen at Longchamp racecourse: a short, ballet-like skirt with a flounced broderie anglaise petticoat, threaded with black velvet ribbon, peeping provocatively out beneath. In London, the first giant pandas to be seen at the London Zoo, installed the previous December, were attracting record attendances. Another animal to become well known later was also making his entry into public life: Dookie, the first of the royal corgis, had become the pet of the two princesses. He appeared with his mistresses and their mother, whose large fox fur cuffs bore an uneasy resemblance to the characteristic corgi ruff.

Princess Elizabeth was also acquiring some new clothes. For her thirteenth birthday on 21 April, her mother gave her a new riding-habit and some silk stockings, though she continued to wear her familiar white knee-socks in public. From her father, she received a diamond-studded bracelet and from Queen Mary a silver dressing-table set. A cine-camera and projector arrived from her uncle David, who put a call through from France to

Windsor Castle to wish his niece many happy returns of the day; they talked for ten minutes, and after thanking him for his present the Princess politely enquired if he was keeping well.

But the highlight of the day was undoubtedly the birthday tea party in the Oak Room, where the two-tier cake, surmounted by thirteen candles, stood in the centre of the table. The Princess managed to blow them all out in one go before cutting the first slice. She must have wondered how much good fortune this would bring: a few days earlier she had taken part with her parents in an ARP exercise at Windsor, where they had learned how to decontaminate themselves after a mustard gas attack (used by the Italians in Abyssinia).

Budget Day on 25 April passed without change in the income tax rate of 5s 6d in the £1. Cambridge won the ninety-first Boat Race, beating Oxford by four lengths in nineteen minutes and three seconds, and in Piccadilly the police put the customary suit of armour round Eros to prevent his demolition by excited supporters. Harrods Man's Shop was advertising shirts from 8s 6d for plain linen crash 'long-sleeved in navy, silver-grey, rust or natural', to 15s 6d for knitted wool or short-sleeved linen piqué sports shirts; and it had pressed into service Scott's verses, 'To mute and to material things/New life revolving summer brings.'

For anyone with the gift of clairvoyance, two other advertisements, both in *The Times* on 3 April, would have caused a shudder of horror. Both were for cruises, then fashionable with young as well as old. The *Jervis Bay*, it was announced, was sailing on 8 April for Colombo, calling at Malta, Port Said and Aden; seventeen months later, on 5 November 1940, by now an armed merchant cruiser, she was escorting a convoy of thirty-eight merchant ships in the Atlantic when they were intercepted by the heavily armed and armoured German pocket battleship *Scheer*. With only six-inch guns and no armour, she steamed across to shield the convoy by simultaneously drawing the Scheer's fire and laying down a smokescreen. She was quickly reduced to a burning hulk but her tactics succeeded, enabling the convoy to scatter and thirty-three out of the thirty-eight ships to escape. From the *Jervis Bay*, sixty-five survivors were picked up; her Captain, Fogarty Fegen – the son of a Vice-Admiral who lived in Tipperary – went down with his ship and was awarded a posthumous VC.

The second advertisement was for the *Arandora Star*. In June 1940, after the French collapse and Italy's declaration of war on Great Britain, there was a mass round-up of enemy aliens. Many had lived in this country for years and, like those in the hotel and restaurant trade, not only earned their living here but also considered themselves part of the fabric of British life. But because of the lack of time and qualified personnel needed to weed out active or sympathizing Nazis and Fascists, combined with panic and a generally antipathetic atmosphere, all were lumped together; and many were put on the *Arandora Star* to be sent to Canada for internment for the duration of the War. When she was sunk on 2 July 1940, 613 enemy aliens went down with her. The 470 Italians drowned included well-known names in the restaurant trade such as Italo Zangiacomi, General Manager of the Piccadilly Hotel for thirty years, Cesare Maggi, Restaurant manager of the Ritz, John (Giovanni) Sovrani, Manager of the Normandie Hotel, the Managers of the Hungaria Restaurant and the Café Anglais, Hector (Ettore) Zabattoni, Banqueting Manager of the Savoy, and Primo Pozzi, the chef of the Monseigneur and many members of their staffs. Cesare Bianchi and Luigo Vergano, head chefs at the Café Royal and Quaglino's, survived, as did the Italian owners of the Monseigneur.

But these tragedies were still to come. For the moment, smart London was fascinated by the prospect of a new gateway to romance. Two young women of twenty-five, both of whom had been presented at Court, were about to open Bond Street's first marriage bureau, clearly aimed at the sort of people likely to stroll down this expensive and socially exclusive thoroughfare. They were Miss Mary Oliver, the daughter of a country parson and Miss Heather Jenner, the only daughter of a brigadier. Miss

Oliver, the brains behind the scheme, had been attempting to start the business for some time; the previous year the London County Council's Public Control Department had refused to license her as a marriage broker but perhaps the coming of spring softened them, for they now relented sufficiently to allow her to offer romance on a cash basis for a probationary twelve months. The Misses Oliver and Jenner charged an initial fee of five guineas and another of thirty guineas for a successful conclusion to their introductions, 'but each client who doesn't like the person they've been fixed up with can have another try at the bureau for the same five guineas'.

On the Friday before the bureau opened, Miss Jenner, painting the walls of their tiny room a cheerful bright yellow for its official opening on Monday 17 April, declared that although she wasn't interested in marriage for herself just yet, she and Miss Oliver were 'already scouting around unofficially on behalf of the few men and women who want us to help them get married'. Three days later, the word 'few' was no longer applicable. From the moment news of the bureau appeared in the press, the girls were bombarded with applications, and by Monday evening they had received 250.

'I knew shy and lonely people would welcome the idea but I never thought so many people in social circles would seek assistance,' said Mary Oliver. What was perhaps even more remarkable was the perspicacity with which the two girls had discerned a new and highly specialized market. Country gentlemen, wealthy widows, the retired planters or soldiers from among Miss Jenner's acquaintance wrote and telephoned. A retired army officer of fifty, 'goodlooking and well set up', wanted to marry a 'goodlooking young girl who is interested in horses and good at games'; a peeress wanted a bride for her son who had 'an income of £2,500 a year but I want him to marry a woman with enough money to enable him to live up to his title when he inherits'.

Most of the men, even then, specified blondes, while women

wanted kindness and security from a man with some experience of the world. Debutantes, among the first to telephone the Bond Street Marriage Bureau, asked chiefly for older men ('I'm tired of the bright young men I meet. Please, please, find an intelligent, reliable man of about 40 to marry me!').

By now, the social roundabout was starting to whirl faster. The flat-racing season was well under way, with Lord Rosebery's Blue Peter winning the Two Thousand Guineas (run on 26 April) from a large field. As usual, the runners were almost entirely English-bred. The sport of kings was then dominated by the old aristocrats and magnates of the turf, whose names studded the race cards of every major meeting. Other owners with runners in the Two Thousand Guineas were Sir Abe Bailey, Lord Astor, Lord Derby, Mr James Dewar of whisky fame, Lady Ludlow, Lady Zia Wernher and the Aga Khan; the winner of the second race was owned by the Duke of Marlborough, the winner of the fifth, by the King.

Two days later, the Season began officially, with the Private View of the Royal Academy's Summer Exhibition, attended by everyone whom the Committee honoured with an invitation. In their top hats and their finery, they queued along Piccadilly to enter Burlington House that morning, to see and be seen, and perhaps to look at the paintings. Among these were the latest portrait of the King, by Mr Francis Hodge, and one of the Prime Minister by Mr James Gunn. This had been viewed early that morning by Mrs Chamberlain, who had come elegantly clad in a leaf green ensemble trimmed with nutria, and a green and brown hat. A portrait of Lord Baldwin by Oswald Birley was also on view and, almost inevitably, another of the beautiful Duchess of Kent, by Mrs Flora Lion. Yes, with the Season well and truly on course, perhaps things were not really so bad. Most reassuring of all to his many readers, Castlerosse was finally making a recovery from his long and tiresome illness. 'It is years since I have had so much kindness, especially from women,' he wrote. 'Most of the ones I know appear to have been born with No on their lips.'

Thirteen

PARTIES IN MAY

By the beginning of May the smart world was back in London. In Bond Street chauffeur-driven cars brought women in furs, their pet pekingeses or sealyhams on their laps, to shop for luxuries: an elegantly-packaged drum of one hundred gold-tipped Black Russian cigarettes, or a three-guinea Sulka shaving smock to save their husband's twenty-guinea silk dressing gowns from blobs of lather. On levee days officers of the armed services in full dress uniforms were to be seen there – MPs bidden to some state occasion sometimes put ordinary trousers on over their knee breeches to go to vote. On one such occasion Chips Channon recorded: 'I forgot my buckled shoes and was ragged about them.' Near the clubs, small flower stalls sold red carnations for the daily buttonholes.

The month began with two dinner parties for the King and Queen before they set sail for Canada on 6 May. Both were semi-official in character, a 'Godspeed' from the representatives of their host countries. On 2 May they dined with Vincent Massey, the High Commissioner for Canada and brother of the actor Raymond Massey, and his wife, at their home in Hyde Park Gardens. 'Ordinary' evening dress was worn: for the men, white tie and tails; for the women, their most splendid evening-dress and a tiara. The Queen was in white satin embroidered with silver, Mrs Massey in ice blue. The hall had been transformed into a bower of red rambling roses, through which they passed on their way upstairs to the green and cream dining room, where the High Commissioner, a keen collector of glass, had ordered some of his finest pieces to be set on the table.

Two days later, they were entertained at the American embassy in Princes Gate by virtually the entire Kennedy clan. A fortnight earlier, the ambassador had received the Freedom of Edinburgh and the honorary degree of Doctor of Laws at Edinburgh University where he had made a stirring speech about the sterling qualities of human nature, talking in vintage Kennedy style of 'Freedom. Faith. Friendship. Knowledge. Courage. The will to serve.' This did not prevent him from privately taking the view that in any war with Germany, Britain would be soundly beaten.

But at that time any expression of these opinions was still more or less confined to confidential exchanges with fellow Americans, and his wealth, energy and easy manner, coupled with the beauty and elegance of Rose Kennedy, made the Ambassador and his wife one of the most glamorous couples at the Court of St James's. Their children were immensely popular. All good-look-ing, with dazzling white even smiles, superbly healthy and bubbling with vitality, the young Kennedys took part enthusiast-ically in all that the English social scene had to offer – though if their English friends had known that Jack, so handsome, friendly and boyish, was writing his senior honours thesis on 'Great Britain's Unpreparedness For War', the warmth of their welcome might have been somewhat abated.

The retardation of the eldest girl, Rosemary, had not yet manifested itself severely enough to keep her from leading a comparatively normal life under the careful eye of her mother; two years earlier, after much anxious thought and preparation, Rosemary had successfully negotiated presentation at Court along with her sister Kathleen. Eunice, presented at the first March Court of 1939 by her mother, was asked to virtually all the debutante parties.

Kathleen, less formal, more friendly, open and forthcoming

than the average English girl, had a retinue of admirers, but by then was in love with Lord Hartington, the eldest son of the Duke of Devonshire, much to the consternation of their families. Both the firmly Protestant Cavendishes and the deeply Catholic Kennedys abhorred the idea of a mixed marriage. So by August, when Kathleen's feelings had become more intense, Rose refused to allow her daughter to return from the villa near Cannes, in which the Kennedy family were staying, to attend Billy Hartington's twenty-first birthday celebrations at Chatsworth. But that spring, with the summer stretching fresh and golden in front of her and the first real love of her life like a beacon ahead, 'Kick' Kennedy found it hard to view the international situation with as much gloom as her compatriots did. 'It's really amazing you can sound so pessimistic about war,' she wrote to a friend a fortnight before her parents' party. 'People over here are absolutely calm compared to Americans.'

Rosemary, Kathleen and Eunice, together with their 'sub-debutante' (an epithet borrowed from American papers for the occasion) younger sister Patricia and brothers Jack and Joseph Junior, attended the royal dinner party given by their parents, albeit seated slightly apart at a small table for six at one side of the dining room. Joe Junior had just returned from Spain, where for three months he had been observing the Spanish Civil War in its last stages, sending back letters that were more like despatches. These, his father would proudly read out – once to an assembled company which included both the Prime Minister and the Editor of *The Times*. (Kennedy had originally refused to allow his son to go to Spain on the grounds that as he held a diplomatic passport this would not be proper. Joe circumvented this parental ban by waiting until his father was visiting the US then going to Paris, where he exchanged his diplomatic passport for an ordinary one, with a journalist's visa to facilitate entry to the more remote and dangerous spots, and departing immediately for Spain.)

Joseph Kennedy and his wife Rose, in a pale green frock

embroidered with green crystal beads, received the royal couple in the embassy hall, glamorously bedecked with pink arum lilies and climbing roses swathed up a glass wall floodlit from behind. Upstairs, a further profusion of flowers awaited them: immense pots of lilies and great vases of apple blossom in the 'French' drawing room, with glimpses in the pine room beyond of bowls of nasturtiums in brilliant oranges, reds, yellows. The Queen, in a crinoline dress of the palest pink satin, its skirt caught with pink bows and pink flowers, a full tulle scarf, large diamond necklace and tiara, sat between her host and Mr William Bullitt, the American ambassador in Paris who had flown over for the occasion, and no doubt bewitched them both with her well-known charm. When, in 1923, her engagement to the Duke of York had been announced, Chips Channon had written in his diary, 'half the clubs in London are in mourning'.

By now the Season was in full swing, and the grand hostesses were giving elaborate parties. These women were a breed of their own. Some gave political parties, like Lady Londonderry. An imposing presence, she would stand at the top of the great staircase of Londonderry House, and her dignified grandeur would be echoed in the classical statues surrounding the hall. But most hostesses entertained not so much for a cause (if the pre-war Conservative Party could be so described) but as a way of life and, almost, a profession. For Syrie Maugham, the daughter of Dr Barnardo and the former wife of Somerset Maugham, it was both. Syrie was the first of the society decorators and the originator of the all-white room – her decorating establishment became known as 'headquarters of the white furniture traffic' – and many of her guests later became clients. So did those of Lady Colefax, also a decorator ('the middle class wife of a middle class barrister,' wrote Conrad Russell to Lady Diana Cooper), whose speciality was artistic and literary stars such as H. G. Wells, André Maurois and Rex Whistler.

Some of these women were hugely rich, like the corncrake-voiced Mrs Ronnie Greville, probably the archetypal hostess of the inter-war period. Born out of wedlock, Maggie Greville's origins were humble: her mother had been housekeeper to her father, the Rt. Hon. William McEwan, PC, for Edinburgh Central. Later McEwan, who as a widower was reputed to have fathered many offspring, married his mistress and made their daughter Margaret heir to his immense wealth. She married Ronnie Greville, a son of the second Lord Greville, who was a great friend of George Keppel, husband of Edward VII's mistress – so at one bound Mrs Greville was at the heart of Edwardian society. She maintained her position as Court intimate throughout three reigns. Queen Mary invited her to luncheon in her box at Ascot, and when she went there one year suffering from phlebitis, her carriage was given permission to draw up at the Royal Entrance to save her undue exertion. As Duke and Duchess of York, the King and Queen spent part of their honeymoon at her house Polesden Lacey and it was the first house they visited after their accession; they frequently went to dinner parties at her London house, 16 Charles Street; in the spring of 1939, they dined there on saddle of mutton, in a party of ten.

Mrs Greville was a forceful personality, cheerful, short and dumpy, with a round face and grey hair. She was famous both for her trenchant, witty and often caustic conversation, which did not spare those near or dear to her, and for her wonderful collection of jewels – emeralds, diamonds, and great ropes of pearls, which she wore with a black lace dress. At Polesden Lacey, a huge building of golden stone overlooking the surrounding Surrey countryside, she had had the long dining-table specially made so that people could talk to those opposite as well as to their neighbours on each side. Against the prevailing trend, she seldom decorated it with flowers, instead preferring the simplicity of superb damask linen, old silver and plain white candles with parchment shades. The tablecloth, like the napkins which bore her monogram, was woven in Ireland, the glass and china were plain and unadorned save for a narrow border of gold round the edges of plates, goblets and finger bowls, but the sixteen silver candlesticks, set in pairs down the table, were heavily chased. Between them stood tankards, goblets and porringers from her collection of Georgian and Carolingian silver.

A constant stream of visitors came to enjoy the paintings by Reynolds, Raeburn and Dutch masters, the marvellous gardens and superb food. Her friends were widely drawn, from the powerful and the political – Lord Willingdon, a former Viceroy of India, and Sir Samuel and Lady Maud Hoare – to the literary and cultured, like Sir Osbert Sitwell. Spangled with such names as Earl Balfour and the Aga Khan, the list of those entertained at Polesden Lacey ready like a between-the-Wars *Who's Who*. That summer, among those who stayed there were Princess Alice, Hector Bolitho, the former Prime Minister of Canada, Sir John Simon, Mrs Cornelius Vanderbilt and the ubiquitous Beverley Nichols. Another guest, whose minute, neat signature appears frequently in her Visitors' Book in the summer of 1939 was Professor Lindemann, Winston Churchill's scientific adviser. A house party in July included the Queen of Spain (who stayed for a fortnight), Lord George Cholmondeley (the younger brother of the Lord Great Chamberlain), and Lady George, Viscount Horne and the Earl and Countess of Abingdon and Lindsay.

International glamour was represented by Mrs Reginald Fellowes, who lived in Paris but took a house in London every year for the Season, and was to be seen anywhere the occasion was sufficiently smart to warrant her appearance. Dark and amusing, Daisy Fellowes was not particularly pretty but she was immensely chic. 'She wore a white frock with a black coat but I found her coiffure more interesting than her clothes,' wrote Corisande of the *Evening Standard*. 'Her hair was drawn up from the back of the neck, and arranged in three curls suspended horizontally from somewhere near the top of her head. One or two were arranged about her forehead. Her hairdresser found the inspiration for this new style of hairdressing in a painting in the National Gallery.' A few days before this breathless comment appeared, Mrs Fellowes had been seen in Bond Street with a new style of handbag that added fuel to her sartorial reputation. Its frame was shaped like a double piano keyboard; by turning a small handle, she set going the musical box inside, so that passers-by heard the sound of tinkling music as she approached. 'Such was her attention to detail,' ran one awed report, 'that the buttons on her black suit were cut in the shape of a piano!'

Another hostess noted for the lavishness of her entertaining was Mrs James Corrigan, said to have inherited a fortune from her husband, an American steel magnate, vast enough to bring in an annual income of £150,000. She had a sporadically imperfect grasp of the English language (she is supposed to have said of a cathedral that 'the flying buttocks were magnificent'), a small pointed face, and stood on her head every day to improve her circulation. She was rumoured to be bald, and to possess a wardrobe of wigs: 'a perfectly set one, a windswept one, a "must go to the hairdresser" one', according to Loelia, Duchess of Westminster. She rented palazzi in Venice which she filled with a constant stream of house guests whose every need was catered for: notes were left on the bedside tables exhorting guests not to tip the servants, buy stamps or cigarettes, pay at the hairdresser, cleaner or for drinks at the Grand Hotel or Lido bar. She brought over bands and cabarets from the Continent to enliven her dances in London, and was the first person to introduce the tombola at parties, and the prizes she gave – one to a man, one to a woman – came from Cartier. One of the most usual was a gold cigarette case. She was also a crashing snob and it was noted by her guests that these sumptuous presents were always won by members of the aristocracy in strict order of precedence. This accuracy was, no doubt, a tribute to her brilliant social secretary.

But Laura Corrigan was no empty head. Although her parties during the Season of 1939 were as splendid as ever, she realized that with the coming of war, grandeur of this kind would go, and she spent much of August giving away silver and household effects to friends. Lady Munster, Lady Weymouth and Lady

Milbanke received silver and linen, large quantities of which she had always kept stored in London ready for whatever house she took – though she kept her personal sheets of pink crêpe de chine – and to those who already had linen, she gave jewellery. True to her principles of aristocratic precedence, the chief beneficiaries were the Duchess of Kent and the Marchioness of Londonderry.

Most famous of all these women, perhaps, was Emerald (born Maud) Cunard, who mixed beauties and politicians, aristocrats of the oldest lineage and the lions of the literary world, ancient enemies and new sparkling talent, to devastating effect. Her wit and inconsequent charm, along with her fluffy yellow hair and little hooked nose caused one observer to describe her as 'a canary of prey', another to call her 'an enamelled bergerette', and the writer George Moore to adore her for years. She eventually directed that her ashes be scattered over the few hundred square yards of London that were for so long the centre of her life, Grosvenor Square. Though she was well read and had a real feeling for literature, her main passion was for music, and in particular, opera. She worked unsparingly behind the scenes to help the cause of English opera, entertained most evenings during the opera season; and her greatest love affair was with the fiery conductor, Sir Thomas Beecham, then at the height of his enormous powers.

Most of these hostesses gave their most important party later on in the Season, the middle of June being the most favoured time. But for the debutantes, there were now dances every night. One of the biggest was given by Lady Astor at her house at 4 St James's Square, for her niece Miss Dinah Brand. This glamorous entertainment was attended by the Duke and Duchess of Gloucester and the Duke and Duchess of Kent, who were among the forty guests who dined with Lady Astor before the dance. Other guests around her oval dining-table, with its unusual centrepiece of an eighteenth-century Chinese pagoda hung with tinkling silver-gilt bells, were the American ambassador and Mrs Kennedy, Miss Eunice Kennedy, the Duke and

Duchess of Marlborough, the Duke and Duchess of Devonshire and Lady Rose Paget, one of the five good-looking daughters of the Marquess of Anglesey. Even in that era of lavish floral decoration, the flowers were exceptional – brilliant gold tassels of laburnum swaying overhead, great masses of mauve, pink and purple flowers in the ballroom itself, white gardenias and pots of arum lilies in the small sitting-out room whose exotic, languorous scent drifted out to ballroom and drawing-room.

Another big dance was given by Mrs Charles Hambro for her step-daughters Cynthia and Diana Hambro, at which everyone wore white, with the occasional coloured shoulder-straps. Most of the debutante dresses had the Winterhalter look of off-the-shoulder bodices above wide skirts, popularized by the Queen, though many of the older women still favoured the sleeveless, scoop-necked chemise styles fashionable earlier in the thirties.

Not all the evening entertainments were for the debutantes. Almost every night, Emerald Cunard could be seen at the Covent Garden Opera in the centre of a large party. On 3 May, Toscanini conducted the London Musical Festival concert at Queens Hall, an event that was social as well as musical. The King and Queen, Queen Mary and the Duke of Kent were there, the Queen and Queen Mary both in diamond tiaras and white fox fur wraps. Beautiful young women were much in evidence, chief among them Lady Elizabeth Paget, the most beautiful Anglesey daughter, dazzling in pale pink satin; also there were leaders of musical and literary London, such as Dr and Mrs Malcolm Sargent, Osbert Sitwell and Mr and Mrs Sacheverell Sitwell.

The following night there was a charity dance at the Dorchester, at which Lady Diana Cooper, asked to pick out the two winning tickets from the raffle for the prizes of a blank canvas (to be painted by portraitist Robin Guthrie) and a jeroboam of champagne, drew out first her own name and then that of her husband, Duff Cooper (he was a former Secretary of State for War and First Lord of the Admiralty and had been the only member of the Cabinet to resign in protest against the Munich

Agreement). Mr Guthrie must have been delighted, for he had always wanted to paint Lady Diana. The same night the indefatigable Lady St John of Bletsoe gave a huge cocktail party for around five hundred people graced by many of her protégées, some daringly in black, others in printed summery frocks.

On 5 May there was a notable party of a very different kind for an older age group, to celebrate the Golden Wedding of the Duke and Duchess of Portland. He was eighty-three and she was eighty; both were tall, handsome and distinguished-looking. The Duke, born in 1857, had first seen the Duchess, then Miss Winifred Dallas Yorke, the beautiful daughter of a country gentleman, at a railway station. There and then he swore he would marry her; and their wedding took place in 1889. Their union had been blissful: 'The best thing that ever befell me,' he said, 'was when the lady who is not only queen of my heart but queen of all hearts wherever she goes and wherever she is known, consented to be my bride.' The Duchess's recipe for married happiness was simple: 'If I have ever been rude to my husband during the day, I go to him before night and tell him how sorry I am.'

At the time of their marriage he was not a rich man, but when as a subaltern he succeeded his cousin, the fifth Duke, he inherited nearly 200,000 acres. At the Golden Wedding Dinner for members of the family on 11 June at Welbeck Abbey, near Worksop, all was splendour and magnificence. Dinner was served on the famous gold plate service given to the Duke as a wedding present; the Duchess wore the Portland diamonds (valued conservatively at £10,000) and, although it was Sunday, Worksop's post offices were specially opened to receive greetings from all over the world, including a telegram from Queen Mary.

The Duke was known for his grand manner, and there were many stories told about him. Once, when staying with a friend in Norfolk who had an excellent partridge shoot, he appeared so exceptionally cheerful that the head keeper remarked to the Duke's valet (who was loading for him): 'His Grace is in good form!' 'He certainly is,' replied the valet. 'He did a thing this morning which to my knowledge he has not done for twenty years. He put on his own braces.'

Fourteen

NEGOTIATIONS AND FRIVOLITIES

At the end of May, the newspapers contained a disconcerting mixture of the sinister and the mundane. Lord Castlerosse, recuperating in Paris, pronounced it a pleasanter place than London, 'the reason being that the French do not believe war is imminent'. The 500-year-old Dunmow Flitch contest to find the happiest married couple, interrupted only once previously in its history (by the 1914–18 war), was cancelled again, this time because those who ran it were too busy with national defence work and recruitment to organize it.

The negotiations with Russia, which had been initiated two months earlier and were to drag on the whole summer, were already proving troublesome. The Prime Minister was not the first, and certainly not the last, to feel the bewildering, exhausting effect of prolonged encounters with Soviet Russia. On 21 May he wrote to his sister Ida: 'I have had a very tiresome week over the Russians. Their methods of conducting negotiations include the publication in the press of all their despatches, and continuous close communication with the Opposition and Winston. I wish I knew what sort of people we're dealing with. They may be just simple straightforward people but I cannot rid myself of the suspicion that they are chiefly concerned to see the "capitalist" powers tear each other to pieces while they stay out themselves.

'It appears that we shall have to take the fateful decision next week, whether to enter into alliance with them or break off negotiations. Those who advocate the former say that if we don't agree Russia and Germany will come to an understanding which to my mind is a pretty sinister commentary on Russian reliability. But some of the members of the Cabinet who were most unwilling to agree to the alliance now appear to have swung round to the opposite view. In the end I think much will depend on the attitude of Poland and Rumania. If bringing Russia in meant them running out I should think the change a very disastrous one.'

Draft proposals that Great Britain, France and Soviet Russia would co-operate immediately in defence if any one of them was made the target of a (European) act of aggression, or 'if any of them is involved in war as a result of fulfilling assurances given to other states in Europe', were finally sent to Moscow that week. *The Times* of 27 May noted approvingly that such an agreement would be wholly defensive and, anyway, embodied the principles of the League of Nations Covenant. With the ball now in Russia's court, the Prime Minister, writing on 28 May, felt more cheerful:

'At the present time I am in a happier mood. The worst times for me, and the only ones which really cause me worry, are when I have to take a decision and don't clearly see how it is to come out. Such a time was the early part of last week. Halifax had written from Geneva to say that he had been unable to shake Maisky in his demand for the three party alliance. Daladier had insisted that it was necessary. Poland had raised no objection. The Dominions were divided. It seemed clear that the choice lay between acceptance and breaking off of negotiations. There could be no doubt that the latter would rejoice the heart of Berlin and discourage Paris and everyone. There was no sign of opposition to the Alliance in the press and it was obvious that refusal would create immense difficulties in the House even if I could persuade my Cabinet.

'On the other hand, I had and have deep suspicions of Soviet aims and profound doubts as to her military capacity even if she honestly desired and intended to help. but worse than that was my feeling that the alliance would definitely be a lining up of opposing blocks and an association which would make any negotiation or discussion with the totalitarians difficult if not impossible. The only support I could get for my views was from Rab Butler and he was not a very influential ally. In these circs I sent for Horace Wilson [Permanent Secretary to the Treasury, and Chamberlain's *eminence grise*] to see if I could get any light from discussion with him and gradually there emerged an idea which has since been adopted. In substance it gives the Russians what they want but in form and presentation it avoids the idea of an alliance and substitutes a declaration of our *intentions* in certain circumstances in fulfilment of our obligations under Article XVI of the Government . . . as soon as I had this idea clearly worked out in my mind I recovered my equanimity and have retained it ever since.

'It still remains to be seen what the Russians have to say but I think that they will find it difficult to refuse. All the information goes to show that we need not expect any coup at present but that preparations are being made to effect one (in Danzig) when a favourable moment arrives. We are therefore still in the danger zone but I myself still believe that Hitler missed the bus last September and that his generals won't let him risk a major war now. But I can't yet see how the detente is to come about as long as the Jews obstinately go on refusing to shoot Hitler.'

The phrase 'Hitler missed the bus' must have remained in Chamberlain's mind, for he used it with disastrous consequences the following year. In a speech made at the Central Hall, Westminster, on 4 April 1940, he said that he was ten times as confident of victory as he had been when the War began. Asking why it was that Hitler, in spite of all his long preparation for war, had not at the outset tried to strike a knockout blow at Britain and France, the Prime Minister said that, whatever the reason, one thing was certain: 'He missed the bus.' Five days later, Hitler invaded Denmark and Norway, carrying all before him. Chamberlain's opponents fastened on these words as evidence that he was quite unfit to conduct the war and had no grasp of the military threat; he resigned on 10 May. By 21 June, the British army had been ejected from Europe and Hitler had subjugated Denmark, Norway, Holland, Belgium and France. Those unhappily chosen words must have continued to haunt Chamberlain in the few months remaining to him – he died on 9 November 1940.

The legislation to introduce conscription was moving slowly through Parliament. The Labour Party stated that, though it must and would oppose the Bill, this policy would not prevent the Party attempting to amend the Bill at the Committee and Report stages in order to 'improve efficiency, break down class privileges, provide for the men's dependants, and assure full and fair safeguards for conscientious objectors'. (There were to be sixty thousand of these – almost four times as many as in the 1914–18 war.) But the Labour opposition on Second Reading was finally defeated by 387 votes to 145 and the Third Reading of the Bill was carried on 18 May by a triumphant 283 votes to 133. The following day the General Council of the Trades Union Congress, defending itself for co-operating with the Government, was handsomely supported by a thousand delegates.

Plans for evacuation of children from large cities were well advanced and suitable billets had by now been found throughout the country. The RSPCA held a conference of vets, horse-owners and drivers of horse-drawn vehicles to decide how best to protect their animals in the event of 'national emergency' – a phrase often employed to avoid mentioning the stark word 'war'. There were forty thousand horses in the Metropolitan area alone, and it was thought the bombing which all the experts forecast would drive them so mad with terror they would rampage down streets to the danger of themselves and those they encountered. Westminster Abbey was now open by night as well as day, so that people could keep a Vigil for Peace.

In the drawing rooms of London, the dancing gathered

momentum. On 17 May, Queen Charlotte's annual Birthday Ball at Grosvenor House saw the usual parade of debutantes; 228 of them, eight abreast, followed the huge iced birthday cake behind Lady Willoughby de Broke, slim and erect in white satin and diamond tiara. Down each side of the room was a 'guard of honour' formed by 108 debutantes of the two previous Seasons, and the cake was cut by Princess Helena Victoria (a granddaughter of Queen Victoria), attending the ball in Lord and Lady Howard de Walden's party. The tiara'd chaperones, who included five duchesses, were seated at tables all around the room, proudly watching the progress of daughters and nieces.

The social climax of the month was Derby Day, run that year on 24 May, and televised for the first time from start to finish by the BBC. The main commentary was by Freddie Grisewood, but during the race itself viewers were treated to another by the ever-popular Commander Thomas Woodroffe. (On the face of it this was perhaps an odd choice. Two years earlier the gallant Commander had won immortality for himself when he was commentator on the Coronation Review of the Fleet. His task was to put into words for listeners the spectacle of the illuminated fleet, with every ship dressed overall with fairy lights, and the moment at which they were to be switched off simultaneously. But earlier in the day the King had ordered 'Splice the mainbrace!'; the combination of alcohol and the cool night air of late May had had their effect, and the only words which emerged were 'The fleet'sh lit up – the fleet'sh lit up – I mean with fairy lights.' A moment later the lights were switched off and 'Tommy' Woodroffe further regaled listeners with 'Now the whole ruddy fleet'sh gone. Disappeared. I mean, can't shee it any longer . . . the whole damn – sorry – the whole thing'sh gone . . .' At which point the BBC faded him out.)

For the Duke of Gloucester, the King's representative while he was away, Derby Day started with a levee which he held at St James's Palace. The Duke of Kent and Lord Harewood were also present; then, with the Princess Royal, they all went on to see

Queen Mary at Marlborough House. The Queen Mother had just suffered a wretched accident: her car had collided with a lorry, and overturned at the junction of Wimbledon Park Road and West Hill Road, and her eye had been cut on a sharp edge of the car's woodwork. Among the four eminent medical men who rushed to Marlborough House to examine it was Sir John Weir, the first homeopathic doctor to be appointed by the Royal Family, and a physician to the King. The damage was rather more serious than the various bulletins issued by her doctors indicated – at one time there was doubt as to whether the sight of that eye could be saved – bruising was extensive, and she was suffering considerable pain. She bore it with her usual bravery and stoicism and all her family rallied round; as well as visitors, every afternoon she received a cable from the King and Queen in Canada, to whom she returned cheerful messages. Marlborough House was also besieged by so many members of the public anxious to show their sympathy by signing the Visitor's Book there that the police had to institute special traffic controls.

After visiting Queen Mary, the royal party set off for Epsom in three cars. It was a glorious day (the temperature rose to 77°F) and smart racegoers dressed to match. Once again the Duchess of Kent was pre-eminent ('even in mourning she is more elegant than other women,' Chips Channon had once written), in a white crêpe dress and jacket patterened with a soft red and edged with fine white pleats, a small white straw hat and tulle veil setting off her dark hair. Her semi-tailored style was echoed by other women. Mrs Anthony Eden wore a navy blue crêpe dress, short jacket and poppy-red turban with long streamers hanging down the back; the Duchess of Gloucester was in a pale pink wool dress and jacket. Other women wore crisply cut, printed silk dresses with small straw hats or turbans; their more romantic, floating dresses and picture-hats were waiting in the cupboard until Ascot.

As with all pre-war racing, there were no starting stalls but a flag start. Also as usual, the owners were British, with the exception of the popular and enormously wealthy Aga Khan, whose runner that year was Dhoti. Lord Derby had entered Heliopolis; Sir Abe Bailey, Farnstone; Sir John Jarvis, Admiral's Walk and Mr Edward Esmond had secured the leading jockey of the day, Gordon Richards, to ride his Fox Cub. The race was won by Lord Rosebery's Blue Peter, ridden by Ephraim Smith and the seven to two favourite after his earlier win in the Two Thousand Guineas. The prize money was £10,550 10s. Lord Rosebery, whose father had won the Derby three times, took his victory with exemplary calmness. He arrived in the paddock, said Castlerosse, 'as unmoved as a divorce court judge, despite the fact that Blue Peter must now be worth at least £100,000 to him'.

That night, Lord Rosebery celebrated his win with a Derby Dinner at the Savoy, to which he invited all his racing friends, owners and jockeys and their wives and everyone who was connected with Blue Peter's victory. His party dined privately in the Pinafore Room, round which a Blue Peter flag was draped; there were pink and yellow flowers on the tables, and during dinner a slow motion film of the race was shown. In contrast to his unmoved demeanour on the course, Lord Rosebery spent most of dinner walking from table to table to joke with his guests and receive their congratulations. After dinner he took his party through to dance in the main restaurant, where his triumph was being celebrated in a similar way. It too was almost smothered in pink sweet peas, guests were given favours in the Rosebery colours of pink and primrose yellow and sat at tables decorated in spun sugar confections in the same shades. They ate a special thirty-shilling Derby menu – le Consommé Sportif, le Suprême de Sole Blue Peter, Le Filet de Surrey Epsom, and Le Parfait Glacé Lord Derby. They danced to the music of Carroll Gibbons and the Savoy Orpheans, supplemented that evening by Geraldo and his orchestra; and Lord Rosebery led the Duchess of Norfolk, in a blue frock embroidered with silver and diamante, on to the floor. At midnight pink and yellow balloons tumbled out of a great jockey cap suspended above the dancers, and even the cabaret was a comedy act with an equestrian theme, whose players, almost needless to say, wore the Rosebery yellow hooped in pink.

At Grosvenor House, the Derby Ball marked the beginning of the most socially intense weeks of the Season. Organized by Lady Welbeck and Mrs Peter Pleydell-Bouverie, it was attended by virtually everyone 'in Society' (except for those included in Lord Rosebery's party), from the Duke and Duchess of Kent – the best dancers in the royal family – to Kathleen Kennedy. By now, so crowded was the calendar of debutante dances and so bored the chaperones at the endless hours of waiting and watching, that several of the more daring began to bring their knitting to smaller dances. And there they sat along the walls, tiaras nodding incongruously over needles – but conscious that they were at least doing *something*.

Fifteen

HEALTH AND PANACEAS

The streptococcus which travelled down from the throat to the lungs of Sir Philip Sassoon, finally carrying him off on 3 June 1939, was an enemy to which no real defence had yet been found. Without antibiotics, then unknown, infections lingered on and the state of health of well-known persons was a frequent subject for bulletins in the newspapers, sometimes in the social column of *The Times* or sometimes, with more detail, in gossip pages. One typical entry read: 'Mrs Euan Wallace, considered the most popular of all politicians' wives and the best listener in London, is lying ill with glandular fever.'

These snippets were not mere frivolous reportage, but a subject of very real interest. Thousands of men and women died young every year, either from infections which post-war generations would regard as comparatively mild, or from diseases which have now been virtually wiped out. As recently as 1937 a patient had had to have her leg amputated after puerperal fever following a home confinement, and she took the case against her doctor all the way to the House of Lords. The *Lancet*, a faint note of outrage apparent in its report, called this 'a high water mark in patients' actions against their physicians'.

Thanks to sulphonamides, the incidence of many infections had dropped dramatically. The main venereal diseases, for example, were showing a steady decline. The number of cases of syphilis, it was reported at the ninth Imperial Social Hygiene

Congress on 22 July in London, had dropped from 42,800 in 1920 to the provisional figure of 18,034 in 1938; and gonorrhoea was also declining.

But many other diseases still remained killers. One was pneumonia. Despite M & B, this illness remained immensely dangerous – witness the deaths from it, within thirty-six hours of each other in the spring of 1939, of the distinguished anthropologist Dr Leonard Buxton, the Bursar of Exeter College, Oxford, and his wife, both in their forties.

Up to two thousand children still died every year of diphtheria, a state of affairs by then regarded as a scandal. 'The 60,000 or so schoolchildren in London could be made completely safe from diphtheria at a cost of about £70,000,' said a report from the Medical Research Council, and Sir Edward Mallund pointed out in the Robert Mead lecture at Cambridge on 28 April that 'diphtheria could soon be cleared out of England by the immediate preventative inoculation of infants and children, as has been done in Ontario'. The following year, a nationwide programme of immunization was launched.

But undoubtedly the most lethal of the diseases subdued or vanquished since the war was tuberculosis, which accounted for approximately one-third of all deaths from disease among young adults. In 1938, it killed a total of 26,176 men, women and children in England and Wales. One reason was that pasteurization of milk was not compulsory, and new cases often developed from drinking milk containing the TB bacilli. The real root of the problem, however, was appalling housing, in damp, crowded conditions; worst afflicted were the poorest districts of Wales. 'Racial susceptibility per se is a minor factor,' said the *Lancet*, pointing out that 'in many areas there are deplorable conditions in regard to housing, nutrition and conditions in schools'. Most at risk were children who had been subjected to the possibility of infection since birth and those who had to spend the greater part of their time inside these damp, rotten houses. Hence, not surprisingly, the disease took its greatest toll of girls between the ages of fifteen and twenty-five, an age-group in which both these factors overlapped. In Wales, the female death rate in this group was sixty per cent higher than that among Welsh men – and sixty-seven per cent higher than in any English group.

Without antibiotics, surgery was slower and more dangerous. This was especially true in reconstructive or plastic surgery, which frequently involved a whole series of operations with skin-grafts, each of which had to recover from sepsis before the surgeon could continue with the next one. Until penicillin became available during the war, treatment for those burned or facially disfigured was long drawn-out and often agonizingly painful.

In 1939, cosmetic surgery was comparatively rare (the famous 'face lift' that had wrecked the looks of Gladys, Duchess of Marlborough, was in fact a series of wax injections above the bridge of the nose, designed to give her a straight Grecian profile. But reconstructive surgery was about to make a major leap forward. Hardly known before the 1914–18 war, it had become a specific and recognized branch of surgery as a result of the great number of men returning from the trenches with terrible facial injuries.

The 'father' of modern plastic surgery was Sir Harold Gillies, a New Zealander whose work during the 1914–18 war established many of the techniques in use today. By about 1920, most of the wartime casualties had been dealt with, the American, Dominion and Commonwealth doctors who had worked with Gillies had gone home, and the demand for reconstructive surgery had dropped dramatically. Gillies himself, knighted for his work in 1920, dominated this specialist field in the UK between the wars. In the early thirties, he was joined by his cousin Archibald McIndoe and later by a third New Zealander, Rainsford Mowlem, and an Englishman, Thomas Pomfret Kilner, all of whom trained with Gillies. These four men were the only recognized practising plastic surgeons in the country.

When, in 1938, war appeared imminent, it was anticipated that a high proportion of military and civil casualties would involve facial wounds and the Ministry of Health decided to establish four maxillo-facial units under these four men. At the outbreak of war, Gillies himself was established in Queen Mary's Hospital, Roehampton, Mowlem worked at Hill End Hospital near St Albans, Kilner's unit was in Oxford, and McIndoe had finally found the site he was looking for at the Queen Victoria Hospital, East Grinstead.

Because plastic surgeons were skilled at skin-grafting, they had for a long time been called upon to deal with serious burn cases. One of the great problems was the administration of general anaesthetics, which in the thirties often involved masks or other external appliances. These, of course, were impossible to use on the appallingly burned faces of Battle of Britain pilots and other wounded. In the 1914–18 war Gillies's anaesthetist had devised a technique of passing a tube into the trachea that caused no interference with breathing, and subsequently this became standard practice.

But infection was not so easy to counter, and reconstructive surgery that required several skin-grafting operations meant long spells in hospital or on leave as the patient waited for the infection to disappear. 'The smell of the bandage under my nose became so powerful that I took to dosing it liberally with eau de cologne,' wrote Richard Hillary, after a skin-graft by McIndoe to give him a new upper lip. (When Hillary was shot down during the Battle of Britain, he was badly burned before he could parachute out of his Spitfire.)

In ordinary life, because so many infections could develop into lethal illness from comparatively small beginnings, initial symptoms were treated with far greater respect than they are today. Taking the potential invalid's temperature, for instance, had an almost mystical importance – especially in parental eyes – and half a point above 'normal' was enough to ensure a minimum of twenty-four hours in bed. Among the comfortably off, the well-equipped house had several thermometers in case one broke at a time of crisis; and more nervous individuals had personal thermometers reserved for their own exclusive use to avoid any chance of 'germs' – that malignant, invisible army waiting to pounce at the slightest hint of unwariness. Nannies took the temperature of their small charges at the first sniff, as a matter of routine (under the arm, in case the child bit the thermometer, swallowed the mercury and was poisoned) and woe betide the doctor who failed to do the same thing immediately on arrival at a child's bedside. Apart from Nanny's disapproval, fearsome enough in itself, he risked word getting round that he was either ignorant, uninterested or in too much of a hurry to be bothered.

The cult of the thermometer meshed in well with another important item of medical belief: the importance of bed rest. This was considered a vital part of most treatments – indeed, it often *was* the treatment. Illnesses suffered at home, such as influenza, generally meant a long and boring convalescence, first in the bedroom and later on a sofa. Once in hospital, most people remained for many weeks, often developing catarrh as they struggled free of pneumonia, while elderly people suffering, for instance, from a fractured femur, died of the pneumonia they caught from staying in bed. In many ways, it was more dangerous to go to bed with a complaint, especially if comparatively mild, than to ignore it and struggle on.

The helplessness of the medical profession in the face of much serious illness was largely hidden from the public by an impenetrable fog of jargon. When over half of those found TB-positive on first diagnosis in actual fact already had this killer disease in advanced form, no doctor wanted to add to his patient's fear by mentioning its proper name openly. It was termed 'Cock's bacillus' (a man called Cock had discovered the tuberculosis organism), which did not carry nearly the same charge of dread. 'Visceroptosis' covered most inflammation of the internal organs. The placebo was a valuable weapon, Tinct. Lavand. Co. (tincture of lavender compound) being a particular favourite; many swore by the efficacy of this pretty pink water. With little in the way of drugs in his pharmacopoeia, the doctor of 1939 had to use what he could find, and a patient's faith in his abilities was all-important.

In 1939 there were 61,109 doctors – of whom fewer than 6,000 were women – on the British Medical Register, a figure which worked out at roughly one for every 800 people. The 16,000-odd National Insurance doctors who served the poorer communities and who received nine shillings a year for each individual on their list, averaged a 'panel' of 1,000 patients. The smaller practices of those days, combined with the limited pharmacy of drugs available, meant not only fewer 'prescription' visits by patients but also more time for talk. In the fabric of pre-war life, the good family doctor held a position analogous to that of a lay priest. In a country practice, he knew most of the intimate secrets of his patients, and discussion of their worries was just as much a part of treatment as the inevitable bed rest. At Christmas, presents of food – game, eggs, or vegetables – would arrive at the surgery. He usually had a fairly good idea of each patient's income, and graded his bills accordingly, often 'forgetting' to send them to the poorest. In a small community, this system of medical care generally worked well, though it was a different matter in the poor, crowded districts of large towns where practices were not so attractive and there was less money to pay for what treatment was available.

In those days, when income no less than effective treatment depended on a good bedside manner and a high reputation, it was important for most physicians not just to care but also to be seen to care, to be overcautious rather than take the slightest risk. A doctor would confirm that indeed 'another day in bed wouldn't do her any harm, Nanny', and would be sure to follow all the rituals that patients or those around them expected and found reassuring – especially when it came to the prevailing medical orthodoxy.

One of the cornerstones of this was the Theory of Focal Sepsis, developed by Sir Arbuthnot Lane. When Sir Arbuthnot, one of the most powerful personalities on the medical scene between the wars, evolved this idea, he instilled in several generations of doctors the belief that trouble in one place – a bad tooth, say – was a focus for infection that then filtered through the whole body, leading to a general deterioration of health. Conversely, unexplained disorders could be put down to one of these foci: track it down, said Sir Arbuthnot, whip it out, and presto! the patient would be as good as new.

Thus tonsils and adenoids, so often inflamed or enlarged during childhood, were frequently found guilty and removed without further ado. Although 1931 was the peak year of what became known as the Great Tonsil Rush, few middle-class children escaped the thirties with their throats intact. Many of these operations took place on the kitchen table at the hands of the family GP, who also gave the anaesthetic. Inexperienced or less confident doctors brought along a partner to handle the bottle of chloroform or ether used at that time. In the country, the distance from the nearest hospital was one reason for this 'kitchen surgery'; another was the natural wish to avoid frightening a small child by removing it from home rather than allowing it to convalesce in its own bed. Coming round from an operation was bad enough in any case: vomiting, often violent, was universal after anaesthesia, with jaundice a common side-effect after a long operation. Anaesthesia techniques in hospital were also primitive and, because of the risks, surgeons operated as quickly as they could and few operations lasted longed than two to two and a half hours.

Another popular excision was appendectomy. The swallowing of cherry-stones, pips from grapes, oranges or, in the more timid households, apples, was thought to lead to appendicitis. Rich food and drink was considered another cause. 'Appendicitis may be a good argument for plain living, as people in prisons, lunatic asylums and other institutions rarely suffer from it,' observed one writer, 'and whereas wild apes do not get appendicitis, the rather pampered zoo ones do.' Certainly, the American death rate from appendicitis (or more significantly, the operation to remove the appendix) had dropped during the Great Depression. It was believed that in cases of acute appendicitis, death would result failing an immediate operation and, as acute abdominal pain was quite often wrongly diagnosed as appendicitis, a high proportion of upper-class stomachs wore a fine but unnecessary diagonal scar. At one London hospital alone, over one thousand of these fashionable excisions took place in 1938, and some people even took the precaution of having their appendices removed when planning a long sea voyage.

No organ, however, came under closer scrutiny than the gut, regarded with particular suspicion by Sir Arbuthnot because of the large number of bacteria found there. His view was taken to heart by the general public, largely owing to the fact that any malfunction was so readily apparent. Anyone could tell if his gut was in good working order, or not. No specialist knowledge was required, no examination by another person necessary to know if Sir Arbuthnot's one vital criterion for a healthy colon – a regular daily motion – had been met. Every true-born Briton, of whatever age, social class, sex, or metier, was able to tell almost without thinking whether he or she had had 'a movement' that morning.

Such was the power of Sir Arbuthnot's proselytizing that the alternative spelt – quite literally, for many – doom and despair. Almost every complaint that did not actually kill was laid at the door of the sluggish bowel. Constipation, ran the accepted wisdom, caused not only migraine, lethargy, indigestion, halitosis and a poor complexion, but also more esoteric conditions such as difficulty in childbirth, depression, permanent fatigue, frigidity and impotence. Liquid paraffin sold by the gallon, and no bathroom cupboard was complete without a wardrobe of laxatives, frequently compared as to taste and effectiveness.

Children were sent to the lavatory after breakfast to 'go', and were asked immediately afterwards if they had 'been', a metronomic punctuality being held up as the medical version of the Platonic ideal. The same system was followed away from home.

At some preparatory schools, boys had to put a tick or cross against their names on a notice board, and thus it followed that everyone knew the state of his neighbour's bowels – information which occasionally followed them inconveniently into later life. In the greater delicacy of girls' boarding schools, those unable to mumble or nod the required affirmative were summoned that night to matron for a spoonful of Milk of Magnesia, Syrup of Figs or, in recalcitrant cases, a foul-tasting dose of castor oil.

In the profession itself, the former blind faith in Sir Arbuthnot's creed wore off towards the end of the decade, and argument was raging. At a meeting of the Medical Society in London on 13 February 1939, there were several lively exchanges after Sir Arthur Hurst's talk on 'The Use and Abuse of Purgatives'. Two-thirds of the patients who came to doctors with a definite syndrome resulting from the use of purgatives were women, and all complained of constipation, he told the assembly. Some had even had their appendices removed in an effort to avoid it, others had taken gigantic doses of popular remedies such as sennapods – 'up to 60 a night'. But paraffin, he declared, was not a purgative.

Mr Gordon Brown said that surgeons found it very difficult to stop the nursing staff – clearly as convinced as the rest of the population of the virtues of regular daily evacuation – giving either purgatives or paraffin at their discretion. Continuous paraffin drinking, he thought, might be responsible for chronic disorder of the colon. Mr J. E. Roberts said heatedly that the long-suffering public had been abused in this way by several of the speakers present. He himself believed that Sir Arthur Hurst was responsible for the sale of paraffin 'in half gallon bottles'.

But this was nothing compared to the remedies advertised in the popular press. Nowhere was Sir Arbuthnot Lane's influence so apparent as in the advertisement columns. If the Fuehrer had studied these, he could have been forgiven for thinking the entire British nation was so obsessed with its bowels, let alone so incapacitated by constipation, as to render the rumble of war a mere irrelevant twittering on the sidelines.

Manufacturers, leaping onto the bandwagon of the clean colon, used every ounce of persuasion, suggestion and authority at their command. Some delicately avoided the word 'laxative' – though their meaning was unmistakable to their attuned and expectant audience – while others were bluntly medical in their language. It was possible to pick these latter ones out even at a distance, as they were invariably illustrated with the picture of a doctor or a nurse – sometimes several at once. A further embellishment was a neat diagrammatic sketch of the lower bowel.

'How your colon gets furred up like the inside of a kettle,' began one advertisement for Kruschen Liver Salts that appeared regularly in the daily papers and was, presumably, designed to be read over breakfast, 'Sixteen doctors prove how to overcome constipation!' It continued with a detailed description from which the following is the sentence least likely to put the squeamish off their bacon and eggs: 'Stagnant waste matter decays and spreads poison to every part of the system like the poison from a decaying tooth . . . you get headaches and twinges in back and limbs, you puff on stairs, you sleep badly, you lose your appetite, get indigestion, feel consistently tired, flat, fit for nothing.'

Others, such as the manufacturers of Bile Beans, adopted a more positive line, promising love, life and laughter to those intelligent enough to take their product. Still others aimed at the best of both worlds, using a combination of dreadful warning and shining inducement. Eno's Fruit Salts, a popular fizzy morning 'tonic', ran a campaign featuring Mr Can and Mr Can't and their wives, Mrs Can and Mrs Can't. 'What I suffer from is a lack of energy,' sighs Mr Can't, a fat man in a grey homburg, notable also for his miserable expression. 'What *you* suffer from is lack of Eno,' counters Mr Can – younger, better-looking, and wearing a smarter hat. Even the advertisements for Brooke Bond tea carried the word 'digestive', and breakfast cereals were sold not on their taste, vitamin value or ease of preparation, but on their laxative effect: Kelloggs launched their new breakfast cereal with a tiny diagram of the intestines accompanies by the slogan, 'Eat it every day and never miss a day!'

The message of such advertisements was backed up by stirring editorials in magazines such as *Woman and Home*, pointing out the evils tight bowels could cause in the family. The costive colon was seen as a potential homewrecker, cause of everything from juvenile delinquency to broken relationships. One contemporary health pamphlet declared roundly: 'What is known as frigidity in women – that is, indifference or actual aversion from marital relations – is often traceable to just one cause, habitual constipation.'

Many preparations were advertised with the implicit claim that they could cure loss of virility. 'Phyllosan increases your vital forces!' 'What is it in These Drops of Phosferine that Gives Them such Rejuvenating Power! Sustain Your Fortitude with Phosferine!' 'A million Years of Youth Set Free by Gland Therapy!' shouted another. Glandular therapy, as it was more often known, was a particular craze of the pre-war years, tried by Noel Coward and Somerset Maugham among others. But it was not only celebrities seeking to preserve their youth and vitality who allowed themselves to be injected with extracts of monkeys' testicles. In 1939, Portsmouth football team were among those who submitted themselves to this treatment. In their case, it was to improve their position in the First Division – Glandular therapy, it was said, had been responsible for the earlier success of Wolverhampton Wanderers.

Patent medicines, of course, reflected the preoccupations of the day, from catarrh, deafness, indigestion and anaemia to that vague but peculiarly female complaint, 'nerves'. Before the age of tranquillizing drugs, panaceas in the popular press promised freedom from anxiety in dramatic, full-page terms ('Mother of four was nervous wreck. "What a relief I got after taking Yeast-Vite – I could not carry on but for it!"').

An alternative preferred by many was the cigarette, soothing, handy, and cheap. For the tobacco industry those were halcyon days, when its advertising focused chiefly on the low price of cigarettes and smoking had tacit government approval. It was, however, recognized that in times of stress one smoked more and that this was vaguely A Bad Thing. Thus one advertisement depicts a stockbroker with his top hat on the back of his head, standing on the floor of the Stock Exchange and examining the tickertape, with a thought bubble saying 'Mr Conscience! Better mark that smoking down a point or two, hadn't we?' The message below points out reassuringly that this will be unnecessary . . . 'if you smoke Cooltip, a Virginia cigarette by Abdullah, at 10 for 6½d, 20 for 1/1'.

Although the connection between smoking and lung cancer had not been made, 'smoker's cough' was a recognized affliction of the heavy smoker. Most of these were men; women smokers were both less numerous and more socially circumscribed – no well-brought-up young woman smoked in the street, and many others only smoked in private houses. Few people, for example, knew that Queen Mary smoked heavily, as she was never seen to do so in public. When Sir Thomas Beecham rebuked a woman for smoking at a broadcast concert of the Royal Philharmonic Orchestra, everyone around her applauded his stricture vigorously – and the BBC listeners heard the whole thing.

Sixteen

MAY – GRAND HOUSES

By mid-May, Queen Mary had begun her annual round of early summer visits, staying at the various country houses of her friends, many of whom locked away their more precious bibelots. The Queen had a habit of directing a longing gaze at some particularly choice *objet*, and of then voicing her admiration with remarks such as 'What an exquisite little snuff box! I wish I had enamel of that shade of green in my own collection.' She would repeat this routine until her hostess would finally say in desperation: 'Perhaps Your Majesty would allow me to present it to you.'

In pre-war England, many of these grand country houses, with their armies of servants and vast numbers of rooms, still managed to maintain much of the magnificence that characterized such private palaces in the days before 1914. At Eaton Hall, the Duke of Westminster's enormous house in Cheshire, there was room for sixty guests, along with their maids, valets and chauffeurs. Wentworth Woodhouse, Lord Fitzwilliam's house in Yorkshire, could accommodate sixty-two. Wentworth Woodhouse, with its 240 rooms, 1,000 windows and 200-yard frontage – the longest in England – was incongruously surrounded by lawns black with coal dust from the adjacent mines from which all this splendour derived. Inside the house, as Margaret, Duchess of Argyll, recalled 'the corridors were so long that when the footman showed us to our rooms he actually unwound a ball of string to enable us to find our way back to the reception rooms'.

The guest who had dressed for dinner and had managed, Ariadne-like, to find the drawing-room again, would join the procession that wound its way through various magnificent salons until the vast green dining-room was reached, where a liveried footman stood behind each chair. 'Everything on the dining table was gold, including the knives and forks. Ornamental gold plates were also on all the tables around the walls underneath the Fitzwilliam family portraits.'

Some of these great places specialized in the political house party. At Trent, Sir Philip Sassoon entertained weekend guests such as the Churchills, the Edens, and the Vansittarts. Sir Robert Vansittart, removed from his post as head of the Foreign Office in December 1937, had then been given the empty title of Chief Diplomatic Adviser to the Government. Although his advice on European affairs and the menace of Hitler was subsequently vindicated, it was never accepted by Chamberlain, who thought him deeply and unjustifiably anti-German.

Trent, when bought by Sir Philip's father, had been a large and ugly building of purplish stone; Sir Philip tore it down and had it rebuilt in pretty red brick. Trent was known for its wonderful park, with its azaleas, greenhouses, Japanese garden and the lake on which swam a collection of about four hundred ducks and exotic wildfowl. Sir Philip had also installed a swimming-pool, tennis courts and a nine-hole golf course; tennis and golf professionals were on hand to coach any guests who wanted it. His other main house, Lympne, where guests found a dry martini, a carnation for a man's buttonhole and an orchid for a woman's corsage awaiting them in their bedrooms when they went to change for dinner, was even grander. Built just before World War I, in red brick, it had a miniature Spanish patio in white marble and a garden sloping gently down towards the sea, tended by more than twenty gardeners. Its chief features were the herbaceous borders, described by those who saw them as an explosion of colour. These borders were twice as wide as usual and planted so as to be at the peak of their glory in July and August, the months when Sir Philip came down most frequently.

At Leeds Castle in Kent, Lady (Olive) Baillie also entertained politicians. Lady Baillie, the eldest daughter of the first (and only) Lord Queenborough, was half-American, and her money came from her mother, a daughter of the Hon. C. Whitney, former Secretary of the US Navy. Sir Adrian Baillie was her third husband. Leeds Castle, one of the oldest inhabited fortresses in Britain, beautifully refurbished with American money and according to American standards of warmth, plumbing and comfort, and was enormously popular with those lucky enough to be asked. Her closest political friends were David Margesson, Winston Churchill and Chips Channon. Here, too, there was a nine-hole golf course as well as croquet lawns, tennis courts, and billiards and gambling at night. At weekends there were seldom less than thirty people staying, with a fair sprinkling of the young, frivolous and beautiful.

But probably the most famous house parties of all took place at Cliveden, the beautiful Italianate mansion overlooking the Thames near Maidenhead and Windsor that was the home of Lord and Lady Astor. These weekends gave a name not only to a group of people but also defined a specific political outlook.

Entertainment was in any case Nancy Astor's passion. From the moment she became chatelaine of Cliveden on her marriage in 1906, few weekends passed without a sizable house party, with additional guests increasing the numbers at luncheon and dinner. She mixed old and young, aristocratic and self-made, with a deft and determined hand. Here Edward VII had stayed with Mrs Keppel discreetly occupying an adjacent bedroom; here Charlie Chaplin had lectured Lloyd George on the need for slum clearance; here Rudyard Kipling, Henry James and George Bernard Shaw had held forth over the immense and beautiful dining-table brought from Versailles. In large part, Cliveden's special atmosphere of intimacy, comfort, brilliance and an often daunting sophistication was a reflection of Nancy Astor's own qualities. Beautiful, highly intelligent, sharply witty, and gifted with enormous charm, she combined a deep respect for the institutions of her adopted country with a healthy scorn for its more pointless traditions. She was also a brilliant mimic (her niece, Joyce Grenfell, later became famous on the stage for her monologue characterizations). As a hostess, her exceptional generosity was marred by only one flaw: a deep belief in the virtues of total abstention. The only drinks found in abundance at Cliveden were non-alcoholic cider and ginger beer.

Nancy Astor had become Britain's first woman MP in 1919, and from then on the political flavour of her house parties was to become ever more pronounced. Fittingly, Cliveden itself had a strong political provenance. It had been built for the Duke of Sutherland in 1850, by Charles Barry, the architect who had designed the Houses of Parliament; round the topmost course of the house ran its history in Latin, drafted by Mr Gladstone himself. It was conveniently close to London for the politicians who flocked to it and, once inside its great hall-drawing room, the visitor was immediately conscious of luxury and comfort, from the generous warmth of central heating to the superb flowers everywhere – pots of gardenias, lilies, every variety of geranium.

As the dark years of the thirties passed, a stroll through Cliveden's four hundred acres, with their azaleas and rhododendrons, their woodland hazy with bluebells in the spring, provided senior politicians and public figures with ever more welcome opportunities for private, off-the-record discussions. In the quiet of the wood-panelled library (which was always known as the Cigar Box) foreign ambassadors could exchange unofficial views or discreetly indicate the attitudes of their governments.

By 1939, the Astor parties were regarded as such a centre of power and influence that their *habitués* had been dubbed 'the Cliveden Set', a title first bestowed towards the end of 1937 by Claud Cockburn, editor and publisher of the political journal *The Week*. Whether the Cliveden Set was actively promoting certain policies, or whether its members were simply people who thought alike and met constantly at the same house, is open to conjecture; but certainly their positions were influential and their views were similar and frequently expressed not only in Parliament but also in speeches, lectures and through the columns of two of the most influential newspapers of the day. Those of the Prime Minister himself were, of course, well known; other frequent guests were Geoffrey Dawson, the editor of *The Times* (then owned by Major John Astor) and his chief leader writer Barrington Ward; and J. L. Garvin, the editor of the *Observer* (also an Astor paper). Both of these newspapers supported the appeasement policies of Chamberlain. Another frequent guest was Lord Lothian who, according to Michael Astor in his book *Tribal Feeling*, 'believed in the power of good even to the extent of believing he could reform Hitler and the Germany that supported Hitler'.

Whatever the political viewpoint, however, one thing was constant. At all such houses, luxury reigned supreme. The bedside table alone contained almost everything the sybarite could want: a Thermos flask of iced water and a box filled with an assortment of digestive, Marie and dry biscuits, Turkish and Virginian cigarettes, matches, ashtray, and a batch of the latest novels. Fresh flowers, often matching the chintz, adorned the dressing-table or stood on a chest of drawers, and the writing-table, with its small square writing-tray for those guests who preferred penning their numerous letters and notes of thanks in bed, was supplied with writing-paper, envelopes, fresh blotting-paper in the leather blotter, pens and ink. Once up and dressed, the guest could choose anything from shooting, hunting or dry fly fishing during the season, to squash (made more fashionable when the Prince of Wales installed a court at Buckingham Palace earlier in the decade), riding or golf – some hostesses booked caddies in advance so that they were always available.

For the non-athletic, there was always that thirties speciality, the jigsaw puzzle. Laid out on a table in the hall or in the drawing-room – sometimes for months when singularly unidentifiable pieces of blue sky had to be filled in – few of those passing by could resist pausing long enough to fill in at least one missing piece of these huge and panoramic scenes (The Durbar, The Charge of the Light Brigade and, of course, The Coronation). As well as occupying an idle quarter of an hour, or providing an excuse for mild flirtation over some particularly tricky corner, the jigsaw in many a country house offered a refuge for anyone left stranded without a conversational partner and too shy to seek one out. For the younger members of a house party, it was all too easy to feel nervous, shy or overawed. When eighteen-year-old Valerie Cole experienced her first weekend house party at Cliveden, her uncle Neville, chaperoning her (Mrs Chamberlain, in bed with a cold, was forced to remain behind), wrote:

'She was naturally rather alarmed at the prospect but she seems to have settled in comfortably. And out of the corner of my eye I can see she is producing devastating effects on the younger and not only the younger members of the party. The fact is that she is an exceptionally pretty girl with a very attractive smile and people want to talk to her. There are a terrific number of people in the house including the Geoffrey Dawsons, Lothian, Devonshires, Dick Cavendishes, Lindberghs and many others.'

Not every girl was fortunate enough to have the Prime Minister as her uncle – or a come-hither smile. But whatever else they lacked, all were expected to have a full share of social poise. In other respects, though, these delicate flowers were treated rather as parcels that might easily go astray. A 1939 debutante describes one such visit: 'You were taken to the station by the chauffeur and put into the train and you always travelled with a maid looking after you. Somebody would have bought the tickets – always first class – and handed them to the maid. I always used to go with my friend. I had our parlourmaid and she had her old Nanny. They wore black dresses with a little pin at the collar.'

On arrival, the two would be met at the station by the host

family's chauffeur or under-chauffeur. 'Being motored up those long winding drives to a strange house at the other end and wondering whether one would get lost and be late for dinner and what one's hostess and especially the other guests would be like was pretty terrifying at 17. My friend and I were usually given rooms opposite each other, with a bathroom somewhere near. We would arrive about teatime and our maids would be whisked away to unpack, lay out our evening clothes and run the bath while we were downstairs breaking the ice over tea.'

Breakfast the following morning was perhaps the worst ordeal. This meal took place punctually at nine o'clock no matter how late the guests had been up the previous night; and everyone was expected to be up and dressed for it. Only older, married women were allowed the luxury of breakfast in bed. In winter, our debutante was woken by the housemaid entering her room to light a fire which, with luck, would soon give off enough heat to take the chill off the freezing air and allow her to dress – one feature of the pre-war country house was its extreme cold. Immense log and coal fires made pools of warmth in the large rooms but, without the central heating possessed so far only by a few, avoiding hypothermia was a major concern of the winter months. In some houses it was so cold that fire or no, girls wriggled into their jerseys and thick tweed skirts under the protective cover of a dressing-gown or a fur coat.

Once downstairs in the chilly hall that fires had not yet had time to warm, the nervous seventeen-year-old would pause, shuddering slightly, outside the dining-room door until she summoned up the courage to open it. 'Inside, you knew it would be mostly men, who at that time of the morning didn't want to talk to you – they'd have their papers propped up and would peer over the edges or be looking at the racing pages. One or two of these rather terrifying beings would get up and say "Shall I help you?" – there were no servants, you see, like at other meals.' On a large sideboard there might be porridge, with cream in a silver jug nearby, kidneys, kedgeree, sausages, bacon and eggs all in silver dishes with spirit lamps underneath. There would also be toast, marmalade, honey, coffee and tea and fruit, and on a side-table ham, and game if in season. Most of this food came from the home farm, or the hothouses in the kitchen garden where peaches, nectarines and grapes were grown.

Food featured very largely indeed in all country-house entertaining, whether this was on a grand or comparatively modest scale. Because the food was strictly seasonal, its freshness and quality were matters of nice timing, judgment and constant interest. None of those to whom this abundant and delicious food was served could themselves cook, so every meal contained elements of surprise, anticipation and, on occasions, apprehension or drama which, reinforced by the brisk exercise most people took, resulted in a hearty appetite. The exception to this extravagant consumption were the Lenten meals in strict Catholic households, where only one complete meal a day, called a 'collation', was served. The most stringent hosts, such as the elderly Lord Bute, weighed out their Catholic guests' portions on small scales. One, whose son was then at Cambridge, was heard to remark to a pretty young guest: 'Michael has got to pass his exam, so he can have more food. But *you* have to have the ration.'

Luncheon at these weekend parties was never less than a four-course affair: soup, entrée, meat dish and pudding or cheese. At 5.00 p.m. there was tea, with all its paraphernalia of silver kettles and teapots and profusion of delicious things to eat, and at 8.30 or 9.00 the climax towards which the whole day had been building – dinner.

The approach of dinner was signalled by the dressing-gong, anything up to an hour beforehand so that everyone had their turn in the bathroom, a room that in the larger, older houses was often the equivalent of a Chamber of Penance. Although the Great Bathroom Revolution, with its concepts of piping-hot water, sybaritic luxury, and at least one bathroom for every three people in a house, swept over from America earlier in the thirties, it had not effectively penetrated beyond the capital (it was thanks to both the Astors' American parentage that there were plenty of bathrooms at Cliveden). At St John's College, Cambridge, for example, there were only six baths for 450 undergraduates. ('What's all this fuss about baths?' asked one don. 'Terms only last eight weeks.') So while Lord and Lady Louis Mountbatten might have an exotic seven bathrooms to the eighteen bedrooms of their duplex penthouse above Park Lane, in the average country house a hot bath was more likely to be a matter of luck, timing and occasional unscrupulousness. For the huge old baths on their claw feet in a converted spare room at the end of some corridor required so much hot water to produce even a moderate temperature that the antiquated boiler was often not up to the task; and only those who had nipped in at the head of the queue could be relatively sure of the joy of a hot bath. 'The young man who took all the hot water' was the subject of a Punch joke – and one of the least popular of guests.

For large, formal dinners the *place à table* was written outside so that everyone could see whom they were taking in or being taken in by; when dinner was announced, in they went, arm in arm, the woman on the man's left, the host with the senior lady, the hostess with the senior man, in strict order of rank and precedence. As it was also customary to sit next to the person who took one in, this meant that the debutante who happened to be a duke's daughter was invariably landed with her host, instead of the normal ration of one young man on each side. It was exactly the same below stairs. 'At all the houses we stayed in,' says one 1939 debutante, 'the butler took in my friend's nanny because she – my friend – was the daughter of a duke.'

Dinner was at least five courses: soup, fish, meat, pudding, and the savoury which was a regular course on all formal and many informal menus (cheese was served at luncheon but not for dinner). Savouries could be as simple as mushrooms on toast; two popular ones were Angels on Horseback (bacon wrapped round oysters and then grilled), and Devils on Horseback (bacon wrapped round a prune stuffed with anchovy and almond and, again, grilled). Both were served on toast. After the savoury, which was supposed to clear the male palate for port drinking, the ladies withdrew, frequently having to wait a considerable time before their men joined them again.

The only exception to this separation of the sexes was Sunday supper, always cold 'to save the servants' – though it still had to be prepared and set out, the table laid and later cleared and the dishes washed. In most houses, Sunday meant no driving for chauffeurs unless there was an emergency. Catholic girls staying in a Church of England household, where the nearest Catholic church was probably some distance away, had to nerve themselves to say yes when asked if they wanted to go to Mass, as this meant that their host not only had to drive them there but also had to return afterwards to pick them up. In the more old-fashioned and stricter households, games, from croquet to cards, were banned on Sunday.

Otherwise, games were a great feature of the country house weekend, and of country life generally. Card games were played constantly, even after smart dinner parties – Margot Asquith, for one, was a great bridge player – and parlour games were popular. 'Dined in London with the Henleys; after dinner played vingt-et-un and French and German games,' wrote David Verey in his nightly diary in February; and on 13 April, 'Dinner party at Barnsley. Played paper games – English, American and French – afterwards.' Vingt-et-un was a favourite, as a lot of people could play it at once. Partly for the same reason, so was The Game, a form of charades then at the height of its popularity. In The Game, the company split up into two teams, each person taking it in turns to act out silently the title of a book, film, or play. Older members of the party departed to the billiard-room but few of the young were allowed to play ('might cut the cloth'), though sometimes they played a hand version of billiards called Pockets or another known as 'Freda', after Freda Casa Maury (formerly Freda Dudley Ward, the mistress of the Prince of Wales) who had invented it. If enough young people were staying, the carpet might be rolled back in the drawing-room for dancing to the gramophone – in some households, this seemed to be on all the time, playing Benny Goodman, Jelly Roll Morton, Fats Waller, Louis Armstrong or songs like 'Oh! Johnny' and 'I Get Along Without You Very Well'.

There were also a great many games of which the common denominator appears to have been a licence to say what you thought of everyone else in the room in lightly veiled terms. Describing someone first in terms of architecture, then as an animal, next as a vegetable, tree, piece of music ('I see X as the Losd Chord') could result in gales of giggles and some embarrassment, while the Truth Game was often torture to the young and unsophisticated.

Other such amusements were more active. Though many sound like children's games, in that age of sexual innocence any excuse for legitimate physical contact, however fleeting, was welcome. A rather rowdy game called Rescue which consisted of tearing round the house 'rescuing' with a tap on the hand those frozen to the spot by the villain, mopped up a lot of surplus energy. Murder, and Sardines, two games which involved turning out the lights and plenty of feeling around in the dark, plus the chance of hiding in a remote and preferably cramped cupboard with an attractive member of the opposite sex, were highly popular for a different reason. Occasionally, of course, there would be a scandal – a bedroom door would be found locked and a girl would be inside with a young man. No hostess who valued her reputation as a chaperone of the young would ever ask either of them to her house again.

Seventeen

SERVANTS

In a great country house, there were servants to do everything required for their employer and his family. It was possible for the children to grow up without knowing where to buy a stamp or ever sticking one on a letter – they would simply put their letters in to the letter-box on the hall table, to be removed later by the butler, stamped, and posted. There were also servants to look after other servants. In the sort of house grand enough to have a stewards' room (often known simply as The Room), upper servants like butlers and lady's maids and their visiting equivalents were themselves waited on by a junior maid or footman.

The idea of having someone else to do all the dirty or dislikable chores stretched the whole way down the social scale. House-holds that today would be described as 'humble' boasted a cook-general, while gentlemen's households seldom had fewer than three or four servants and often far more. One widow of a prosperous manufacturer living in the West Riding of Yorkshire had, for example, a butler, a footman, a cook, a kitchenmaid, a lady's maid, a parlourmaid, a housemaid, a chauffeur, four gardeners and a pigman (this functionary looked after the two Jersey house cows and the pigs which provided pork and home-cured ham and bacon). With the exception of the footman and the kitchen-maid, all the staff were elderly and almost all of them had been in service in the same house for twenty years or more. Their mistress never gave dinner parties and the only people who came to stay were her children and their families, so for large portions of the year there were thirteen people looking after the simple needs of one old lady.

Most of the domestic servants in 1939 (about 1,300,000) were women – long gone was the Victorian bias towards male servants. In a house with a staff of three, a likely line-up would be cook, parlourmaid and housemaid or – one step down in both status and wages – cook-general, house-parlourmaid and between-maid or 'tweeny'. If the house ran to four servants, a working butler or manservant would be a possibility. As in all pre-war jobs, he would be paid more than his female equivalent. A working butler could expect £100 a year and a valet who could also chauffeur, £125. An experienced cook could expect about £80 a year, an experienced lady's maid around £60 (and her mistress's cast-offs), a head housemaid £65 and a junior one about £45 a year. In smaller houses, a cook-general or house-parlourmaid earned about £1 a week. If the family was very small, this point was used as an inducement in advertisements to show that the new employee would not be run off her feet. 'Good temporary cook, 40 shillings, required . . . Staff four, family two.'

On both sides of the green baize door there was a fairly clear idea as to what was expected. The cook, who was always given the courtesy title of 'Mrs', reigned supreme over the kitchen, usually planning the everyday menus herself, though discussing any for entertaining with her mistress. Sometimes she would also do all the ordering, though more often this, too, was done in conjunction with her mistress. In one large Kensington house, for example, every evening the cook brought up a list of what was needed, and this was copied directly into a Harrods' order book, the carbon beneath each order page serving as a household record. Posted that night between 9.00 and 10.00 (needless to say, by one of the servants), the order was delivered by Harrods' van the following morning before 9.00 a.m. Daily ordering of this type was common because many houses did not have a refrigerator. However, they all had a larder with cool shelves of slate or marble, and little muslin circles edged with beads were used to protect bowls or jugs of liquid from flies.

A butler or manservant would valet his master and male visitors, as well as doing the usual pantry and dining-room work. He answered the telephone and the front door, taking letters and visiting cards to his employers on a salver. If his integrity and sobriety were unquestionable, he held the key to the cellar, and decanted the wine – though this responsibility was too heavy for some, and alcohol problems among butlers were fairly common. He was also in charge of the silver; as most houses had a fair amount – trays, photograph frames, silver ornaments, cigarette and match boxes as well as the table silver – keeping it cleaned and polished was almost a full-time job in itself.

In many houses, a parlourmaid took the place of a butler, waiting at a table or answering the door in her afternoon uniform of black silk dress with its white muslin apron and frilly white cap. She looked after the cellar, the silver, the telephone, the valeting, and saw that drawing-room and morning-room were swept and dusted, and fires laid or lit before the family came down to breakfast. She also did light mending for any gentleman unfortunate enough to have ripped a button off or torn a pocket. The ideal parlourmaid was described as having 'the bearing of a Guardsman and the discretion of a diplomat'.

The housemaid spent much of her day cleaning. Scuttling round the house in her cotton print dress, she could be recognized by her cleaning-box, its basket-like iron handle grasped firmly in her hand; it held paper and kindling in the bottom section, with cleaning-equipment, polishes and duster in a tray on top. From time to time, she would dart into bedrooms while their occupants were enjoying a leisurely luncheon or dinner to tidy dressing-tables or pull curtains and turn down beds, lay out night things and remove the shoes that she would later clean. (If the house was grand enough, this task was performed by the bootboy or odd-job man.)

Rich households also had footmen, who would wait at table,

valet younger male members of the family or male guests, and generally understudy the butler. On formal occasions they wore livery – Lord Cholmondeley's was a stylish yellow and black with silver buttons, Sir Philip Sassoon's footmen wore blue uniforms with red waistcoats and gold buttons, with knee breeches as well as white stockings. Ideally, footmen were tall and of soldierly bearing to display this elegance to its best advantage; many of the men employed as footmen in 1939 had in fact served in the 1914–18 war, and wore their medal ribbons on their livery.

Ladies' maids had to be expert needlewomen, and skilled at washing and ironing delicate fabrics. Some were excellent dress-makers, but their dressmaking talents were usually confined to the wardrobes of the daughters of the house. Though maids would mend or alter their mistress's clothes, most women rich enough to employ a lady's maid had their clothes professionally made by a London dressmaker. For many women, their lady's maid was their best friend; the deadpan witticisms of Lady Jersey's maid ('Will you wear your best fur, M'Lady, or are you going to a private party?') were regularly passed around her mistress's circle.

Servants were frequently regarded almost as another piece of personal property and anyone attempting to 'poach' a good cook, butler or maid, as the moral equivalent of the cat burglar. It was not quite so bad if the current and prospective employers did not know each other, but to lure away the cook or nanny of a friend was considered an act of the basest treachery. This attitude appeared to receive the sanction of the law when, in March 1939, a judgment was given in favour of a woman who sued another for enticing away her maid.

For some women, life without their personal maid was unthinkable. Helen, Lady Adare, went as far as trying to bribe a driving examiner to ensure that her maid Sullivan passed the driving test and could act as chauffeuse to her mistress on a continental trip. As the date of departure loomed nearer, it looked as though Sullivan was as yet far too inexperienced to have any chance of passing. Accordingly, when she arrived for her test at the Government Driving School in Hendon, she carried an innocent-looking envelope. She handed this to the Senior Examiner, who opened it to find inside two pound notes and a letter presenting the compliments of Helen, Viscountess Adare, to the Senior Examiner, Driving Test, and explaining Lady Adare's urgent need to travel. The key passage was a mixture of imperious pleading, reassurance and straightforward bribery that was unthinkable, even through the filtering formality of the third person:

'So it was now or never. And even if she is a little behind standard you need have no fear that Lady Adare will let her drive only on quiet roads, until she has more practice. So please pass her if possible. I believe it is very unorthodox to give Christmas Presents to Government servants but perhaps you have a wife who could buy herself a present with the enclosed in memory of this great event.' Alas, it cost the hapless Viscountess a lot more: she was fined fifty guineas, with ten guineas' costs.

Not surprisingly, 'the servants' were an endless topic of discussion, argument or anxiety and, in less happy households, of difficulty or despair. Those from the servant-keeping classes regarded the moral if not the emotional or physical welfare of the girls or women who worked for them as their responsibility, dictating not only what time they came in after an evening off, but also who they saw and, if possible, what they did. For even after one major war, the question of 'followers', as male admirers were still often called, troubled many mistresses. Others took a more enlightened view. Here is Dr Edith Summerskill (later the Labour MP and life peeress Baroness Summerskill), on how to run a happy house:

'Mistresses must satisfy their maids' desire for friendship with young men. The mistress herself is usually married but often prevents her maid from having opportunities of meeting young men who might become possible husbands. The attitude of many is "My maid can have her young man in the kitchen as long as she is going to marry him." But they forget that they allow their maids no chance of becoming engaged. In many households, particularly where only one maid is employed, girls see only the errand boy in the morning.'

Dr Summerskill, who promoted legislation to introduce limited hours and provide a minimum wage for domestic workers, advocated that mistresses should allow maids more fresh air and more outings, otherwise they became depressed from being cooped up all day.

Other employers put their faith in labour-saving devices and generally seeing that their servants were not overworked. One pointed out that she never had any bother getting maids because in her advertisements she always stressed that in her house there were no fireplaces to clean, fires to be laid, coals to be carried, metals that required polishing, but glass-lined bathrooms that were easy to clean and modern equipment in the kitchen.

Where modernity and convenience were concerned, however, the nonpareil was the marvellous penthouse flat, six floors above Park Lane on the top of Brook House, that belonged to Lord and Lady Louis Mountbatten. The kitchen was acknowledged to be the most wonderful in London. It was L-shaped, with five large windows giving on to the roof terrace on which the Mountbattens frequently entertained, and had gas ovens that would cook forty chickens at a time, special sinks for vegetable preparation and cupboards with glass doors so that stocks could be assessed at a glance. Its rubber floor, patterned in black and white draught-board checks, made standing more comfortable and moving about quieter. Because it was so practical, the chef – formerly an assistant in the Buckingham Palace kitchens – needed 'only' two kitchen maids and a scullery boy to help him.

While many families felt genuine concern and much affection for their servants, the idea of improving the facilities and general comfort of their staff did not always strike them. Younger women were often quicker to appreciate how much sheer hard labour was involved in trivial tasks, such as bringing a cup of tea in response to a summons by bells. The Honourable Mrs Denys Lowson, married a few years earlier at the age of seventeen, described how she had provided a flat for her maids on the first floor of her new house in Campden Hill – 'and they have their own bathroom' – moving the nursery quarters up to the second and third floors instead. She chose this unusual position to save them unnecessary running up and down stairs, but she was the exception. Most servants had small rooms at the top of the house, usually with iron bedsteads, linoleum on the floor instead of carpet or rugs, deal rather than mahogany chests of drawers, and cotton sheets when the family had linen ones.

Another practical idea advocated by Mrs Lowson was the replacement of bells by a house telephone: 'This saves an extra journey for the main when anything is wanted, as she doesn't have to come and find out what it is before going back to fetch it.' Foot hassocks ('only cost 2s 6d and a godsend to weary feet during the afternoon rest') were also suggested by Mrs Lowson for the maids' sitting-room, and a gas fire in the pantry to make washing-up and the hours of silver cleaning a less chilly job in the winter.

The other side of the picture was put by a maid who wrote bitterly that she had to dash about between three rooms when she cooked: 'The kitchen is too horrible for words, it contains a huge hearth fire and a table. The larder, a big room, contains besides food, pans, saucepans and kettles, and the scullery, big like a dancing hall, has kitchen cupboards and washing up basins set in it, not to forget the store cupboard standing in the con- servatory. Altogether the cooking space occupies the area of a three room flat, and I have to fetch the vessels, fruit and veget- ables from the larder, potatoes from the cellar, the grocery things from the conservatory, and to prepare the meals in the scullery and cook them in the kitchen. And I mustn't forget to close all the doors between them because the draught is so bad for the hearth fire.'

At the same time, the life below stairs, or behind the green baize door if you lived in the country, often provided much-needed emotional nourishment and companionship for the children of the house, often starved of parental time. Nannies, of course, were a particular source of devotion (alternatively, a few were tyrants whose terrified charges dared not complain for fear of reprisals), and they themselves devoted hours of work to keeping 'their' children immaculate: washing, starching and ironing the numerous pillows in the huge navy blue or black prams they wheeled out every day, smocking little dresses, and airing everything from bath-towels to the ancient teddy on clothes racks in front of the nursery fire. Though discreet, their uniforms – usually a grey coat and hat – were unmistakable. The grander ones, who met in Hyde Park or Kensington Gardens, had 'their' seats and a strict precedence based on the rank of their charges. This social circle reached its apogee at Madame Vacani's Thursday dancing class for tiny children at the Hyde Park Hotel, the boys in velvet shorts and silk shirts, the little girls in bouffant-skirted party-dresses and the coral necklace given them by a godparent, their party shoes brought along in a shoebag. If there was a nurserymaid as well, she might accompany Nanny on these outings – especially if there were several children.

But all this cosseting carried a hidden sting in its tail. As the summer passed, the younger and fitter of the menservants disappeared to join the armed services, first as volunteers and then as conscripts. When war came, all but a few of the vast army who had cared for these privileged classes left the households they had maintained for so long; the men to join up, the women to join the women's services, work in factories, or become land girls. Suddenly, women to whom boiling an egg had been on a par with the Eleusinian mysteries found themselves temporarily helpless as they struggled with recalcitrant stove or the demands of the blackout. Many, chained to a domestic routine that had hitherto required several pairs of willing hands and that had now been made more difficult than ever by the shortages and improvisations of wartime, found themselves virtual prisoners in their own homes.

Eighteen

THE ROYAL TRANSATLANTIC VISIT

The suggestion that the King and Queen should visit Canada was first mooted in 1937 when the Canadian Prime Minister Mackenzie King came to London for their coronation. When President Roosevelt heard of the idea, he asked his special envoy in London, a former ambassador named James Gerard, to propose that, if the King and Queen did accept the invitation to go to Canada, they should also visit Washington.

The Canadian tour was announced officially on 8 October 1938, and on the same day the King replied to President Roosevelt's letter of invitation.

'The Queen and I appreciate most sincerely your kind invitation to visit Mrs Roosevelt and you in the United States in the event of our going to Canada next summer.

'I can assure you that the pleasure, which it would in any case give to us personally, would be greatly enhanced by the thought that it was contributing in any way to the cordiality of the relations between our two countries . . . Although the suggestions which you make for a visit sound very attractive, I am afraid that we shall not be taking the children with us if we go to Canada, as they are much too young for such a strenuous tour.

'With all good wishes and many thanks for your kind invitation.
'Believe me,
'Yours very sincerely.
'George R. I.'

Despite the uncertain international situation, there was no serious thought that the King and Queen should not go – even though there was a distinct possibility that they might be trapped on the other side of the Atlantic should war break out unexpectedly. This visit far transcended in importance any other state visit of recent years. At a time when Britain needed all the friends she could get, it was unthinkable that the King and Queen should miss the chance to consolidate bonds with a Dominion, and to influence American public opinion by appearing in both the political capital of Washington and the most important city in North America, New York.

The original plan was that the sovereign should travel across the Atlantic in a warship, as befitted the head of a maritime nation. Specially decorated cabins were set aside in the battle cruiser *Repulse* (destined to be sunk by the Japanese in the China Sea in December 1941, along with the *Prince of Wales*). But the Royal Navy's careful preparations were to go to waste. As international events grew ever more ominous, the King was increasingly worried at the thought of temporarily removing one of the country's most powerful warships from the Home Fleet. In particular, he feared that this would be read on the Continent as a sign that Britain was taking neither the threat of war nor her own preparations for it seriously enough.

He finally persuaded the Admiralty of this and, a mere week before departure, a liner was chartered instead. This was the 42,000-ton Canadian Pacific *Empress of Australia*, which had taken his brother, then Prince of Wales, to Canada. For the duration of the trip she would become almost an honorary naval vessel, being rated a royal yacht and sailing under the White Ensign, with the King himself in supreme command. Her crew of five hundred was augmented by Royal Navy ratings and signallers, and HMS *Repulse* was to escort her halfway across the Atlantic before turning back at midpoint.

The King and Queen had the same two suites that the Prince of Wales had occupied. The King's was decorated in red and gold, the Queen's in green and fawn. The furniture in the Queen's bedroom was upholstered in her favourite shade of blue but, true to the spartan traditions of the navy, the King insisted that plain enamelled iron bedsteads be brought from the royal yacht. There was, however, nothing abstemious about the Queen's wardrobe, packed in huge trunks for which two whole cabins on the lower deck of *Repulse* had originally been allotted. She devoted the whole of the last three days before departure to final fittings for her Canadian and American wardrobe, details of which were already intriguing the American public – one New York paper was reputed to be offering $1,000 for sketches of her new dresses. An important part of the King's luggage for Canada was the Imperial State Crown, leaving Britain for the first time in its history (a departure only made possible by the passing of the Statute of Westminster in 1931).

The royal party left London on Saturday 6 May, the King and Queen having spent their last day quietly with their children at Buckingham Palace. 'Remember,' said the Queen to her eldest daughter, 'I want everything to go on as if I were still here.' There was a Guard of Honour of sixty Sea Cadets from the Navy League Establishment at Kingston to see them off at Waterloo Station, and the Prime Minister postponed his usual Friday night departure for Chequers.

'We waited over till Saturday morning to see the King and Queen off,' he wrote. 'They had a brilliant morning for their start, and I think they went in good heart, though the King is naturally worried at leaving the country at such a time. But I told him I didn't think anything would happen while he was away and I believe I was justified in doing so, though we can never exclude any possibility with the dictators.'

At Portsmouth, the Keys of the Fortress were presented to them, the first such presentation since 1890, when they had been offered to Queen Victoria. But a far more magnificent farewell awaited them at sea. Two hours after the *Empress of Australia* had left Portsmouth, she was met by ships of the Home Fleet, formed into two lines: to port were the battleships *Nelson* and *Rodney*, the aircraft carrier *Ark Royal*, the cruiser *Newcastle* and the destroyers *Boreas*, *Echo* and *Express*; to starboard the cruisers *Aurora* and *Sheffield*, the destroyers *Punjabi*, *Mashona*, *Bedouin*, *Tartar*, *Encounter*, *Escapade* and *Esk*. The *Empress of Australia* steamed along between the two lines, while the ships' companies lining the rails cheered the two small figures on her bridge as they passed. As the liner broke free of the last warships, a royal salute of twenty-one guns was fired and three Fleet Air Arm squadrons and a Royal Air Force fighter squadron flew over, dipping their wings in salute and final farewell as the ship disappeared towards the open Atlantic, her escort in position around her.

Things quickly changed for the worse. The voyage was bedevilled by freezing fog and icebergs, which for the first time for many years mysteriously appeared much further south than usual. But first came gales. Four days out, the King and Queen were gamely watching Walt Disney's *Fox Hunt* and *Charlie Chan in Monte Carlo* – both chosen by the Queen – as storms whipped the sea and the Atlantic rollers heaved and tossed. Earlier in the evening, the King had even managed a set of deck tennis before the weather had brought his game to a halt. But despite the high winds which caused her to pitch and toss hideously, at who knows what discomfort to those on board, the *Empress of Australia* forged ahead at a steady seventeen knots. On the fifth day, Wednesday 10 May, she reached midpoint in the Atlantic. With no means of wiring pictures or copy, this was the first chance for press reports of the trip so far to be despatched home; this was done by the simple method of throwing them overboard in a wooden barrel (also containing mail), which was picked up as it bobbed on the rough seas by some masterly manoeuvring by *Repulse*, which then turned round and headed for Plymouth.

Worse was to come. Suddenly, the wind dropped, and a muffling, icy mist, harbinger and concealer of icebergs, covered the entire surface of the sea, bringing the *Empress* and her escorts to a standstill. The only sound to be heard was the continual wailing of foghorns. By three o'clock on the afternoon of 11 May, the *Empress of Australia* had spent eight hours motionless on a flat calm sea in a fog so thick visibility was zero. She was about 350 miles south of Cape Race in Newfoundland. In the next sixteen hours, she was able to move only two miles.

The following day, she was able to restart her engines briefly and then, after stopping again, to move forward gently at a cautious five knots in the wake of a faint pencil of light from HMS *Southampton*'s searchlights. Again the fog came down in a thick blanket; equally suddenly, it lifted again momentarily, to reveal the extraordinary sight of *Southampton* ahead, blazing with lights against the wall of dense, greyish-white fog now receding over a flat, steely sea. With HMS *Glasgow* following, the *Empress of Australia* gingerly moved forward once more – only to be stopped again by fog after fifteen minutes. In all, she made above five nautical miles during the night.

But Sunday 14 May dawned clear and still, revealing a sea without a berg in sight, but whose surface was covered with ice floes. Starting her engines, the *Empress* ploughed through these at about four knots, bumping and scraping the immaculate paint-work on her sides. As the going got more difficult, she altered her course southwards in an effort to circumvent the floes, but again ran into fog, although this time it was considered safe to move forward slowly through it. Scheduled to arrive on 15 May, the royal convoy was still only off Newfoundland when it should have been approaching Quebec. It had been a nightmare voyage, especially in view of the fate of the *Titanic*, as the Queen remarked in a letter to Queen Mary:

'For three and a half days we only moved a few miles. The fog was so thick it was like a white cloud round the ship, and the foghorn blew incessantly. Its melancholy blasts were echoed back by the icebergs like the twang of a piece of wire. Incredibly eery, and really very alarming, knowing that we were surrounded by ice, and unable to see a foot either way.

'We very nearly hit a berg the day before yesterday, and the poor Captain was nearly demented because some kind cheerful people kept on reminding him that it was about here that the Titanic was struck and *just* about the same date! . . .'

The ordeal was not over yet. On Sunday afternoon, they ran into yet more ice, this time a belt of pack ice several miles wide through which the *Empress* drove by force. The King stood by the lookout man, filming her stem cutting through the broken, lumpy mass. He too described the scene to Queen Mary, in a letter written after they had landed at Quebec on 17 May. 'Last Sunday when the fog cleared we spent the whole day in loose lumps of ice, and in the afternoon we had to push our way through a quarter of a mile of quite thick and solid ice. We saw several icebergs of varying size.'

The whole incident was a most interesting experience, con-cluded the King, adding philosophically: 'As a matter of fact I have been able to have a good rest on the voyage, and the two extra days are all to the good for me, but I should not however have chosen an ice field surrounded by dense fog in which to have a holiday. But it does seem to be the only place for me to rest in nowadays!!'

The King and Queen's tour was extensively reported in Eng-land. By now, pictures could be flown home rather than sent back by sea. The first transatlantic commercial mail service had just begun, though an attempt to fly non-stop from Moscow to New York failed. Pan American Airways' thirty-seven-ton flying boat, the *Yankee Clipper*, made the first commercial crossing in twenty-six hours and seventeen minutes, landing at South-ampton Water. There had been two stops en route: the first in the Azores to pick up three thousand letters, then a landing at Lisbon on the Tagus. The new air service carried photographs of the King and Queen leaving the Dominion Parliament after the King had given the Royal Assent to legislation.

It was part of an arduous schedule. They began with a banquet on Thursday 18 May in Montreal. On the menus, someone had had the forethought to write a few hints on etiquette for the guests. Chief among these was that no one should speak to either royal personage without first being addressed themselves. The unhappy Mayor of Montreal was heard by the King to mumble 'mustn't speak until I am spoken to'. The King burst out laughing. 'Your Majesty,' said the Mayor, 'this is the first time I ever blushed.' Later he explained he was 'thinking out loud'.

From Montreal they went to Kingston, Ontario, then on to Toronto, where the Queen inspected the regiment of which she was Colonel-in-Chief, the Toronto Scottish. After an afternoon at the races they travelled by train along the shores of the Great Lakes, arriving in Winnipeg on 24 May, where, despite the pouring rain, they were welcomed by cheering crowds. The King made his Empire Day broadcast from Government House and Mr Mackenzie King, the Canadian Prime Minister, presented the traditional furs on behalf of his country. The Queen received her favourite fox furs in the shape of a twin silver fox with gold clasps; there was an Arctic white fox fur for Queen Mary; and sets of marten scarves and muffs for the Princesses.

With hardly a pause they were off again, arriving in Regina, the capital of Saskatchewan, on 25 May, turning up the next day in Calgary, Alberta. Before arriving in the State capital, Edmonton – the most northerly point of their tour – they spent a night in a log cabin, its floors covered with the skins of buffalo, bear and wolf. From there, they set out for Mount Edith Cavell, driving up as far as possible before starting off on foot. Alas, a snowstorm swept down on them whey they were at seven thousand feet and they retreated again to the cabin and a blazing fire of pine logs. Next day, via Banff Springs in the Rockies, they went on to Vancouver where they saw the longest bridge in the Empire.

In Washington the royal couple stayed with the President and Mrs Roosevelt for two nights. They were the first King and Queen of England to set foot on American soil, though Edward VII, when Prince of Wales, had in 1860 been the first member of the royal family to stay in the White House. So much smaller was the White House then, and so great was the demand for beds caused by the Prince's suite, that the seventy-seven-year-old President, James Buchanan, had had to give up his own room and sleep on a sofa.

This time, there were no such problems. The welcome extended by the Roosevelts was warm, lavish, and characterized by a homely charm. 'Well, at last I greet you!' said the President as he grasped the King's hand. 'How are you? I am glad to see you.' Under the windows of the apartments given to the Queen grew country flowers – roses and verbena, their scent fragrant in the warm summer evening. Inside, glinting mirrors reflected the cream satin curtains and the antique daybed with its cushions of finely striped yellow silk.

When the party moved to the President's country house at Hyde Park, this informality even included a certain note of farce: in the middle of dinner a large side-table collapsed with a crash of crockery, and afterwards the butler, unfamiliar with the house, missed the step into the library and fell into the room while carrying the after-dinner drinks tray. Finally, after a long conversation, the President put his hand on the King's knee in a fatherly way and said: 'Young man, it is time for you to go to bed.'

On Thursday 8 June, when the King and Queen were guests of honour at a state banquet in the White House, all was magnificence. Once up the staircase, with its iron balustrade covered with dark green velvet, important visitors were received in the Oval reception room. By a happy chance, the walls here were covered in blue silk of the exact shade so loved by Queen Elizabeth. The same blue was used for the silk curtains and swagged pelmets, and for the satin-covered chairs and sofas. The Oval room also held the world's most expensive piano; this extravaganza was entirely covered in gold lacquer with the arms of the various states embossed on its sides.

The banquet took place in the large oak-panelled dining-room. One hundred and four people could sit at the huge horseshoe table beneath a silver chandelier holding sixty candles. The President sat at the centre of the table's outer side with the Queen beside him; on the inner side, exactly opposite her husband, sat the First Lady, the King on her right.

The menu of calves' head soup, broiled flounder with wine sauce, boned capon and buttered beans, struck horror into the hearts of American gourmets, both for its lack of sophistication and for its failure to represent the best of typical and unique American specialities. 'I doubt very much that the home of the President of the United States has ever presented so unattractive and uninteresting a menu at any State Dinner in its history,' declared the noted cookery writer G. Selmer Fougner. To his mind, the delicacies they should have been served (the ones 'in season in Washington shops just now') included soft-shelled crabs, terrapin, Long Island duckling, green asparagus and new potatoes.

The royal visitors were offered a far more imaginative and delicious selection for a less formal luncheon held in the smaller and more intimate white-panelled dining-room where the Roosevelts ate when *en famille*: jellied soup, soft-shelled crab and spring broilers with Waldorf salad, peas and new potatoes, followed by strawberry ice cream. On other occasions the guests enjoyed ham with barbecue sauce and capons stuffed with rice, okra, shrimps and sliced gherkins – a favourite New England recipe.

They also had a chance to taste the famous White House mint juleps. These were made with very strong bourbon whisky to which lemon juice, ginger ale and fresh mint had been added, and served in frozen glasses, the rims of which had been dipped in sugar. Although the First Lady was a total abstainer this never stopped her serving these drinks to her guests.

Apart from the fact that the Queen herself drank little, there could not have been a greater contrast between the styles of the two women. Mrs Roosevelt was 5 ft 11 in tall – six inches taller than her guest – and a woman entirely without vanity, who boasted she could dress without a mirror. Plain, slightly deaf, the mother of six children and extremely fit, she was used to getting up early, skipping, and then going for a short ride. Despite being very shy, she was a widely syndicated newspaper columnist: 'My Day' was read avidly by millions of her countrywomen.

Queen Elizabeth, on the other hand, was all delicate, smiling femininity, feathered hats and long-skirted dresses in pastel colours, evoking an admiration that was barely short of obsession. In Washington, male society in particular spoke of her in tones of adoring gallantry. 'This pretty face, this wonderful skin!' enthused Representative George Bender of Ohio, adding, after shaking hands with the King: 'Your Majesty shows yourself as a man of most discerning judgment by the beautiful Queen you have selected.' At the Congress Reception, Mr Robert Mouton of Ohio bowed deeply and pressed the Queen's hand to his lips in what he later described as 'a kiss of sincere appreciation', while the Representative for Texas exclaimed, 'You're a thousand times prettier than your pictures – and I mean it!'

The newspapers were equally bowled over, full of such phrases as 'the ever-charming young Queen'; and a pedigree was printed showing the Queen's relationship to George Washington – both were descended from a Colonel Augustine Warner, born in 1611, who settled in Virginia in 1628. As in Canada, Washington women dropped their hemlines to copy her long-skirted dresses, while exclaiming: 'She's mighty pretty!'; and the small daughter of Harry Hopkins, the President's close friend, cried 'Daddy, Daddy, I have seen the Fairy Queen!', as she watched Elizabeth, dazzling in diadem, jewels and crinoline, leave the White House for dinner at the British embassy.

When, to shield her famous complexion from the blazing Washington sun, the Queen raised a white silk parasol lined with dark green over her head, this immediately became a fashion that swept America. By the following day, the managing director of one company had had to order five thousand parasols as a first delivery to cope with this new vogue. Said *Life* magazine: 'To the makers of umbrellas and parasols . . . the reign of George and Elizabeth will ever be the period when a Queen and a Prime Minister raised the parasol and umbrella to unprecedented pinnacles of international significance and chic.' Mrs Roosevelt's tartan chiffon, worn as a compliment to her guest, could not really compete.

'Elizabeth-mania' struck New York with equal fervour. When one of the bands lining their route struck up 'Let Me Call You Sweetheart', the song was instantly taken up by the crowd. 'All New Yorkers are in love with you and you have only been here five minutes!' said the Mayor's Secretary to Queen Elizabeth, who replied, 'What a lovely thing for you to say', and more than three million people lined the route of the eight-mile long drive to the World's Fair (opened at the end of April) to catch a glimpse of the Queen and her husband.

'The Queen looked almost as if she would cry with happiness and the King kept on saying "Wonderful Wonderful!",' reported the *Sunday Express*. New York, town of superlatives – boasting the world's highest building, and more to the point, more Germans than in most large German cities – had taken George and Elizabeth to its enthusiastic heart. 'I knew when Americans saw this very charming man and woman doing a difficult job of work they'd hand it to them,' said Ambassador Joseph Kennedy, explaining why, in spite of his pessimistic view of Britain's future, he had urged the visit of its sovereign. As for the King and Queen, each realized the importance of this visit. It had refreshed and cemented bonds of blood and friendship with the US, and the royal couple themselves had acquired during their trip a greater self-confidence and broader perspective. 'It has made us,' they said.

They left from Halifax, this time in the Canadian Pacific liner *Empress of Britain*, making a brief call at the tiny fishing village of Holyrood on Newfoundland – where, again, the entire local population turned out to greet them enthusiastically – before heading for the open sea.

Mercifully, the journey home was without the danger of the outward voyage. All the original plans were swept aside again, however, when heavy rain, gales and fog forced the fleet to cancel its welcoming of the King and Queen home to British shores. On the morning of 22 June, as the couple were having breakfast, the *Empress of Britain* was nudging her way through the Channel fog at a mere twelve knots, while thirty-one ships of the Home Fleet were streaming out of Portland and Weymouth harbours. But instead of lifting, the fog soon came down so thickly that the *Ark Royal* reported her aircraft would not be able to take off and, from the Commander-in-Chief's ship, *Aurora*, it became impossible to see the two flanking lines of battleships and destroyers drawn up in readiness for a triumphal welcome. Finally, just after 10.00 a.m. the message 'His Majesty the King considers the weather unsuitable for the Fleet Reception and regrets that it must be cancelled' was sent from the royal liner to Admiral Sir Charles Forbes, Commander-in-Chief of the Home Fleet. He radioed back: 'With humble duty, the Fleet congratulates Your Majesties on their safe return from their triumphant tour. The Fleet regrets that the weather has prevented the welcome they had hoped to give.'

Happily, it did not prevent a joyous and touching reunion with their daughters. Up and breakfasting by 7.00 a.m., the princesses had a thrilling day. Smartly dressed in dove grey coats, matching tam o'shanters, and white socks, they were driven to Waterloo past the cheering crowds which were already beginning to gather for their parents' return. At Waterloo they caught the 8.50 train for Southampton, where they were piped on board the destroyer HMS *Kempenfelt*, which took them out into the Solent.

As the *Empress of Britain* approached, the princesses could make out through the fog their mother and father waving to them from the promenade deck; then, still clutching the comics they had been reading, the two little girls scampered shrieking and laughing across the *Kempenfelt*'s gangway and hurled themselves into their mother's arms. Princess Margaret, shouting 'Hullo, Mummy!' at the top of her voice, got there first. Both children hugged their parents and Princess Elizabeth kissed her father, telling him, 'We had a lovely time in the destroyer!' The excitements were not over yet. Two woolly toy pandas, the gift of the crew, presented to them by the ship's smallest page, were quickly discovered by Princess Elizabeth to be nightdress cases. 'How *lovely*!' she said enthusiastically.

By now the fog had cleared and the rain had stopped; as the liner steamed down the Solent, escorted by four destroyers and flights of seaplanes circling in the grey sky, the princesses scampered all round the ship, asking questions. Finally, they were led below protesting that they were not at all cold, and still jumping up and down excitedly as they hung from their parents' hands. The party atmosphere continued when, at 1.30, they went in to luncheon, which the ever-thoughtful crew had laid complete with balloons and paper hats.

The King and Queen finally disembarked at 2.45 p.m., to the strains of 'God Save The King' and the tremendous cheering both from the crews lined up along the bulwarks and from every seaman who could reach a porthole. The whole of Southampton was *en fête*, and all normal work had stopped. The King kissed Queen Mary's hand, and greeted the Dukes and Duchesses of Gloucester and Kent and the Princess Royal and Earl of Harewood. It was noticeable that, far from appearing tired by the 9,000-mile trip, he looked extraordinarily fit, and thoroughly bronzed by the sea air.

In London, the Prime Minister moved an address to Their Majesties in the House of Commons, in which he spoke of the demonstrations of loyalty exceeding all expectations which had taken place in Canada. By evening, a crowd of some fifty thousand people, who had been gathering outside Buckingham Palace ever since the news of their arrival, were chanting 'We want the King! We want the Queen!' Police loudspeaker vans asked them to disperse, but to no avail, and the rhythmic shouting continued. Finally, the King, in dinner-jacket, and the Queen, in a flowing heliotrope evening-dress, came out on to the Buckingham Palace balcony, where they stood for five minutes,

31   Lady Elizabeth Paget and Raimund von Hofmannsthal, married at St Ethelburga's, Bishopsgate

32   Lord Castlerosse (photo Howard Coster)

33   Racing at Newmarket

34   Eno's Fruit Salts – a cure for all ills

35 Sir Henry 'Chips' Channon (photo Howard Coster)

36 Margaret Asquith, Countess of Oxford (photo Howard Coster)

37 Cliveden House, viewed from the south-east

38 George VI and Queen Elizabeth set foot on Canadian soil at the start of their triumphant tour of North America, after a hazardous voyage

39   At the scene of the tragedy, rescue vessels circle the protruding
stern of the *Thetis* in the hope of picking up survivors

40 Mrs Ingleby-Mackenzie with Master Christopher Wynn-Parry

41 Parents at Eton's Fourth of June celebrations – an event of the Season not to be missed

smiling and waving to the crowds. As the cheers rose to a crescendo, men threw their hats in the air and women waved their handkerchiefs.

There was a more official welcome the next day. For once there was no rain as the King, in the full dress uniform of an Admiral of the Fleet, with the Queen by his side, drove in state to luncheon at the Guildhall. This was a traditional occasion of the utmost magnificence. The carriage, with its escort of Life Guards, was stopped at the City Boundary of Temple Bar by two policemen holding a red cord across the road, whereupon the Lord Mayor, Sir Frank Bowater, stepped forward and offered the pearl-handled sword of the City of London, hilt forward, to his sovereign. The King touched the hilt lightly. As they arrived at the silk-hung pavilion on the steps of the Guildhall, where the Lady Mayoress awaited them, they were greeted by a trumpet fanfare, followed by the national anthem played by the band of the Royal Artillery.

Among those at the royal table were Queen Mary, the Prime Minister and his wife, the American Ambassador and Mrs Kennedy, the Canadian High Commissioner and Mrs Massey, the Lord Chancellor and Lady Maugham, the Foreign Secretary and Lady Halifax, and the Lord Mayor and Lady Mayoress. The King and Queen laughed and joked happily together over luncheon; then, when the meal was over, and after smoking only half his cigarette, the King rose to make one of his best speeches. In a firm and confident voice, and speaking without the hesitations which usually plagued him, he told the seven hundred guests of his desire to serve the ideals of Empire, which had inspired his tour. It was his wish to show that 'the Empire's headship exists today as a potent force protecting peace and goodwill among mankind'.

When he mentioned the Queen's name, the guests leapt to their feet and a great cheer broke out, so spontaneous and heartfelt that the Queen's eyes filled with tears. The cheering broke out again when he described their welcome in Canada as 'an expression of thankfulness for those rights of free citizenship which are the heritage of every member of our great Commonwealth of Nations'. As the royal party left the Guildhall, the guests were so affected by patriotic fervour that they broke spontaneously into 'Rule, Britannia! Britannia rule the waves . . .' Fortunately for her future, she still did.

Nineteen

THE TRAGEDY OF THE *THETIS*

June, most beautiful of summer months, opened with horror. In a tragedy that ominously foreshadowed the fate of thousands of other brave men, the submarine HMS *Thetis* sank on her acceptance trials in Liverpool Bay with huge loss of life – out of one hundred and three men on board, only four managed to escape. This terrible accident, which made an indelible impression on anyone old enough to understand it, was played out in front of the entire nation. Every newspaper was filled with pictures of the stricken submarine, its stern protruding from the water and surrounded by naval vessels, tugs and circling aircraft; constant radio bulletins gave the latest news of rescue attempts; and their chances of success dominated all conversations. In Liverpool schools, where children of workers at the Cammell Laird shipyard (where *Thetis* had been built) attended, classes were interrupted with the latest news, and all over the country men and women paused as they passed a church, turned, and went in to pray for a few moments for those on board.

The *Thetis* disaster was the second, and worst, of three submarine accidents within one 23-day spell. On 23 May 1939, the US submarine *Squalus* had failed to surface from a dive off the New Hampshire coast and, though thirty-three of her crew escaped by means of a diving bell, twenty-six were trapped in flooded compartments. On 15 June, the French submarine *Phénix* and her crew of seventy-one were to disappear on a routine practice dive in fifty fathoms of water in the China Seas. (It is believed that she struck a rock on the seabed.)

When the *Thetis* sailed just after 9.30 on the morning of Thursday 1 June for the open waters of Liverpool Bay, to complete her final trial of seaworthiness before acceptance by the Admiralty, she was carrying almost twice the normal complement for her class of submarine. Her own crew consisted of five officers and forty-eight ratings. Also on board were Captain Oram, who commanded the Fifth Submarine Flotilla, the captains of her sister ships *Taku* and *Trident* and the *Trident*'s First Lieutenant and Engineer Officer, eight officials from the department of naval construction at the Admiralty, twenty-six Cammell Laird men, representatives from other shipbuilders, and even two catering employees who were supplying that day's celebratory luncheon.

Although under naval command, because she was not yet commissioned *Thetis* had no naval escort. Consequently, the only vessel to accompany her when she made her first, and last, dive fifteen miles off Great Orme's Head was the tug *Grebecock*, stationed the regulation half-mile away. As the submarine began her dive at 1.40 p.m., it was immediately apparent that she was having great difficulty submerging. To those watching from the *Grebecock*, who included the naval Liaison Officer Lieutenant Coltart, an experienced submariner, this appeared to be due to an extraordinary buoyancy. Finally, and very suddenly, she disappeared beneath the waves.

Following usual submarine practice, *Thetis* signalled her dive to Fort Blockhouse, Gosport, saying that she intended to surface three hours later, between 4.40 and 5.05 p.m. The Duty Chief Yeoman of Signals at Gosport reported at 4.45 that no surfacing signal had been received. From then on Fort Blockhouse called *Thetis* every ten minutes. There was no response.

The Chief of Staff at Gosport was reluctant to put the full-scale 'Subsmash' procedure into operation straightaway for what might be nothing more than a wireless failure. The signal from the *Grebecock* querying the length of *Thetis*'s dive, sent at 4.45, did not arrive at Gosport until 6.15 (*Grebecock* had wirelessed Liverpool, and the message had been sent on by telegram). Five minutes after receipt of *Grebecock*'s message, a full-scale search was under way.

But when the first aircraft and ship arrived on the scene, they were inadvertently fed false information. *Grebecock*, unable to anchor because of the depth of the water, had been pulled about four miles off course without realizing it by the strong tides and so gave a false position. Thus the night search, in bright moonlight, was unsuccessful. Later Captain Oram, one of the four survivors, was to say he wondered why *Thetis*'s distress signal, the indicator buoy and smoke candle, released just before 4.00 p.m., had not been seen.

It was not until 7.50 a.m. the following morning that the destroyer HMS *Brazen*, diverted on her way home from Ireland to search for *Thetis*, finally sighted the submarine. She was nose down in shallow water some four miles from the spot where she had dived, with her stern projecting 18 ft above the surface of the sea at a steep angle.

Almost at once two men appeared in the water beside her. These were Captain Oram and Lieutenant Woods, *Thetis*'s torpedo officer, who were both picked up immediately by the destroyer's whaler. It was not until two hours later, at about 10.00 a.m., that two more men surfaced: Leading Stoker Walter Arnold and Mr Frank Shaw of Cammell Laird. It was the evidence of these four at the subsequent enquiry which clearly established the cause of the tragedy, as well as painting a picture of unforgettable heroism.

What had happened? The cause of the tragedy lay, ironically enough, in *Thetis*'s very newness.

Before opening the rear (inner) door of a torpedo tube to load, or inspect for leaks, it was essential to check that the bow cap was not open or, of course, the sea would flood in. To prevent the opening of the rear door when the tube was flooded (as for firing a torpedo) there were various safeguards: checking the drain valve, which would show infallibly whether a tube was flooded or empty, checking the bow cap indicator dials which told whether the lever that opened the bow cap was at 'shut' or 'open', and checking the pressure gauge.

The final precaution was to use the test cock. When its lever was moved to the unlocked position, two small holes were lined up, giving a minute opening – often called a 'telltale' – into the tube. If the tube was flooded, a fine jet of water would spurt through the holes. When *Thetis*'s torpedo tubes were painted, however, the holes in the test cock of Number Five torpedo tube had been blocked by a skin of paint – or rather, with a tough bitumastic solution applied before final enamelling. *And no one had checked to see that they were clear*.

In addition, the 'closed' position on the bow cap indicator of Number Five torpedo tube – half hidden anyway by a horizontal bar – was, unusually, diametrically opposite to that on the easily-seen indicators of the tubes immediately above it. So, to anyone not used to this quirk of design, all the bow caps could appear closed when Number Five was in fact open.

After the submarine had dived, Lieutenant Woods decided to inspect the inside of the tubes, largely to check if there was any leakage round the all-important bow caps. There was nothing to make him think any of the tubes would be flooded – indeed, quite the reverse: *Thetis*'s unusual lightness, despite her extra passengers, equivalent in weight to about four hundred gallons of water, did not suggest full tubes.

But the procedure he had learned at torpedo school was stringent: the four routine tests must always be carried out to check whether a tube was flooded or empty. When Woods began his inspection shortly before three o'clock, he failed to carry out the all-important drain valve check, which would have indicated that a tube was full.

He looked at the dials and levers, and checked the test cock of Number One tube. Nothing came through its telltale hole, and the rear door opened easily. Completing his inspection of the bow cap, he repeated the procedure at tubes Two, Three and Four.

At Number Five tube, Woods again checked the test cock. Nothing. But when he tried to open Number Five rear door, he found the lever extremely difficult to move. At the time, this did not worry him: many other pieces of mechanism were stiff because of their very newness.

As he finally managed it, the door, now free from all restraint, burst open and the sea flooded in. Woods, still with no reason to imagine the bow cap open (it was never discovered why it was), believed that the tube itself must be fractured and lost the few seconds in which he might have been able to move the bow cap lever back to 'shut'. From this moment, although it was not to be realized for some time, there was no hope.

When the accident happened, Leading Stoker Arnold was in the pumping room. His picture of what happened is graphic:

'There was a rush of air from the fore-end torpedo tube. There was shouting from the control room to surface. Next the lads who were in the fore-head torpedo tube came scrambling out. They got out of that compartment, and then went into the second compartment, into the accommodation space, and then shut the door. We couldn't do it for a few seconds because of the angle of the boat but eventually we managed.

'By then *Thetis* was just hanging in the water at an angle – it was the steepest angle I have ever known for a submarine.

'We knew we were down by then. There was no panic. They were all calm. There was no thought of disaster. Everyone was confident and we all felt sure we should get to the top ourselves in a few hours.'

They tried blowing the main tanks, but this did not bring *Thetis* back to the surface. Escape to the surface through the Davis Escape chamber during the hours of night had been ruled out: with no ships in the vicinity, the combination of darkness and strong tides, and exposure in the cold waters would ensure certain death within a short time. It was agreed after discussion that the next step was to try and close the bow cap, after which the tube could be pumped out.

The first to attempt this was Lieutenant Chapman, who entered the Davis Escape chamber. It was flooded up, but he had to give up through pain and dizziness. Woods immediately volunteered to make the next attempt, and asked for another hand to help him; Mitchell, the torpedo gunner's mate, stepped forward. But they, too, failed owing to the distress suffered by Mitchell as the chamber was flooded. Again the laborious process of draining it, with a chain of buckets passed from hand to hand, took place. By now all the lights were out.

Another plan was devised: to climb a ladder to the forehatch in order to screw it down before attempting closure of the rear door. Again Woods volunteered, cold, shivering and exhausted but insisting that he was all right; this time he took with him Petty Officer Smithers. But the dizziness, and terrible pain round the heart, suffered by Smithers as the chamber flooded up meant that his attempt, also, had to be abandoned. With this third failure, hope diminished. It was now just after 7.00 p.m.

By 4.00 a.m., the submarine had been considerably lightened: over fifty tons of fuel and tons of fresh water had been pumped out, and her stern had risen. Captain Oram was still confident that it could be raised to the surface. By 7.00 a.m. *Thetis* was lying at an angle of about thirty-four degrees – Oram had estimated that at an angle of thirty-five degrees the stern would be showing above the surface.

By then, conditions inside her were serious. Normally, in those days submariners could expect to survive thirty-six hours underwater; with the large number of extra men on board *Thetis* and the consequent consumption of air, it would be more like twenty-four hours. Already, half the air on board had been used earlier to blow the main tanks.

Breathing had become deep, laboured and distressing, many men were retching and their eyes watering. Extreme lassitude had set in, coupled with inability to co-ordinate thought and action. It was imperative that the lengthy process of escape should start as soon as possible if the last men were to have sufficient energy to carry it out.

But first, the submarine's position had to be made known. Captain Oram decided to try to reach the surface himself, in order to act as a living indicator buoy and, if he survived, to help co-ordinate the recovery operation. Oram planned, if the tide allowed him to reach it, to hold on to the submarine's stern or to the indicator buoy sent up earlier. If he failed, as was all too likely, he would be swept away by the tide; to double the chance of success, he asked for a volunteer to go with him. Again Woods volunteered.

Messages were tied to both men giving *Thetis*'s position and saying that the two forward compartments were flooded. In the darkness of the silent ship, Oram and Woods scrambled on their knees up to the stern escape chamber helped by the hands of sailors lying on their backs. The hull was now tilting at an angle of forty-two degrees.

Oram and Woods, still not knowing whether any ships were near or whether they were going to their deaths through cold and exhaustion, aggravated by the effects of the carbon dioxide poisoning from which all were now suffering, stood in the slowly flooding escape chamber, watched through peepholes by those left behind. Just before they pushed the top hatch open they heard three charges detonate. A faint cheer went up from their shipmates: *Thetis* had been found.

Oram and Woods did not find escape difficult. The after escape chamber was only 20 ft below the surface, and they were picked up straightaway by *Brazen*'s whaler. It was now 8.00 a.m., and Oram still hoped with some confidence that all could be saved. He expected that pairs of survivors would now appear roughly every twenty minutes. All on *Brazen* were optimistic: the men on *Thetis* had signalled by tapping that they were all still alive – and surely, her very nearness to the surface, with its life-giving fresh air, must in itself be a good sign?

But another two hours passed, and still no more heads had surfaced. Oram, the only man on the spot who knew accurately the internal layout of the submarine and the conditions inside her, was suffering so badly from carbon dioxide poisoning that he was unable to participate in any discussion until one and a half hours after his escape.

Inside *Thetis*, talk had almost stopped in order to save breath. The men were waiting in their Davis equipment as the second pair of volunteers, a naval rating and a civilian, entered the hatch. Both failed to make it and were brought back into the submarine dead; of a second pair who tried, one died in the hatch and the second shortly after being brought back. All four were found to be foaming at the mouth and had torn off their masks.

The next volunteers were Arnold and Shaw. By now, their growing weakness had made scrambling almost vertically up the escape hatch doubly difficult. Arnold took charge, telling Shaw to breathe naturally, and to open his exhaust cock as he left the chamber.

'I then flooded up. The water came up to our middles. I then opened another valve and water came in quite quickly. Then Mr Shaw pushed the hatch up and went up. Then I went out myself. I got caught in some clips as I left the hatch, and kicked myself free.' They felt sure, he added, that everyone else on board would follow. But no one else appeared.

It was supposed that, in a subsequent attempt, one of the civilians on board failed to follow the procedure correctly, jammed the hatch, and blocked all further exit. Escape was a terrifying enough process even under practice conditions. Before the hatch could be opened, pressure had to be equalized within and without, which meant allowing the water to rise above the head of the man escaping until the chamber was completely full. As Frank Shaw said: 'As the water covers your head, you can hardly see and you've got a feeling you are trapped. Instinctively you put up your hand to shove the hatch open.' But, of course, it would remain obdurately closed and for a young and inexper-

ienced seaman, who was probably a non-swimmer, it must have
been all too easy to panic.

At 10.40 the Sixth Flotilla of Tribal class destroyers arrived
from Portsmouth, steaming in perfect formation across Liverpool
Bay; and, as the senior officer present, the flotilla captain now
took command of operations. At 11.30, shortly before high water,
the diver from the salvage vessel *Vigilant* went down – but only,
as was correct diving procedure, to fix guide lines to the
submarine's hull to assist the divers to follow. By now, though,
there was only one chance of saving the men inside her and that
was by replacing an atmosphere growing more foul and poison-
ous by the minute with fresh air as rapidly as possible. It was
decided to cut a hole in *Thetis*'s stern.

But time, tide and distance were to prove enemies impossible
to overcome. Drilling meant obtaining oxyacetylene blow-
pumps . . . and the tug from Birkenhead bringing the oxyacetylene equipment in response to *Brazen*'s signal did not reach the
scene until 2.30 p.m. Joined by *Vigilant*, she began instantly to
prepare for drilling. Because of the danger of the rising tide
slopping into the opened submarine, the flotilla captain decided
that *Thetis* must be pulled into a more upright position, with a
second cable around her for safety. Gradually her stern rose to an
almost vertical angle; success seemed in sight.

However, the pull of the swirling water was too strong.
Suddenly her stern canted over, hung for a few seconds and, at
3.10, the 3½-inch steel hawser snapped with a pistol-shot crack
and *Thetis* rolled gently over under the water to slide 140 ft down
to the mud of Liverpool Bay. All was over.

The brief official statement came some twenty-five hours after
the air had finally run out. At 4.10 p.m. on Saturday 3 June, it was
announced: 'The Admiralty regrets that hope of saving lives in
the *Thetis* must be abandoned.'

Later, at the enquiry, Lieutenant Woods had the bitter experience of reliving the moment that must have remained with
him all his life, when he had to agree with Counsel that, had he

performed all four routine tests, he would have found out that Number Five torpedo tube was not empty but open to the Atlantic.

A final question was put to Captain Oram. 'Did you see any sign of complaint or panic from beginning to end?' For the first time his voice trembled. 'I would like to make known the very gallant behaviour of all on board. I saw no sign of any panic. Whenever there was any work to be done I heard men talking and joking until the foul air caused them to be quiet. They showed a quiet bravery of which the memory will live with me for ever.'

On 7 June, the Admiralty held memorial services for *Thetis*. At St Martin's in the Fields, the Sea Lords knelt with two thousand Londoners; at sea, HMS *Hebe* carried the mourning families to the spot where the entombed men lay, leaving behind her a wake of flowers strewn over the heaving, sunlit sea as a single bell tolled.

Salvage operations began almost immediately. The *Thetis* was raised, refitted, and commissioned as HMS *Thunderbolt* in October 1940. She was sunk in the Mediterranean on 14 March 1943 by an Italian corvette, one of the eighty-eight British submarines lost during the War. Lieutenant Woods, who won the Distinguished Service Cross, was killed in a car crash in Malta in 1946.

Twenty

FOURTH OF JUNE

The last Fourth of June before the war took place on Saturday 3 June. That year, Eton's annual celebration of George III's birthday occurred on one of the summer's most perfect days, marred only by the tragic news dominating that morning's papers. Brilliant sunshine bathed the chestnut trees, their pink and white candles stirred by a faint, pleasant and – in the words of the Eton Boating Song – 'hay harvest' breeze. Around the ancient buildings and famous playing fields strolled parents, friends, relations and Old Boys, leavened with the inevitable sprinkling of debutantes. With Old Etonians forming a sizable section of those who governed the country and ran its commercial affairs and social life, the Fourth of June was an event of the Season not to be missed.

There were Speeches, luncheons, cricket matches, and exhibitions. There were two Processions of Boats in the evening, one in the early evening and the other at dusk, followed by a display of fireworks as a grand finale.

It was a long day. For masters and boys, it started with Early School from 7.30 a.m. to 8.20, then breakfast, followed by Chapel (then compulsory), after which came the process of smartening up before parents arrived in mid-morning. On the Fourth of June, everyone was allowed some of the sartorial privileges normally reserved for members of the Eton Society – always known as 'Pop' – a self-elected society of senior boys who in effect acted as school prefects. The Captain of the School (the senior King's Scholar) and the Captain of the Oppidans (the senior non-Scholar) were *ex officio* members of Pop, which was otherwise composed largely of the best games players.

Boys who had not yet grown to the necessary 5 ft 4 in in height which required them to wear tailcoats wore an Eton suit. This consisted of short black Eton jacket, black waistcoat and striped trousers; a large starched white Eton collar, worn outside the collar of the jacket, and a black tie, completed the smaller boys' uniform. Their taller friends in tails, who normally wore white collars with tuck-in bow ties and black waistcoats, put on stick-up collars, white evening bow ties, and buff or grey double-breasted waistcoats. Everyone was allowed to carry a rolled umbrella and wear a buttonhole. On other days such refinements were the prerogative only of members of Pop, who could be recognized by the splendour and elaborateness of their waistcoats and their beautiful spongebag trousers, but on the Fourth of June, as Bernard Fergusson wrote: 'Only the braid on their coats and the sealing wax on their hats will distinguish Pop.' Everyone had his top hat specially ironed, a service provided free by the two rival Eton outfitters, New and Lingwood, and E. C. Devereux.

Before lunch there were Speeches in Upper School. These were orations, poetry or drama, often in Greek or Latin as many Collegers were classical specialists. They were learned by heart and declaimed by members of the sixth form, dressed in knee breeches, silk stockings and silver buckled shoes, to the Provost and Fellows and a small invited audience. *The Times*'s description cannot be bettered:

'It was a perfect day for Upper Club or Agar's Plough or the Brocas. Not quite so perfect, perhaps, for sitting on a rather unyielding form in Upper School and enviously watching through the long windows the lights and shades on Lupton's Tower. Yet the Fourth is not the Fourth without Speeches, and he is but half a man who does not joyfully face them . . . As Miss Prism, Hope-

Jones, the Captain of the School, had the true "prunes and prisms" voice and accent and carried the scene to triumph largely on his own back.

'Likewise new and amusing, the game of bridge, from Punch, between Shakespeare, Johnson, Mrs Shakespeare and Marlowe. The conversation is entirely in Shakespearian quotations, such as "I'll call for Clubs!", "I'll double thy folly!" and so on.'

Quite by chance, one of the sixth form speakers had chosen a passage from J. M. Synge's *Riders to the Sea* which, in view of that morning's news, was only too tragically apt. *The Times* continued:

'Yet it must be added that by far the best thing in Speeches came too early and made all that succeeded appear just a little flat. It may be doubted whether the longest memory can recall anything finer on these occasions than Watson's speech . . . in which he was the old woman mourning the loss of her husband and sons. There was no need for the morning's tragic news from the sea to render it poignant. The complete hush which enveloped Upper School attested to its quality. The speaker was very quiet. He stood motionless as a statue. He made no ostensible attempt to add to the beauty of the words and thereby added incalculably to their effect. His brogue – or rather, perhaps, his intonation – it would be an impertinence for an Englishman to praise.'

Old Boys, as was the custom, sent telegrams to the Provost and Headmaster. From Brazil, China, Egypt and the Sudan, from Palestine, Bareilly and Shinyanga, from Tientsin, Shanghai and Malta, from Kenya, Rhodesia, Australia and the Argentine came these tributes to a classical education. The Governor of the Fiji Islands wrote: 'Solus in insulis Fiji Etonenses pie salutant Luke Gubernator' ('Alone in the isles of Fiji, the Governor, Luke, sends faithful greetings to the men of Eton'). The Viceroy of India wired: 'Urbe summa in Indis cenaturi Etonenses duodecim Matrem salutamus. Vicerege praecentori Floreat concinemus et haec nostra cena Himalayensis Esto Perpetua Linlithgow'

('Twelve Etonians, about to dine in the capital city of India, salute our Alma Mater. We shall sing May Eton Flourish! with the Viceroy as our choirmaster and may this, our Himalayan dinner, be celebrated for ever. Linlithgow'). And from Sydney came a distant message of solidarity: 'Tres Togati novemque Oppidani Sydneyi apud guberantorem cyathis centum subtis vigilbusque lucernis ad lucem perlatis salutant Almam Matrem' ('Three Collegers and nine Oppidans at the home of the Governor in Sydney, having taken a hundred glasses and having kept our vigil through the night until dawn, salute our Alma Mater'). From seven Etonians in New York came 'Septem Etonenses apud Novum Eboracum coenantes Almam Matrem salutamus Regi et Reginae propinamus Floreat Etona' ('Seven Etonians assembling together in New York drink the health of the King and Queen and propose the toast to our Alma Mater with the words "Floreat Etona!"').

From seven others in France came the message 'Sept ancients élèves à Paris respectuesement vous saluent. Vive l'Eton. Heseltine, Buckhurst, Lambert, Stanley, Wyndham, Tomkin, Mason.' All were eighteen or nineteen, staying in France to improve their French, and the message was despatched during the course of a Fourth of June dinner at a small restaurant called the Rotisserie Perigourdine at 2 Place St Michel, chosen for its excellent value. Their five-course dinner of crème de champignons, sole meunière, caneton à l'orange, asperges vertes sauce mousseline and fraises des bois à la crème, came to forty-five francs a head (about five shillings). They drank Chablis, Châteauneuf du Pape, Champagne Deutz et Geldermann 1933 and liqueurs. Two of them did not survive the war, Peter Tomkin and Gully Mason, the wildest Etonian of his generation, perpetually on the verge of the sack, who was killed as a Flight Sergeant.

The Princess Royal and Lord Harewood, both of whose sons were then at Eton, were among the hundred guests at a luncheon in College Hall given by the Provost, Lord Hugh Cecil, and

Fellows. The headmaster, Claude Aurelius Elliott, with his wife, gave a separate luncheon party at their house in the Cloisters.

After lunch – picnics for most parents, though some house-masters gave luncheon parties – people perambulated round Agar's Plough and under the magnificent elms of Upper Club, on which the First and Second Elevens were playing the Eton Ramblers – the Ramblers beat the First Eleven quickly and easily by nine wickets – and at 3.00 the Band of the Welsh Guards struck up. Reported *The Times*: 'there was nothing new unless, to some people, the heraldic animals – they may be wyverns, or they may be griffins – which guard the bridge from Upper Club to Datchet Lane and seem rather to dwarf it'.

Soon it was time for those who were going to row in the Procession of Boats to get ready. They wore costumes copied from a George III sailor's uniform, with blue or white duck trousers (for upper and lower boats respectively), a striped shirt, short dark blue jacket and straw hat with gold crossed oars and a few artificial flowers. The colour of the ribbon and the stripes on the shirt varied according to boat; those in the *Alexandra*, for example, wore shirts with pinkish-mauve stripes and a pinky-mauve hat ribbon, for *Monarch* the colour was dark blue, for the *Prince of Wales* golden-brown. Coxes of the Upper Boats were dressed as miniature admirals, and those of the Lower Boats as midshipmen. For a wet bob to receive a letter from one of the Eight saying, 'I would be delighted if you would take an oar in my boat, the *Prince of Wales*, on the Fourth of June', was a moment of supreme excitement and pleasure; not quite so unmixed, perhaps, for the parents who would have to foot the bill at the hosiers. Other boys had their families to tea in their rooms, buying for this occasion ample supplies of strawberries and cream, and Fuller's chocolate or walnut cake. A pot of tea was produced by the boys' maid.

There followed Absence, the roll call in School Yard and Weston's Yard to ensure that none of the boys had sneaked off to London, and the first Procession of Boats on the stretch of river above Windsor Bridge. This did not attract a large crowd, but the families of the oarsmen, at least, attended.

Towards nightfall, there was a gradual drift down to Fellows' Eyot just below Windsor Lock. Spectators found places on the grassy bank and watched the last swallows circling over the water as they waited for the Procession to begin. The boats had been taken downstream, through Windsor Lock to the Windsor Castle Home Park, where supper in a marquee awaited the oarsmen. There was beer or cider to drink, but for most it was a fairly sober affair – it would be difficult enough to stand up in a moving boat without the added hazard of tipsiness. In the gathering dusk, with a band playing and floodlights illuminating the river, the Procession began, the boats being rowed at a fair speed to get way on – essential if they were to be reasonably stable when the oarsmen stopped rowing.

The first boat was always the ten-oared *Monarch*, full of school heroes such as the Captain of the School, the Captain of the Oppidans, the Captain of the Eleven, and the Master of the Beagles, many of whom could not row at all. It was followed by two other Upper Boats. As each one came into view, its crew stood up two by two, finally taking off their hats in salute to the spectators. The Lower Boats had a greater ordeal: in addition to standing up, each pair of oarsmen had to hoist their oars to an upright position. This exercise had to be perfectly synchronized, otherwise the boat would become unbalanced and the oarsman, or even the whole crew, would topple into the Thames.

That Saturday, when the sixth boat, the *Thetis*, glided out of the darkness into the floodlights, it was seen that around their hats her crew wore neither coloured ribbon nor flowers but a simple black crêpe band. The chatter and laughter ceased, the watching crowd rose to their feet and stood in silence until the boat had passed.

The day, as always, ended with a half-hour fireworks display on the far bank of the river. There was every kind, huge catherine wheels, crackers that leaped about like maddened grasshoppers, maroons, 'acrobats' that swung round parallel bars faster and faster as they burned ever more fiercely, but perhaps the most popular items were the magnificent rockets. These exploded with successive bursts of coloured stars – first red stars, then red followed a split second later by blue stars, then red, blue and silver stars. By this time, the audience, most of whom knew what was coming, were counting enthusiastically. Excitement rose until the final rocket produced six different, dazzling showers of coloured sparks, and the display closed with two tableaux. The first showed the faces of King George VI and Queen Elizabeth, which surmounted the words 'God Save The King!' and the second, the college arms above the motto 'Floreat Etona'.

Not everyone was able to enjoy this display, however. An unwritten rule had been broken and the next issue of the *Chronicle* carried a letter from an aggrieved but anonymous Old Boy, who signed himself merely 'O.E.'

'It may seem pernickety to offer any proposal for improving the Fourth of June arrangements after a Fourth that will live long in memory as one wholly delightful and successful. But I should like to make one suggestion: i.e. that one or two representatives of authority might walk about Fellows' Eyot during Fireworks, to ensure that people really *do* sit down. I write as one who happened to be not very far from a young man and a young lady who absolutely refused to sit down in spite of many protests – some kindly, some acid – from behind. I can hardly believe that he could have been an O.E., so carelessly regardless was he of the enjoyment of those behind him!'

Of that year's Eton Eight, four were to be killed in the war. J. M. H. Wilson was killed serving in the 10th Hussars. *Thetis*'s captain, John Skinner, was killed when serving in the Indian Cavalry (his younger brother was also killed; they are commemorated by a bridge in the playing fields). Derek Mond, the captain of the *Alexandra*, was killed as a pilot in the Fleet Air Arm. Henry Maudslay was a Squadron Leader serving in 617

Squadron (the Dambusters) and died with all his crew when, twenty minutes after the destruction of the Mohne Dam, his bomb hit the top of the secondary target, the Eder Dam, and exploded just under his Lancaster.

Twenty-One

FLAMING JUNE

'During these last two months of summer the apocalypse was shadowed ahead as certainly as the twilight signals the night,' Diana Cooper was to write many years later. Blazing sunshine and heat fit to buckle railway lines gave a slight air of unreality to the first of the ARP exercises held in the West End – an effect heightened by the doggerel concocted by someone in the Lord Privy Seal's Office to describe the correct course of action indicated by the various air raid signals.

> *Wavering sound . . . go to ground.*
> *Steady blast . . . raiders passed.*
> *If rattles you hear . . . gas you must fear.*
> *But if handbells you hear . . . then all is clear.*

There were slit trenches in Kensington Gardens, barrage balloons floated above the London parks, posters everywhere described how to recognize mustard gas and decontaminate oneself after an attack. Hotel and restaurant windows were sandbagged; the Savoy, particularly vulnerable in its position on the river, had already fortified itself before the Munich crisis with thousands of feet of steel tubing and timber beams reinforced with concrete in its main restaurant and reception rooms. But the implied peril did not put off the usual throng of visitors arriving from the United States for London's most fashionable months –

regulars like Douglas Fairbanks and Mary Pickford, Mr and Mrs Sam Goldwyn, Alfred Hitchcock, the Lunts, Robert Donat, Leslie Howard (later to be killed as a passenger in a civilian airliner shot down by the Luftwaffe on its way from Lisbon to London) and the Armenian-born novelist Michael Arlen, who would retort 'Per ardua ad astrakhan' when teased about his smart new fur-collared overcoat.

The Lords of the Admiralty announced that they had decided to give the Fleet its annual summer leave early, in July, so that ships could be refitted and ready for exercises in August. Cheap milk, at 2d a pint about half the normal cost, was introduced for mothers and young children. Contingency plans were evolved for lessons by radio to avoid chaos in schools flooded by evacuees and, along more practical lines, for a national blood transfusion service. Registrars of marriages were under order to report immediately any notice of a marriage which appeared to have been arranged in order to give an alien British citizenship, an expedient to which German and Austrian women living in Britain were now resorting in increasing numbers.

For those with any drop of Jewish blood, such measures were all too understandable. Stories of Hitler's persecution of the Jews were becoming more common. Eleven thousand living in East Prussia had been told to get out by 20 June, with a further ten thousand Polish Jews given the alternative of leaving at once or being put in concentration camps; and the horrors of these were gradually becoming known. In one article, the *News Chronicle* estimated that at least ten per cent of the prisoners were dying, after appalling whippings and torture. Those who could seized their last chance of escape: ten thousand were believed to have entered Britain in the previous three months. But obtaining permission to stay was not always easy, and pathetic appeals, such as this, in *The Times*, regularly appeared:

'Will kind-hearted person help to get transit stay. Urgently needed; 64 years old Jew from Germany, good appearance; formerly manufacturer; possesses permit to South America. Please help. Box H1349.'

Reservists were called up for two or three weeks of training and younger men were flocking to the colours, though how their fathers felt, who had fought in the 1914–18 war, and their mothers, who had seen their own fathers, older brothers and cousins go off to that wholesale slaughter, can only be imagined. 'Enquired of Robin about my joining the Army, i.e. the new Welsh Guards Battalion,' wrote David Verey on 3 June. A few days later, he played tennis all afternoon and in the evening 'took the under-gardener and a tenant into a Recruiting meeting in Bibury. Captain Gunther who is forming a new Bibury Platoon in the new 7th Battalion of the Gloucestershire Regiment spoke. It all sounded very exciting and Victor joined up. I wished I could.'

In that small section of society known as Society, Savile Row tailors were kept busy making uniforms for the new young officers – a common next step was the portrait in uniform by Vandyck or some other well-known photographer – and so many dancing partners were now at Territorial camps that there was a great shortage of men at debutante parties. (The resourceful Lady St John of Bletsoe had her own remedy: instead of the usual mixed dinner party she asked only men, so as to ensure a squad of partners for the girl she was sponsoring that season.)

For the parties, of course, continued. Frivolous as they seemed to many in view of the events in Europe grinding relentlessly on, they did at least shed a semblance of normality over a country being prepared for the unthinkable as rapidly as possible. And after all, what point would there have been in stopping them? So the young girls danced and chattered as they always had, comparing notes on the bands, the floors, the full-skirted frocks worn by their friends, the strange new floral decorations by Constance Spry, in which turnips mingled with gladioli, or tomatoes and purple green cabbage nestled among the soft mauves and pinks of sweet peas.

At 18 Bryanston Square, Geoffrey Howard's band played at Lady Baillie's dance for her debutante daughter and the house was filled for the night with red peonies. The supper was particularly good, featuring a copious supply of plovers' eggs, a delicacy not always easily come by. (Ever since the Lapwings Act of 1928 it had been illegal to sell British plovers' eggs, though not to eat those found on your land, and consequently most were imported from Holland. In 1939, plovers were either laying badly or managing to conceal their eggs from their human predators, and consignments were small. Fortunately, the eggs of the black-headed gull were almost as delicious and cost far less – only about 3s a dozen instead of anything from 15s to £1.)

The Kents and Gloucesters were among the guests at the Baillie dance, although the Duchess of Kent, looking taller, slimmer and more elegant than ever in peach lamé with a high, pointed tiara, had to leave early to go on to the Rose Ball. Lady Baillie herself wore a 'fender' tiara but, for once, the majority of women guests were bareheaded. For the first time for many years, tiaras were suddenly 'out'; even at a large party in St James's Palace a few days later, where guests were to be presented to the Duchess of Gloucester, only a few women wore them.

The habit of knitting in the ballroom, however, was becoming ever more popular. Needles clicked away merrily among the rows of chaperones sitting along the walls. Lady Acland, responsible for starting the whole thing a few weeks earlier, brought an ambitious piece of work with her to one dance, a wool dress to which she managed to add several inches during the course of the evening. Even so, one chaperone who brought a mauve jumper she hoped to complete during a dance at Claridges did not have the courage to bring it into the ballroom when she realized everyone else was empty-handed, and left it bundled up ignominiously in the cloakroom.

Some people still genuinely believed that the threat of war would recede, while others hoped. On 8 June Lord Halifax intervened in a Foreign Affairs debate in the House of Lords with an important speech on Anglo-German relations. A danger-ous element in the situation, he said, was the possibility of the

German people as a whole drifting to the conclusion that Britain had abandoned all desire for an understanding. And, in one of the many letters with which Margot Asquith bombarded *The Times* at that period, she urged the vital importance of a united front supporting Chamberlain: 'Do the Germans, the Italians, or the citizens of any country in Europe believe that we intend to declare war upon them? I doubt it. If any of these wish to make war upon us they would be encouraged to do so if they read in our newspapers we are disunited.'

There was still the possibility of an agreement with the Russians – the only chance of transforming the whole picture – though the truth was that the Russians, as always, were an enigma even to those conducting the negotiations. 'I can't make up my mind whether the Bolshies are double-crossing us and trying to make difficulties or whether they are only showing the cunning and suspicion of the peasant,' wrote Chamberlain to his sister Ida on 10 June. 'On the whole I incline to the latter view but I am sure they are greatly encouraged by the Opposition and the Winston-Eden-Lloyd George group with whom Maisky is in constant touch.'

Most people believed that, if war did come, it would at least hold off until after the harvest. At that moment, the headlines were dominated by the launching on 14 June of the Japanese blockade of the British and French Concessions in Tientsin. 'There is a brand new and very serious crisis as the Japanese are blockading the British Concession and treating the British in outrageous fashion. This is an act of war, and it is supported by Germany,' wrote David Verey. They were, in fact, threatening to electrify the barbed wire barricades surrounding both Concessions, creating, in effect, the equivalent of concentration camps – and inflicting rough handling and systematic humiliations on British and French subjects. Several were stripped naked, ostensibly for a customs search, at one of the Tientsin barriers; after one such incident, the Japanese commander, General Homma, blandly denied intent to cause indignity by telling journalists, 'We Japanese do not regard nudity as disgraceful,' citing, as an example, the Japanese practice of mixed baths. As a clincher, he smilingly suggested that he strip there and then to prove his point, a proposal which was not taken up by the assembled members of the Press. The Government debated the matter urgently; representations were made to the Japanese government, which failed to reply; food ships were despatched to Tientsin; finally, towards the end of the month, Tokyo gave a hint that it was ready to talk.

Meanwhile, life went on. England won the Test Match against the West Indies, with Headley scoring his second century; and at Wimbledon, attended by Queen Mary in a snowy white dress with powder-blue parasol, the American Alice Marble beat twenty-five-year-old Kay Stammers from St Albans to win the Ladies' Championship. Shipping companies reported a cruising boom after the slack days of April, when it had seemed that war might break out at any moment. The Blue Star, Canadian Pacific and Orient and Peninsular lines all reported better business than in 1938 for their various cruises to Norway, the Mediterranean, and the Atlantic isles.

But anyone who had picked up a German newspaper would have sensed that the sands were rapidly running out. The German press campaign against Britain had now become vitriolic, she was invariably referred to as Perfidious Albion and the humiliations of the British and French at the hands of the Japanese were reported in gloating detail. On the penultimate day of June, Lord Halifax, in a speech at the Royal Institute of International Affairs, replied with his gravest warning yet, emphasizing his country's determination to resist aggression by all the forces at her command.

By now, a strong public campaign was being waged for Churchill and Eden to be included in the Cabinet. Both were recognized as men whom Germany would take more seriously when they spoke in this way. 'I fear war is coming and I believe it will be in September,' wrote Marie Belloc Lowndes to her daughter on 25 June. 'I mean by that Hitler will "take a chance" at Danzig, hoping that Chamberlain will again give in. Then there will be war. I can't understand how anyone can doubt it considering the way Hitler and his gangsters are going on.'

Twenty-Two

~

ROYAL ASCOT

Royal Ascot, the most fashionable race meeting of the social calendar, began on Tuesday 13 June. That year it was a trifle short on glamour: as the King and Queen were on their state visit to North America, their place was taken by the Duke and Duchess of Gloucester and there were no daily state carriage processions down the course. No preparations had been spared, though, to make this elegant meeting as splendid as possible. During the drought which preceded Ascot Week, millions of gallons of water had been pumped on to the course, which unfurled like a velvety green ribbon against the dried-up, paler tones of the surrounding countryside. The renovation of the stands had been completed and, at a cost of £500,000, a tote built.

Despite the large amounts of money that changed hands at Ascot, there was very little criminal activity. It was the only race-course in the world with a police court actually on the premises, where cases were dealt with almost immediately. It had been set up as a result of an act of *lèse-majesté* in the nineteenth century, when a bottle was hurled at the head of King William IV. The court was presided over by the Chairman of the local Bench and the Chief London Magistrate, Sir Rollo Graham Campbell. His task was an enviable one, as between cases they were able to watch the racing from the royal enclosure. Sometimes they managed an almost uninterrupted day's racing.

'The vogue for Ascot house parties has returned. Entertaining will be on the grand scale and if only the King and Queen were here, everything would be perfect!' lamented one correspondent. For only Windsor Castle, not used by any member of the Royal family while the King and Queen were away, was without its customary house party.

Almost every house of size in the neighbourhood was full. Just as some who lived in Leicestershire or Rutland would let their houses for the hunting season, so non-racing people near Ascot, Sunningdale or Bracknell would rent out their homes for Ascot Week. For these few days, rents of £100 – then an enormous sum – were commonplace. Those who preferred not to turn out of their houses sometimes rented out their drives only, as car parks; for some of the richer, this was a means of raising money for local charities.

Sometimes temporary owners would bring in their own household staff, though invariably the resident gardener was retained, as the only person who could be relied on to produce ripe strawberries or hothouse peaches at their peak, or to forecast when Cook could rely on perfect young peas to accompany the salmon. Sometimes a condition of renting was that the house should be fully staffed, and the tenants would bring with them only personal servants such as a lady's maid or nanny. Meanwhile the owners, a handsome profit in their pockets, would be enjoying a holiday elsewhere.

For the community round about, Ascot was a tremendous moneyspinner, putting thousands of pounds into the pockets of local tradesmen. One local butcher's main worry was wiener schnitzel. 'Veal done in a foreign style seems to be a craze this year,' he said. 'You have to cut it thin as paper, which makes a lot of work.' He preferred straightforward orders for sirloin of beef or saddle of mutton. On the course itself, there was a catering innovation: the introduction of a lunch costing five shillings, with as many helpings as anyone could eat.

Even for racegoers who came down for the day, Ascot was an expensive business. No one seriously social would dream of attending unless they were in the royal enclosure, vouchers for which cost six guineas a day for a gentleman, four for a lady, with a box at thirty guineas. The price, though extraordinarily high even by the standards of the time, was no deterrent: on 14 April, the first day the Ascot Office in the courtyard of St James's Palace entertained requests for vouchers, several thousand letters arrived.

Entry to the sacred turf of the royal enclosure was not, however, simply a matter of handing over the necessary fee: no one who had been divorced, or made bankrupt, was eligible for entry, and anyone caught passing on or selling a ticket the Ascot Office had been gracious enough to grant would certainly have been banned. With so many keen to attend, there was always a certain anxiety that applications might have arrived too late, been overlooked or simply been unlucky in the queue for tickets. But somehow the bulky envelope marked 'Master of the Horse' in the corner always did arrive, and the same familiar faces were seen year after year.

Once sure of being among those strolling on this select and sacred lawn, every woman attending concentrated on finery that would make her the cynosure of male eyes – and the envy of all women. This could be a much more costly affair than dressing for a Court: a different frock for each day of the meeting could add up to £200 – without counting the shoes, hats or handbags needed to go with them. Lesser mortals, however, could have a splendid day's racing for a guinea, with the spectacle of their 'betters', togged up to the nines, thrown in. Or as the *Daily Mail*'s social correspondent put it: 'At certain times, men and women from the Royal Enclosure, dukes, marquises, admirals, generals, millionaires and Mayfair beauties, each compelled to bear his or her name plainly displayed on a badge pinned to the coat, poured into the Guinea Enclosure.'

But for the last Ascot before the war, the parade of fashions was sadly missing. The sunshine of the previous weeks vanished, and the weather went from bad to appalling. On Tuesday, the

Opening Day, a chilly wind meant that the pretty, colourful flowered or printed dresses in silks and chiffons were quickly hidden beneath warm wool coats in serviceable shades like navy, grey or beige, with the inevitable fox furs wound round necks. Silver fox was in the minority; instead, many women appeared with the newly chic red, blue and platinum varieties. The Duchess of Gloucester was one of the few who did wear silver fox, as did the Duchess of Kent, who sported a short and stylish jacket over a pink flowered dress. Soon even the wintry glamour of furs disappeared. As the afternoon wore on the rain came down, causing further shrouding of finery.

On Wednesday, despite the chilly temperatures, women made game efforts towards chic. Filmy ankle-length dresses in pastel shades defied grey and lowering skies, and a blustery wind, which blew skirts against ankles and nearly tore off the coquettish little veil on the Duchess of Kent's hat. The royal ladies, like a bed of neatly planted delphiniums, were all in summery blues; the surrounding hats maintained the indomitable English garden-party spirit. Young girls wore bonnets and wreaths of flowers, older women donned flowered and veiled straws or eye-catching novelties – platters of fruit tipped forward on the head, a tip-tilted saucer full of white camellias, cock's feathers dyed black and bound to the forehead like the antennae of an insect, or curled ostrich feathers held over one eye by a thin ribbon tossing wildly in the breeze. By Gold Cup Day on Thursday, it was clear the weather had won. Women were dressed much more warmly. The Duchess of Gloucester wore a dusty (then known as 'dirty') pink dress and coat and a small burnt-straw hat, the Duchess of Kent was elegant as ever in a dress of deep caramel crêpe with two long red fox furs. This time her hat was close-fitting, a confection that from a distance looked as if it were made entirely of small butterfly-like bows. The cold weather did not, however, deter Mrs Corrigan from serving the drinks at her usual Gold Cup party out of doors in the flagged garden of Englemere (the large house she was renting from Sir Archibald Weigall for Ascot

Week) as well as in the drawing-room. Nor did it affect the high spirits of her guests: Lord Dudley arrived on horseback, everyone danced the popular Lambeth Walk and the Duke of Marlborough, as he had done at her previous parties, led the band round the garden.

She was only just in time to make the most of the gardens at Englemere. On Friday morning the rain began to fall, and it continued relentlessly. Only as the last race started was the sun finally glimpsed, its watery beams gleaming down on sloshing puddles, sodden grass and mud, and the umbrellas and mackintoshes of those staunch enough to remain to the bitter end.

There was nothing in the racing, either, to cheer spectators. Earlier in the week famous English racing names had featured, with Lord Lonsdale's Snowberry, ridden by Gordon Richards and trained by Fred Darling, winning the Queen Mary Stakes and Sir Abe Bailey's Caerloptic the Hunt Cup. But in the steadily increasing downpour of Friday afternoon, all the honours of this most English of meetings went across the Channel. The French won the Windsor Castle Stakes by what the judge believed was the shortest of heads (there were, of course, no photo-finish cameras). Worse was to follow: they also took the first three places in the Queen Alexandra Stakes, at two miles six furlongs and seventy-five yards (a mile more than the St Leger) the longest race run under Jockey Club rules. No wonder *The Times* summed up Ascot 1939 as 'the most miserable known within recent years'.

Few would have disagreed. Even the clothes were the dullest for years. 'There wasn't a single freak fashion in the paddock or the royal enclosure,' noted one expert in a tone that managed to combine approval with disappointment. However, Margaret Whigham had been there. The top debutante of her year and so famous for looks and social lustre that Cole Porter featured her in his song 'You're The Top', she had recently married the US golfer

Charles Sweeny and was later to become Duchess of Argyll. And, as the *Tatler* remarked: 'No Ascot could possibly be called dowdy if Mrs Charles Sweeny is there.'

Twenty-Three

OXFORD AND CAMBRIDGE

June was also party month for England's two most ancient universities. Many of the undergraduates were, of course, on the list of eligible young men invited to debutante dances (to the detriment of their studies, as their tutors believed); but the Oxford Commem and the Cambridge May Week balls in June were the highlights of the undergraduates' social year. For all except the wealthy, buying a ticket represented a considerable outlay. At Cambridge, for instance, a single ticket for the Clare Ball cost two guineas (buyers were urged to 'Reserve your garage space for May Week now!'), while Downing had secured Victor Sylvester and his band for its ball the following night, and was charging thirty-five shillings for a single ticket, three guineas for a double. The dancing went on all night, interspersed with romantic interludes on lawns or in punts, and the party wound up with breakfast at dawn, perhaps in Grantchester.

There were concerts, bumping races, picnics, a garden party at Newnham and a fête at Girton, and a girl undergraduate's twenty-first birthday party held in someone's rooms in the all-male college, St John's. Above all, for both universities, there was the river: alluring romantic, pleasurable, threading through days and nights, scene of parties in punts – food brought in hampers, harmonicas and accordions playing the hit tunes of the moment – backdrop for the intimacies of friendship or the heady exultation of first love. But the stench of war underlay the perfume of youth, gaiety, ardour and friendship. It was the last chance to play and those who could seized it. Fortunately, most could afford to.

For though state scholarships had been introduced at both Oxford and Cambridge some time earlier, the great majority of undergraduates were still ex-public schoolboys whose parents considered that university was a natural part of a gentleman's education, and could afford not only the fees of around £200 for a year's residence but also the necessary allowance to cover both enjoyment and living expenses. Entry standards for most universities were not particularly high – doing well ('matriculating') in School Certificate did away with the need to take an entrance examination. Put simply, if you were comfortably off, male, and reasonably intelligent, going to university was a matter of choice rather than competition. In any case, the emphasis was on assimilating the breadth of vision, mental expansiveness and, with luck, some of the culture which exuded from the ancient stones and the more eccentric, brilliant or witty dons, rather than on absorbing learning as a form of vocational training with a particular job in view. Indeed, many future employers placed more stress on athletic than academic ability; at least one, an international oil company, preferred Blue to a First (though not, possibly, the half-Blue newly introduced by Cambridge for judo).

The life of an Oxford or Cambridge undergraduate was a mixture of the spartan and the sybaritic. He lived in college for at least a year and during this time servants looked after most of his needs – yet baths were few and far between. At Balliol, for example, the only baths were in the basement of one staircase at the far end of the second quad. 'Apart from the 200 yards in the open air to reach a bathroom, you really had to book well in advance to be sure of it,' recalled one undergraduate. Breakfast could be sent across from the college kitchens (at Cambridge this cost 9d), 'scouts' or 'gyps' (male) or 'bedders' (female and elderly) looked after his rooms; the college servants waited at lunch and dinner in the hall.

In character, the two universities were different then as now, Oxford being more mondaine, political and arts-orientated, Cambridge more reclusive and scientific. At Cambridge, about a fifth of the undergraduates were reading scientific subjects, at Oxford only about one-tenth.

Although the tradition of the academic woman was by now established, the male staff of both universities were still fighting a strong rearguard action. In all sorts of ways, the woman undergraduate was made to feel at best that she was there on sufferance, at worst that she was some unappealing freak of nature which, if ignored, might simply disappear. Lecturers still tended to treat women as if they did not really exist; one, the eminent Sir Arthur Quiller-Couch, or 'Q' as he was known, invariably began his lectures with the word 'Gentlemen'. When the class of another eminent professor dwindled to six women and one lone man he was reputed to have started 'Sir . . .'

This anti-female bias emerged more strongly at Cambridge, where there was a much smaller proportion of women undergraduates: only five hundred (as against almost six thousand male undergraduates) compared to Oxford's eight hundred (with just under five thousand men). At Oxford, women undergraduates wore the same academic dress and obeyed the same rules as the men, whereas Newnham and Girton girls were not regarded as members of the university. They could not wear caps and gowns although they attended the same lectures as the men (to which the Girton girls were taken in a special bus) and their degrees were only titular. They were also excluded from most of the Cambridge Clubs and, though they were allowed to sit in the gallery of the Union, they were expected to listen to the debates in total silence, and were reproved by the Chair if they applauded. Decorum ruled: men had to be out of Girton by 6.30 p.m., though they could return at 7.45 after dinner until curfew time at 10.00 – the time at which women also had to be out of men's colleges. Undergraduates at St John's were leading a campaign to get these rules altered. They hoped for an extension until midnight.

Not being a 'proper' undergraduate held only one advantage for a woman: she did not come under the jurisdiction of the Proctors. These formidable beings were responsible for enforcing most of the rules of the university, and walked around the town keeping order. Proctors, who were young dons, wore gowns and 'squares' (mortar boards); each was accompanied by two college servants called bulldogs ('bullers') in top hats and tails coats, chosen for their fleetness of foot, stamina, and general fitness.

Penalties were administered on a kind of sliding scale, and usually consisted of fines. One of the regulations was that an undergraduate who went out into the town after dinner in hall had to wear cap and gown. If an offender was spotted – most undergraduates wore tweed coats and grey flannel trousers, so any who broke this rule were fairly easy to pick out – the Proctor would send over a bulldog. If the undergraduate made a bolt for it, the bulldogs gave chase and only a good runner who was sober had a chance of getting away. If, as more commonly happened, the undergraduate realized any attempt to escape was a waste of breath, the bulldog would advance with the time-honoured formula: 'Excuse me, sir, but the Proctor would like a word with you.' Walking up to this dignitary, the miscreant would be asked, 'Are you a member of this university, sir?' and, on confessing that he was, he would be required to give his name and college. A few days later he would receive a note containing an invitation from the Proctor to call on him in his rooms, a visit that usually concluded with the undergraduate departing poorer by 6s 8d – or, for persistent offenders, 13s 4d or even £1. This ritual was known as being 'progged'.

Undergraduates could stay out until midnight, but after 10.00 p.m. 'gate money' had to be paid. Anyone out after midnight, when the gates were finally locked, either had to climb over the wall of his college or be caught by prowling bulldogs. The bulldogs were men of initiative and determination, and were not easy to outwit or shake off even on a dark night – especially if an undergraduate had several pints of beer inside him. Undergraduates who were not living in college were similarly circumscribed, for they had to live in approved lodgings whose landladies reported them if they were late in. Proctors and their attendant bulldogs also kept an eye on places that were out of bounds. 'Fifteen proctors swept up to the Rex ballroom in taxis last Saturday at 11.00 p.m., catching 76 undergraduates who were endeavouring to escape,' reported *Varsity*. 'Top hatted bullers moved about among the dancers, bullers guarded the French windows and a proctor climbed the fire escape.' One resourceful undergraduate locked himself in a cupboard thus avoiding the £1 fine all his fellows paid.

Dancing was highly popular generally. Rich undergraduates gave tea dances in their rooms, and dances with live bands ('Dorrien Hill and His Swing Band', for one) were a regular Saturday night feature of hotels in Oxford and Cambridge as they were in seaside holiday towns. But there was plenty of entertainment of a more cultured variety. The Chairman of the Oxford University Labour Club, Denis Healey, whose ambition then was to write 'the world's greatest book on aesthetics, the philosophy of beauty and art', and Colin Judd (a great friend of Richard Hillary's) had founded the New Oxford Arts Society a year or two earlier. It put on one of the first surrealist exhibitions, invited Anthony Blunt over from Cambridge to talk about Poussin and, in 1939, held a Picasso exhibition where some of the etchings were on sale for £5. Healey also organized a series of lectures on Greek tragedy which were given by speakers of the calibre of Professor Gilbert Murray, the Regius Professor of Greek at Oxford, and E. R. Dodds, the Professor of Greek at Birmingham, a Marxist and a great friend of Louis Macneice.

There were also visits by touring theatre companies and the ballet; after one matinee Miss Margot Fonteyn and Miss Pamela May were interviewed for *Isis* by Richard Hillary. 'Wednesday saw us desperately climbing up the tortuous staircase of Boswell

House to the flat, way up in the roof . . . Miss Fonteyn, holding an egg-whisk and with soap on her nose, was as attractive a mountain flower as any tired climber could hope for.' She informed Hillary that Oxford audiences were more discriminating and less vociferous than those of Cambridge, but that Cambridge had better parties. 'Oxford parties – misery!' she said. 'Death,' added Pamela May. Nevertheless, the representative of *Isis* managed to lure both dancers out to lunch the following day.

For the literary, there was great excitement when an honorary degree was bestowed on P. G. Wodehouse, over from his home in France to be made a Doctor of Literature by Oxford. It was an extraordinarily popular gesture, as Arthur Bryant recorded:

'The outburst of applause which greeted his appearance before the Vice Chancellor far exceeded that accorded to any of the eminent public men and famous savants who received honorary degrees at the same time. It was an unconscious tribute to the gratitude all human beings feel towards those who have helped to make them happy . . . Dr Wodehouse, as we must now learn to call him, has conferred nothing but pleasure.'

The following year, Wodehouse was to destroy the uproarious, affectionate innocence of that day by a piece of crass misjudgment. Caught by the German advance into France, he was interned in the Adlon Hotel in Berlin. His captors, realizing his value in propagandist terms, asked him if he would like to make a broadcast to assure his friends he was all right. He accepted, explaining in a Bertie Woosterish way that the Germans had really treated him very decently. This broadcast, and the five others that followed, showed so clearly that he had no conception of the nature of Nazism, and he displayed such a lack of understanding of Britain's peril that he was bitterly attacked, first by the *Daily Mirror*'s famous columnist Cassandra and then by Duff Cooper, Churchill's Minister of Information. Wodehouse was released soon from internment, though he was not allowed to leave Germany during the war. He remained so shattered by the public reaction to his broadcasts that he never lived in England again, making his home in America. Shortly before his death in 1975, he was knighted on the recommendation of Harold Wilson, who as a young Fellow of University College had perhaps been one of those applauding the new D.Lit.

Above all, it was the heyday of the two Unions. Cambridge might have won the 1939 Boat Race by a good four lengths but they lost decisively in the oratorical stakes, despite the fact that the President of the Cambridge Union that summer was Elwyn Jones, the future Labour Lord Chancellor. The standard of Oxford's debating was so much higher that the National Students' Federation of America for the first time confined to Oxford alone their invitation to tour the States for debates at various universities. The two undergraduates selected by Oxford to represent them were the President of the Union, Hugh Fraser (brother of Lord Lovat; later a distinguished Conservative MP and Junior Minister), and his predecessor of the Hilary Term, Teddy Heath – as the future Prime Minister Edward Heath was then invariably known.

Oxford's oratorical high point was reached with the valedictory speech of the Union's star performer, Monsignor Ronald Knox. This charming, urbane, witty man was giving up his post as the university's Roman Catholic chaplain to retire to Aldenham, Lord Acton's great house, where he intended to think and write (it was at Aldenham that he later produced his translation of the Vulgate). The motion was that 'This House congratulates the Press on keeping the home fires burning', and *Isis* reported: 'Nine times now Ronald Knox has been expected to make the best speech at the Eights Week debate. Nine times he has done so, until his speeches have at the Union become an institution and their success a legend. Legends tend to disappointment, but on Thursday there was none . . . Ronald Knox's speech was not a success but a triumph.' Evelyn Waugh recalled that Monsignor Knox 'performed a memorable pantomime of reading a newspaper in a railway carriage'. (Waugh's own speech was described by *Isis* as more of a literary than an oratorical affair. 'Mr Waugh has a moderate delivery, and . . . he had on Thursday a contempt for the slowness of his audience, and refused to labour home the nicer points of his speech, with the result that it received a mere echo of that applause and appreciation due to its wit, form and argument.')

Many of the best debaters were leading lights of the political clubs. Teddy Heath, at Balliol on an organ scholarship, was Chairman of the Oxford University Conservative Club; he had been one of the undergraduates who, in opposition to Quintin Hogg (the newly elected MP for Oxford), had denounced the Munich Agreement. The Labour Club was chiefly Marxist, Healey recalled: 'We were not close to the Labour Opposition. Many on the left wing were Communist. Roy Jenkins and Tony Crosland, both a year behind me, never joined the Communist Party although in those days Tony would have described himself as a Marxist.' One of the most active on the Labour side was John Biggs-Davison who had, in March, successfully proposed the motion 'That this House deplores the recognition of Franco'.

As everyone at Oxford and Cambridge was of an age to fight, conscription was naturally one of the chief subjects. At one debate early in the year the motion 'That the time has come for the enforcement of the principle of universal and compulsory training for national service', proposed by L. S. Amery and opposed by Liddell Hart, had been defeated in the Cambridge Union; shortly afterwards, Julian Amery, with the support of Randolph Churchill, avenged his father's defeat by carrying a similar Motion in the Oxford Union. But all, including those who had voted against conscription, were in little doubt that the golden days of their youth would end with war and that theirs was the generation, like that of 1914, destined to bear the heaviest burden of slaughter. This view was aptly if gloomily summed up by Arnold Toynbee at the St Catharine's night dinner at Balliol: it was very appropriate that St Catharine was the patron saint of Balliol, he said, because their fate, like hers, was to be broken on the wheel.

Twenty-Four

~~~

A TENSE JULY

July opened with a significant reminder of what war might mean. The first of the month was the twenty-third anniversary of the beginning of the Battle of the Somme, when Kitchener's army went to their deaths; one of the thirty-four In Memoriam notices on the front page of *The Times* commemorated twelve officers of the First Battalion of the Hampshire Regiment (the 37th Foot) killed on that day. Now, there was the additional expectation of terrible mass bombing and gassing of both soldiers and civilians.

There was nothing to do but wait. A frozen, uneasy calm lay over those first days of July. The situation was clearly worsening, with the country teetering on the edge of war; yet actual developments were few. The traditional rule, that war was never declared until the harvest was in, appeared to prevail.

There were, of course, plenty of pointers. Without explanation, the Italians gave all the British, Swiss, French and Dutch residents in the province of Alto Adige, South Tyrol, forty-eight hours' notice to leave; the respective governments of these involuntary evacuees did little more than 'consider' the situation, for fear of triggering something worse.

The British Government published fifteen million copies of Public Information Leaflet No. 1; this told householders what to do if war came, describing air raid signals, fire precautions and plans for distribution of food, and gloomily urged everyone to carry identification labels 'which should be made to last'.

In Paris, the French foreign minister handed a solemn warning to the German ambassador to leave Poland alone; it was felt that this, combined with the hoped-for conclusion of an Anglo-French pact with Russia, might just steer both countries safely past the looming iceberg of war. To the German newspapers, however, this was just another victory in the war of nerves. 'The utmost anxiety as to the possibility of a coup in Danzig prevailed in London and Paris and proved to be entirely unjustified, thus showing that the Western powers are losing their nerve,' they crowed, adding that France and Britain suffered from 'galloping nervous consumption'.

Later, the German verbal offensive was carried a stage further, when letters in green envelopes with German stamps arrived at a number of British golf clubs. They contained Germany's rebuttal of English attitudes under the heading 'Reply to English propaganda by Reichsminister Dr Goebbels' in bold type across the top.

Whenever a day passed without blood-curdling threats from Germany, the headlines reflected two other areas of concern. The first was the aggressive attitude of Japan. The Sino-Japanese war had entered its third year. Taking advantage of the British and French preoccupation with the threat of war in Europe, the Japanese had instituted a blockade of the international concessions in Tientsin. The French and British communities in the city now lived in virtual isolation and the Japanese were still busy stripping civilians, though so far only men.

Nearer home, there was the IRA's sustained and mounting campaign of terror. This, the so-called 'S' plan of blackmail by bombing, had been launched in January as a protest against the London Agreement which Chamberlain and the Irish Prime Minister De Valera had established in 1938. The Agreement had settled some outstanding financial questions and the United Kingdom had given up her right to use certain ports in Southern Ireland as naval bases (a concession which was to cost her dear in the coming Battle of the Atlantic). But Partition remained; and the IRA demanded the instant withdrawal of troops from Northern Ireland. By April, its terrorist activities were occupying the attention of 10,000 police.

No one knew where the bombers would strike next. In London, Hammersmith Bridge was closed for the whole of March because of the damage caused by a bomb; on 1 April, Boat Race Day, five others exploded in various parts of the capital while several more were found and defused. At the beginning of April seven terrorists – the youngest a labourer of only seventeen – were caught before they had planted their bombs, but a few days later, on Maundy Thursday, there were more explosions, this time in Birmingham, Liverpool and Coventry.

In June one bomb went off in Madame Tussaud's and another twenty-seven letter-bombs blew up in the familiar scarlet letter boxes throughout the capital. There were explosions in sorting offices in Manchester, Birmingham, Lincoln and Leicester – several post-office night workers were burned about the face and hands – and one quick-witted railway guard flung a smouldering bag out of the mail van window to see it explode as it landed on the railway bank.

The Prevention of Violence Bill was rushed through the Commons, becoming law on 9 July; in Ireland, De Valera declared the IRA illegal. It was not before time: since January, there had been 127 separate bombing incidents, sixty-six Irishmen had been convicted, and the police had seized enough explosive – 1,500 sticks of gelignite, 1,000 detonators, two tons of potassium chloride and oxide of iron, seven gallons of sulphuric acid and four hundredweight of aluminium powder – to cause, they said, at least 1,000 deaths and millions of pounds worth of damage.

On 24 July, the Home Secretary, Sir Samuel Hoare, asked for more powers to cope with the terrorist campaign. This request was viewed with suspicion by the Opposition, who feared such a measure might infringe civil liberties. Yet even while the debate was taking place the IRA struck again: a bomb exploded at King's

Cross station, killing one person and wounding fifteen. This act effectively put an end to the scruples of more tender consciences, and on Friday 28 July Sir Samuel signed nineteen expulsion orders. Many others did not wait for possible interrogation: that night, bookings for the Irish Mail to Kingstown (Dun Laoghaire) were so heavy that the train had to be run in three sections.

Other trains were carrying a different cargo. Six weeks before the outbreak of war, the first group of thirty thousand conscripts (known as militiamen) reported for six months' training at camps and depots all over the country, and the Army's Director of Public Relations, Major General J. H. Beith (the novelist Ian Hay, recently recruited for this purpose by Hore-Belisha), announced that nearly a million men would be under arms by August. (Although all were issued with the new battledress, a year later many were still short of arms.) Twelve thousand officers and men of the Naval Reserve were called up to man the Reserve Fleet for exercises during August and September. The seventeenth and last warship to be salvaged of the seventy-strong German High Seas Fleet, scuttled twenty years earlier in Scapa Flow, was raised from her resting-place bottom up on the seabed twenty-six fathoms down; the steel thus obtained was used in naval rearmament. Doctors were assigned the posts or responsibility they would immediately take up in the event of war.

Adventurous British youth was joining the RAF, in which almost every day there were new and exciting aeronautical developments – in gliding alone, Britain had just set the record at 14,200 feet, and the new fighters could do well over 300 mph. The fastest fighter in the world, the Vickers Supermarine Spitfire, delivered to a few RAF squadrons the previous year, had just gone into mass production; it could do 362 mph and could climb to 11,000 feet in 4.8 minutes. Only just behind it at 335 mph was the Hawker Hurricane, developed in 1938. Together these machines were to save their country from invasion and defeat during the Battle of Britain in 1940.

At the universities, Air Squadrons were being trained by

experienced RAF instructors. Among those who spent several afternoons a week at the Oxford flying field was Richard Hillary, the Rupert Brooke figure of his generation, who was later to write, in *The Last Enemy*:

'In a fighter plane, I believe, we have found a way to return to war as it ought to be, war which is individual combat between two people, in which one either kills or is killed. It's exciting, it's individual and it's disinterested . . . I shan't get maimed: either I shall get killed or I shall get a few pleasant putty medals and enjoy being stared at in a night club . . .' Alas, he was to be maimed, when he was terribly burned in his Spitfire. Later he was killed when he returned to operational flying.

There was still a pretence of normality. British and German sailors were competing at Kiel in the International Sailing Competition for the Hindenburg Cup (it was won, on 15 July, by two British naval officers); holiday traffic to Europe remained steady and *The Times* was still giving lists of wedding presents. But it also gave details of naval movements, noting on 22 July that a large floating dock, travelling at four knots an hour, had left Portsmouth for Singapore.

While the whole of Europe hung on the difficult, inconclusive and protracted negotiations taking place in Moscow, calls for a national, or at least a more warlike, government were increasing. A letter to *The Times* on Saturday 15 July, from Mr Harcourt Johnson, summed up the opinion of many when he wrote that he could not help thinking that the exclusion of Mr Churchill and Mr Eden from the Cabinet might encourage the dictators to believe that 'violent attacks on British statesmen can secure their non-employment. Certainly this was the impression created in Italy at the time of Mr Eden's resignation.'

Many MPs shared this view, among them Harold Macmillan, who wrote that 'unanimity can best be demonstrated by the formation of a truly national government on the broadest possible basis, including the most prominent and able figures in Parliament, regardless of personal or party differences in the past.'

Neither the Opposition nor his own party really believed that the Prime Minister had the necessary toughness of mind or uncompromising courage to convince the rest of the world that Britain would fight in the event of further aggression. But everyone knew that Churchill and his supporters meant exactly what they said. Some expected another Munich – except that, this time, could peace be bought at *any* price?

If they had been able to see into the Prime Minister's mind, they might have felt even more uneasy. For even at this stage Chamberlain appears to have believed that Hitler had seen the warning light and decided to call a halt. As late as 23 July he was writing to his sister Ida:

'. . . Hitler has concluded that we mean business and that the time is not ripe for the major war and therein he is fulfilling my expectations. Unlike some of my critics I go further and say the longer the war is put off the less likely it is to come at all as we go on perfecting our defences and building up the defences of our allies. That is what Winston and co never seem to realize. You don't need offensive forces sufficient to win a smashing victory. What you want are defensive forces sufficiently strong to make it impossible for the other side to win except at such cost as to make it not worth while. That is what we are doing, and though at present the German feeling is it is not worth while *yet*, they will presently come to realize that it never *will* be worth while. Then we can talk.' But the time for talk had not yet come, he concluded, 'because the Germans haven't yet realized they can't get what they want by force . . .'

Less than twelve months later, force had gained for Hitler everything he wanted except the defeat of Britain and Russia.

42   A summer picnic in the grounds of Cecil Beaton's country house, Ashcombe. *From left to right*: Cecil Beaton, Diana Cavendish, Bridget Parsons, Tony Herbert, Tilly Losch, Teresa Jayman, Betty Smith, Caroline Paget, David Herbert

43   Mr Alfred and Lady Diana
Duff Cooper, with spaniel Noel,
at Bognor

44 Tuesday, 13 June. With impending rain and a chill in the air, racegoers arrive at Ascot armed with mackintoshes and coats

45 Despite the weather, women still made brave attempts to keep fashion on course: here, Miss Peggy Hamilton (*left*) and friend

46　The victorious Harrow team of 1939. *From left to right, back row:*
J. L. Paul, D. F. Henley, R. M. Boustead, G. F. Anson, J. L. Crawley;
front row: L. E. W. Byam, F. C. Boult, A. O. L. Lithgow,
E. Crutchley, P. E. F. Prideaux-Brune; and D. C. H. McLean

47 Lady Sarah Spencer-Churchill, whose dance at Blenheim was the grandest of the Season

48 The Saloon, Blenheim Palace (photo Edwin Smith)

Beauty marches on . . .

it's her duty to face the future calm and unruffled. Beauty—like business—must go on. The wise woman, in a period of strain and crisis, will keep up her regular night and morning routine of Cleansing, Toning and Nourishing—with Elizabeth Arden's famous Essential Preparations—Cleansing Cream, Skin Tonic and Orange Skin Food or Velva Cream—to which her skin owes its freshness, smoothness and delicacy, her features their clear-cut and youthful outline. On this basis, her beauty is securely founded. To remain beautiful she regards as an obligation to herself and her friends.

Cleansing Cream, 4/6 to 22/6   Skin Tonic, 4/- to 80/-   Orange Skin Food, 4/6 to 35/-   Velva Cream, 4/6 to 22/6

Elizabeth Arden

25 OLD BOND STREET LONDON W 1

49   Perms kept hair neat above the collar of a uniform, while make-up, by now an essential article of elegance, helped women 'face the future'

50   Captain Lord George Scott
in his uniform of the 10th Royal
Hussars, painted by Lady George
Scott (Molly Bishop) in 1939

51   The eight gun, single-seater Vickers-supermarine Spitfire

Twenty-Five

THE ETON–HARROW MATCH

The Eton and Harrow Match at Lords, world headquarters of cricket, was an important event in the social calendar. It was attended by the wives, families and friends of Etonians and Harrovians past and present, by debutantes and their mothers, and by cricket-loving Old Boys from both schools who travelled up from the country, while the parade of fashions made it one of the recognized 'set pieces' of the Season.

The match that opened on 14 July 1939 was remarkable for two things. Harrow beat Eton for the first time for thirty-one years; and more top hats were destroyed that afternoon than would have come to the end of their useful life in a normal decade. To appreciate the significance of this, in an age of public decorum when physical assault – let alone at one of the most elegant occasions of the year – was rare, it is necessary to understand the extraordinary chauvinism of the public schools. And in particular, the traditional rivalry between Eton and Harrow (the best-known public school after Eton), carried on only half-jokingly up to and including Cabinet level.

All over London, Old Etonian and Old Harrovian dinners had been arranged, to celebrate or mourn the outcome of the match. At the Dorchester, for instance, the Old Harrovian dinner included eminent Old Boys like Lord Baldwin, who had been Prime Minister during the abdication crisis; Sir Walter Monck-ton, the ex-King's confidant, friend and lawyer, who drafted the

Instrument of Abdication; Winston Churchill; Leopold Amery – the former Conservative minister whose speech in the Commons in May 1940 was to force Chamberlain to resign; Sir Samuel Hoare; and Captain Euan Wallace, a distinguished Conservative MP. The Savoy served 1,400 dinners or suppers that night. One party of Harrovians had telephoned that morning to book a table, explaining they had no evening clothes with them in London. Would they be allowed in with morning coats? The answer was icily negative.

On this of all days, partisanship was honed to a fine edge. In the words of the then Head Boy of Harrow, Peter Wyld, 'Whether you belonged to Eton or Harrow was almost racial in connotation. It wasn't until I went up to Magdalen in October and realized that my literary friends there simply weren't aware that they'd not been at Harrow that the whole thing dropped away from me.

'But it meant so much then that my father, who had made 81 when he played for Harrow and was passionate about both the school and cricket, gave up coming to Lords in 1938 because the anguish of watching Harrow constantly defeated was too much for him.'

Wyld himself watched the victory from the family carriage outside the Tavern. (In Victorian times, many families drove to Lords and parked their carriages on the boundary, sending their horses back to the stables while they watched the cricket and entertained their friends from their carriages. In 1939, this tradition was still maintained, especially by those who had strong links with one or other school, so that a number of carriages were brought to the ground and parked on the boundary in front of the Tavern, the inn where spectators could obtain refreshment.)

The match started without any particular hint of the sensation to come. Eton won the toss and elected to bat first. Although Crutchley – whose father had been largely responsible for the Harrow victory in 1908 by taking eight wickets for 46 runs – made 115 in Harrow's first innings on Friday, there was no reason to think that the long spell of defeat was about to be dramatically broken. In fact, everything seemed exactly as usual. That is, hardly a soul was actually watching the cricket and most of the seats were empty, except for those in front of the pavilion, where sat elderly gentlemen who had once played for one side or the other and the few others passionately interested in cricket.

Everyone else was perambulating round the tarmac behind the stands and pavilion, so intent on meeting and greeting as many friends as possible (encountering the same ones for the third or fourth time was the signal to reverse direction) that it hardly mattered that for long spells the cricket itself was hidden from view. Yet that year, it was almost as though the dramatic finale of the match was unconsciously anticipated, for the number of coaches, wagonettes and even old-fashioned victories was greater than at any time in the past ten years.

Though a little rain had fallen in the morning, the weather had cleared by lunchtime and the afternoon was warm with brilliant sunshine. Most of the women wore floating, garden party dresses and flowery hats, many in the partisan colours of pale or dark blue — the Duchess of Gloucester, for example, who with the Duke was lunching in the Duke of Buccleuch's box, was in pale blue crêpe, and pale blue swathed her wide brown straw hat. Lady May Abel Smith, on the other hand, wore a dark blue coat and blue printed dress, with a silver fox fur. Except for those who came at five o'clock or so from their City offices to watch the last of the cricket, men wore morning coats and grey top hats.

There was, of course, an enormous number of schoolboys, as attendance at the match on one of its two days was compulsory for both schools. Those from Eton wore their school clothes, but with a double-breasted waistcoat in buff or grey instead of the usual black (unless the boy in question was a member of Pop, in which case waistcoats of anything from brocade to shot silk were permissible). The ensemble was completed by a black cane with a silver top and light-blue tassel, and a pale blue carnation. The usual method of achieving this was by standing a white flower in inky water, which often presented a rather curious mottled appearance.

The Harrow boys, whose usual weekday uniform included dashing straw boaters, wore their Sunday top hats with either morning or Harrovian cutaway coats, and the lavender-grey or coffee-buff waistcoats normally worn only by 'Bloods' (those in the Eleven, the Harrow Football Eleven, or the rugby team). But their similar silver-topped canes were decorated with two dark blue tassels and a buttonhole that even Etonians admitted was superior: a single cornflower of a deep, pure, even blue. Traditionally noisier than Etonians ('Rugby may be more clever, Harrow may make more row,' wrote A. C. Ainger in the Eton Boating Song), they would give voice to a long-drawn-out, deep 'Harroo-oo-oow' from the grandstand and on the Mound when goings-on on the field seemed to demand it.

At close of play on the Friday, Harrow had been within three runs of Eton's total, with three wickets still to fall. But when the second Eton innings opened at noon at Saturday 15 July, Fiennes, the Eton Captain, in partnership with Barton, was batting so confidently and steadily that half an hour later the score stood at sixty-six for one wicket. So impregnable now seemed the Eton position that the few cognoscenti actually watching the cricket thought it likely that Eton would have to declare to have any chance of getting Harrow out and winning the match.

Then the Harrow captain, Lithgow, put on Henley at the Nursery end. In two overs this magnificent bowler took three wickets; soon after that, the Eton Captain was caught off him . . . and four wickets were down for sixty-nine. Moments later, another wicket was taken by Byam, the bowler at the other end.

Suddenly the whole picture had changed. With the Eton batting seemingly collapsed, the chance of a draw dwindled – and victory was in sight for Harrow. A buzz of excitement went round the ground. The *Eton Chronicle* later summed up this dramatic moment:

'Old Harrovians from all parts of England began chartering aeroplanes. Spectators who had always regarded Lords as a clearing-house for family gossip even went so far as to face the cricket and enquire earnestly which side was batting; old gentlemen in the pavilion who generally reckoned on a peaceful two hours' nap between the lunch and tea intervals, blew up their air cushions and brought a score card.

'These reactions were not without effect on the Eton batsmen, with a record of 30 years' standing to keep or lose with one careless flick outside the off stump. But they did not flick. They chose more obviously suicidal methods. For perhaps two overs, they would play safe and correct cricket and add half a dozen runs. Then a sudden hush in the Mound or the sudden clatter of yet another rudely-awakened member in the pavilion would stir them to action.

'This invariably coincided with a straight, good-length ball, and each time it meant another wicket . . . the innings closed for 156 with a run-out which aptly reflected the state of nervous tension and left Harrow with 131 to win in more time than a Test Match would demand.'

Nevertheless, this knife-edge situation did not curtail one of the main amusements of the day, the between-innings fashion parade. With the wicket roped off, spectators flooded discreetly but firmly on to the pitch where the latest creations could be displayed to full advantage and viewed easily and unhurriedly. The unfortunate Harrow opening pair had to wait at the wicket until those more interested in glamour than cricket had finally sauntered off.

Henderson and Wallace opened the bowling for Eton. At eighteen, one wicket fell – but it was only a temporary setback. Steadily the runs mounted, while the excitement and tension all round the ground was almost tangible. When one of the opening pair was dismissed at fifty, with the score at ninety-six, Crutchley went in. George Lyttelton, the Eton Housemaster, reported in *The Times* that the cheers from Harrow were now 'the shout of them that triumph, the song of them that intend shortly to feast without stint or misgiving.' Finally, and fittingly, the captain of the Harrow Eleven, Anthony Lithgow, hit the winning shot, a straight drive to the Pavilion from the far end.

Instantly, the sedate grounds of Lords erupted. As Lyttelton put it: 'The drought is over, the Arctic night is past, the chains are burst, the clouds have lifted from the Hill. No metaphors can do justice to the feeling of long-depressed satisfaction with which lovers of cricket in general and this match in particular saw Harrow beat Eton by eight wickets.'

Physical action was clearly the only possible culmination of thirty years of pent-up emotion. A race between the groundsmen and police, and most of Harrow, was won by the latter; half a dozen of the bigger Harrow boys – including Wyld, who sprang from the top of his carriage over the boundary rope – reached Lithgow and carried him in in triumph above the heads of the crowd. Here, as women stepped hastily out of the way, top hats were bashed, and umbrellas broken. Soon ties, braces, button-holes, or anything else bearing the once tauntingly superior blue of Eton, were ripped off and torn to shreds by triumphant Harrovians past and present.

By all accounts, this rough-housing did not start with the boys, largely because there were too many masters about; they joined in only after about twenty minutes, so that for a while it was the older men alone who indulged themselves in this form of score-settling. Next day the *Sunday Express* lamented: 'When the winning run was scored, Lords became a bear garden, and it wasn't the boys who started it, but their elders, pillars of county society, figures on the stock exchange, grey-haired businessmen. Elderly men took off their toppers, which were kicked from their hands. One distinguished-looking Old Etonian punched a cler-ical Old Harrovian. Two other Old Harrovians set upon their school enemy. He was thrown to the ground, his tie torn off and his coat lifted, exposing light blue braces . . . in a few seconds he was debagged.'

The mêlée was thickest in front of the pavilion, where Old Harrovians and Old Etonians rolled about on the grass scuffling, and it spread into the Tavern, to the annoyance of drinkers who had been to neither school. Finally, the police cleared out the combatants, but both sides continued to support their champions. 'Etonians assured their Eleven, with unconscious but appropriate irony, that it was "Jolly Boating Weather",' wrote George Lyttelton, 'while in the opposite camp the strains of "Forty Years On", according to a sardonic and undaunted O.E., celebrated in anticipation Harrow's next victory. Then the lowing herd wound slowly o'er the lea. Soon nothing remained on the scene of Harrow's splendid and deserved success save a raffle of Old School Ties and what, 48 hours earlier, had been new school hats.'

In the opinion of some, though, the outcome of the match had been dependent entirely upon Eton's decision to bat first. This, they believed, was the sole reason for her downfall: since 1901, out of the twenty-one matches completed only five were won by the side batting first. A letter to the *Chronicle* explained it thus:

'The Eton and Harrow Match is the big game for both sides. There is general nervous tension, even among those who have played at Lords before   which affects a batsman far more than a bowler, as the former's first mistake is going to be fatal, while the latter can make several at little cost. The fielding side thus gains an initial advantage which it does not lose, since time heals the nerves of all and no advantage is likely to be gained in this way later in the game.' The other explanation, of course, is that Harrow, a far smaller school, was quite simply much the better side.

Twenty-Six

JULY PARTIES

The last few weeks of the Season exploded in a pyrotechnic burst of parties. *The Times* gloomily reported that although the prospects for grouse were good, the international situation had had a serious effect on the letting of Scottish grouse moors and deer forests; nevertheless, most of the festivities – save for the last and most important, the Buckingham Palace Garden Party – were jubilantly successful. Tiaras were brought out for a final flourish and dresses were rushed through workrooms, if not for the parties then for the last two Courts in mid-July. Dance bands vied with each other to put a new gloss on hits like 'Little Sir Echo', 'Three Little Fishes', the 'Beer Barrel Polka', and 'Boomps a Daisy' – the new 'action' dance tipped to become as popular as the Lambeth Walk.

By now there was a serious shortage of men at the debutante dances. Quick-witted girls would book partners for one another in advance, working in pairs, with the first to arrive filling the cards of both. At dances which included more of the older generation, this imbalance was not, of course, so marked.

Some of the grander parties were attended by the King and Queen, both of whom enjoyed dancing. On 6 July they dined with Lord and Lady Ilchester at Holland House before Miss Rosalind Cubitt's debutante dance there (the Ilchesters had lent Holland House to Mrs Michael Cubitt for her daughter's coming-out). The thirty-six guests sat at three round mahogany tables in the Long Library, and the party was notable as the first public confirmation that the youthful-looking Queen, a month away from her thirty-ninth birthday, had begun to slim – although her regime could hardly be called arduous. Since her return from America, five courses instead of six were served at Palace dinners, puddings had to contain fruit of some kind, and she had cut down on that favourite Scottish meal, afternoon tea.

It was an impressive occasion. The historic Elizabethan house, surrounded by its seventy acres of gardens and woodland, resembled the grandest and stateliest of country houses. When the dance began after dinner, the elm-bordered drive was so packed with cars that it took nearly an hour to travel the few hundred yards to the imposing front door, and almost as long in the queue leading to the top of the staircase where the hosts were receiving. 'When I finally entered the stately white and gold ballroom it was midnight,' wrote one of those there that night. 'The orchestra had just stopped playing and the King and Queen, about to go down to supper, were standing in the middle of the room talking to Noel Coward.' The Queen wore a white crinoline dress with diamonds and rubies; another royal guest, Queen Ena of Spain, also in white, was festooned with ropes of enormous pearls that hung to her waist. Mrs Ronnie Greville, arrayed in pale blue silk and her magnificent diamonds, was still recuperating from a bout of pneumonia earlier in the spring, and had to be carried up the stairs in a wheelchair by two of her footmen. Supper was taken in the magnificent 'Joshua' room, hung with portraits by Sir Joshua Reynolds (under the portrait of Charles James Fox was a receipt, signed by the artist, for one hundred guineas). The only disappointment was the weather: teeming rain prevented anyone taking the air on the floodlit terraces outside the great ballroom windows, or strolling among the massive yew hedges of the formal Italian garden below.

At the Scottish Office, quite a different sort of party was going on, given by Mr and Mrs John Colville for Scottish peers and

MPs. Because Dover House was such an old building, floors of the rooms where the party was to be held had to be specially shored up. This party was notable for the impromptu cabaret given by the host: halfway through, Mr Colville, an expert on the bagpipes, could no longer stand watching others perform. Borrowing a set of pipes from one of the Scots Guards pipers, he began to play. His guests were treated to the sight of the Secretary of State for Scotland marching round the room to a lilting air, the tails of his morning coat swinging like the kilt.

The last two Courts took place on Wednesday 12 July and Thursday 13 July respectively, part of a busy week for the King, who had dined on Tuesday night in the Painted Hall in Greenwich, and had held Investitures on the mornings of both Courts. There was the usual rush to finish Court dresses in time, final stitches being put in place literally only minutes before the hired Daimler rolled up. At the first, Rose Kennedy, wife of the American ambassador, presented another of her seemingly endless brood of glamorous children, seventeen-year-old Eunice. Both, as usual, were conspicuously well-dressed, Mrs Kennedy in close-fitting ice-blue satin with diamond tiara and white ostrich-feather fan, her daughter in an ivory satin and tulle crinoline with ivory satin train, by Paquin – the Kennedy women frequently crossed the Channel to shop.

Despite the threat of war, other Americans were paying their regular summer visits to London. The socially and financially impeccable Mrs Cornelius Vanderbilt joined her son Cornelius Vanderbilt Junior at Claridges. Americans were also strongly in evidence at Henley, where a record number of overseas oarsmen competed. Harvard won the Grand Challenge Cup – the first time they had entered for it since 1914, when they took the Cup back to the US for the duration of the war – and a sculler called Burk, of Penn Athletic, won the Diamond Sculls. Corpus Christi College was beaten in the finals of the Ladies' Plate by Clare College. Henley itself, with its fairs and sideshows, took about £10,000 in fees and meals during the four days of the Regatta. A sizable proportion of this came from the punts and canoes hired out to spectators. 'The day Eton rows at Henley,' said the *Chronicle*, 'sees 700 Etonians steering wobbly courses in hired boats.'

Over in Paris, there was racing at Longchamp, with its typically Parisian mixture of sport and exotic, extravagant chic. Gala fashion shows were a feature of the Sunday night fixtures at Longchamp, where some of the smartest women racegoers wore long dinner-suits topped by hats festooned with towering ostrich feathers.

Many Parisians crossed the Channel in their turn to attend the party given by Laura Corrigan for 'some young friends' at Dudley House. For arch-snob Mrs Corrigan the party, given for Lady Sarah Spencer-Churchill, Lady Elizabeth Scott, Lady Mairi Stewart and Miss Mary de Trafford, was in all senses a triumph: she succeeded in securing Prince Frederick of Prussia (the first name on every List), lured the Infanta Maria Christina over from Paris, and managed to see that the tombola was won by her landlord's eldest son, Lord Ednam. Her young guests enjoyed themselves too: after a huge dinner party for 150, spread over three rooms, there was dancing upstairs on a terrace roofed with glass, where white-coated chefs cooked supper dishes to individual order.

At Sutton Place, where the Duke and Duchess of Sutherland had often entertained the then Prince of Wales, the Duchess gave a dance for her debutante niece, Miss Elizabeth Leveson Gower. Like most of these later parties, it was designed just as much for the enjoyment of their older friends as for the ritual launch of their niece. Thoughtfully, they had devised a system whereby guests – most of whom came from London – would find their cars waiting for them as they emerged from the front door to leave at the end of the evening.

Most brilliant of all (and acclaimed afterwards as *the* ball of the Season), was the seventeen-year-old Lady Sarah Spencer-Churchill's coming-out dance at Blenheim Palace. All was splendour, magnificence, glamour, with the great golden façade of the palace, lit by powerful floodlights, gleaming in the distance as the guests drove towards it down dark country roads. As they approached, the light grew stronger, bathing the ornamental gardens, making the silvery fall of the fountains coruscate and glitter, illuminating the terraces and lawns, gilding the classical statues and sweeping over the lake up into the woods and glade on the far bank.

Over a thousand people entered the palace courtyard through the great bronze gates, everywhere there were footmen with powdered hair and the scarlet Marlborough livery. At the dinner party for fifty-six beforehand it took four relays of servants to carry each huge silver dish from the distant kitchens to the enormous long mahogany table. The dinner included strawberries in wine, a favourite dish of the first Sarah, sometime friend of Queen Anne and wife of the great Duke of Marlborough. Afterwards, there was dancing in the Long Library, the largest room in the palace. Outside, musicians in Tyrolean costume walked about singing on the famous terraces; supper, cooked by white-coated chefs, was on the West Terrace, and all the women guests were given shawls in case the night was cold. 'I have seen much, travelled far and am accustomed to splendour,' commented that veteran party-goer Chips Channon, 'but there has never been anything like tonight.'

Other parties were given in gardens, like Lady Zia Wernher's at Saumarez House in Regent's Park. There, among the lily ponds, blue-tiled loggia and flower beds filled with yellow and bronze antirrhinums, tea-tables were set all over the lawn and gypsy musicians played. At the Independence Day garden party given by Mrs Joseph Kennedy at the American embassy residence in Princes Gate, the theme was flowers. Almost all the women carried posies and the Kennedy men wore red carnations as well as their usual wide, white smiles.

The King and Queen were less lucky. The Buckingham Palace Garden Party of Thursday 20 July was literally washed out by a storm so intense it deprived two counties of electric power. Until the last minute, officials and guests alike hoped against hope that the weather would clear up, or the rain at least lessen slightly. The palace gates opened punctually at 3.15 p.m. but such were the floods of water from the skies that some people simply swung their cars around and turned away without going in at all. Others were more optimistic. But at 3.30 the rain was still pelting down and thousands were sheltering disconsolately in the salons overlooking the sodden lawns and deserted terraces. A quarter of an hour later the decision was finally taken, the palace gates were closed and guests were told: 'The party is cancelled but if you wish you may take tea in the marquees before leaving.'

The braver ones opened their dripping umbrellas, hung mud-spattered organdie skirts over their arms and made a dash for the two marquees at the far end of the lawns to enjoy tea, cakes, and raspberries and cream. Royal servants, mackintoshes over their scarlet liveries, carried the golden tea urn and silver plate from the royal table back into the palace where the King and Queen took their tea in their private apartments. Eventually they appeared at a window to wave to their damp but loyal subjects. The two princesses were also seen, waving but clearly disappointed.

For one of them the following Saturday would prove in days to come a far more momentous occasion. With the rain still tumbling down, the royal yacht *Victoria and Albert*, built in 1899, set off on what turned out to be its last voyage. With the King, the Queen, the princesses and Lord Louis Mountbatten on board, she dropped anchor in the River Dart, opposite Dartmouth College. It was the King's first visit to the college since, as Prince Albert, he had left it still a cadet, to join the cruiser *Cumberland* at Devonport on 17 January 1913 (he was appointed Midshipman later that same year).

The party landed on the college steps on the afternoon of 22 July in a downpour. Mumps and chickenpox were raging through the college, though mainly among the younger cadets – many of whom hung out of their dormitory windows to wave at the royal visitors – and the risk of infection was considered sufficient to prevent the princesses from visiting the college or accompanying their parents to morning service the next day. They spent most of their time in the house of the college's captain, Admiral Sir Frederick Dalrymple-Hamilton. Brought in to entertain the two girls was Lord Mountbatten's nephew, Prince Philip of Greece, at tall, fair handsome and dashing senior cadet of eighteen. It was the first meeting of the future Queen Elizabeth II and the Duke of Edinburgh. Together they munched ginger biscuits and drank lemonade while playing with the model railway laid out on the nursery floor. When a weak sun came out, they played croquet in friendly rivalry on the lawn. Later in the day, after the princesses had walked round the grounds of the college and looked admiringly at its swimming pool, several of the cadet captains, including Prince Philip, were invited to dine on the yacht – but Princess Elizabeth, still bound by the nursery timetable, had already gone to bed.

The following morning the *Victoria and Albert* steamed slowly out to sea, escorted as far as the harbour mouth by the 110 boats – rowing, motor, sail and steam – belonging to the college. So enthusiastically did the cadets follow that the King eventually asked the officer commanding the royal yacht, Sir Dudley North, to signal them back. Most turned round at once, but one lone dinghy continued, its oarsmen appearing not to hear. Finally, after being shouted at through a megaphone, Prince Philip, raising first one oar and then the other in salute, turned back as well.

Twenty-Seven

AUGUST

The last sporting event of the social calendar was marred by a ferocious dispute. At the beginning of Cowes week, Mr 'Tommy' Sopwith, owner of the twelve-metre yacht *Tomahawk*, claimed a foul against *Vim*, the crack US yacht owned by Mr Harry Vanderbilt. The dispute was no doubt exacerbated by old rivalries: Sopwith had raced against Vanderbilt in the America's Cup five years earlier, and both raced regularly against each other in their huge 'J' class yachts. These, abandoned as unsuitable for racing in 1936, were enormously expensive. They cost a minimum of £40,000 to build – the price of a spare mainsail alone was £1,200 – and Vanderbilt's *Rainbow* ran to a staggering £150,000. The twelve-metre yachts to which both men had switched, were cheap by comparison at £4,000.

There were only three entrants for the 1939 twelve-metre yacht race, for these handsome yachts required not only sizable initial outlay, but also constant and expensive maintenance. The foul occurred at the start. *Vim*, beautifully positioned for a flying start, had come speeding up alongside *Tomahawk* just before the starting gun sounded – but as it boomed out, she had suddenly altered her course, almost forcing *Tomahawk* on to the rocks on the Castle side. *Tomahawk*, immediately hoisting her protest flag, saved herself, but at the cost of valuable minutes, and it was some time before she could set off in pursuit of *Vim* (the third twelve-metre, *Evaine*, was so late starting it was virtually a two-yacht race) but finished half an hour after her. However, the Committee of the Royal London Yacht Club, after debating the matter for two and a half hours while a large crowd of yachtsmen waited outside, disqualified *Vim* and gave the prize to Sopwith.

The Season was over. It was time for the next stage in Society's ritual annual sequence: holidays. On Friday 4 August, the twenty-fifth anniversary of the outbreak of the 1914–18 war, Parliament went into recess although the international situation was, to say the least, bleak. Twenty-four hours earlier, Japan had concluded a military agreement with Italy and Germany; the only glimpse of hope was that the Russians had invited the British and French governments to send a military mission to Moscow. The House of Commons devoted the last day before its official summer holiday to discussing the continuing outrages in Tientsin, where British subjects were still suffering assault, abuse and humiliation. The Japanese continued to hold Lieutenant Colonel Spear, the British Military Attaché in China, in solitary confinement in a small, dirty room, not allowing him to take outdoor exercise.

Argument about the date the House should reassemble was heated, the Prime Minister moving that it should adjourn until 3 October. Mr Arthur Greenwood, for the Opposition, attempted to amend this to 21 August, declaring that he did not think it safe to leave the premier free from the attentions of Parliament for more than three weeks at a time; but the motion was carried by a majority of 116.

By now, the nation was attuned to thoughts of war. Stocks of wheat and petrol had been laid in, arrangements made for controlling the supply of fuel and foodstuffs, some of the pleasure-steamers on the Thames had been converted into ambulances and about four hundred owners of private motor boats had offered these as small patrolling water-ambulances, along with their own services. Petrol rationing, based on horse-power, was ready to go into immediate effect; plans were complete for the evacuation of all children from danger areas, six million Anderson shelters had been erected, and all over the country anti-aircraft gun emplacements, sandbags, trenches and balloons were now to be seen.

To add to this depressing picture, the weather was appalling, though the storms, wind and pouring rain did not stop those who could from going on holiday – if only because it might be their last for many years. Some of the unlucky ones were fifty boys from Eton, in quarantine for ten days because two members of their House, Marsden's, were in the sanatorium with infantile paralysis, as polio was then called, probably caught while bathing in the Thames (Eton was one of the few large public schools not to have its own swimming pool).

In Deauville, where the August race meeting had just started, a tennis match was held between English and French MPs; in Monte Carlo the big excitement was the new sport of water-skiing. Others of the smart set sunned themselves at Eden Roc. Vichy and Biarritz were packed and Le Touquet offered golf, polo and constant galas.

Although the weather during the August Bank Holiday was the dullest for years, with Bank Holiday Monday particularly dismal, seaside towns were packed. At Southend, people slept on the beaches and in south-coast towns like Hastings and Dover, there was such an invasion of holidaymakers from across the Channel French could be heard everywhere. At Blackpool, where more than seven million people a year took their holidays – most sitting fully dressed in serried rows of deckchairs along the beach – the scene was one of desolation. Holidaymakers either remained indoors or wandered disconsolately along the windswept pier. Even if the weather had been fine, the sea would have been comparatively empty. The previous year, according to Mass Observation, only three out of every hundred on the beach actually went into the sea.

Others went to the new and increasingly popular holiday camps. Butlin's, set up in 1935, boasted a total of sixty-five thousand visitors to its Skegness camp, where the routine as well as the air was bracing. For three and a half guineas a week, men and women started the day with physical jerks, and could go on to rollerskate, box in the gym, play tennis, ride on the sands (for an extra two shillings an hour) or swim in the heated pool. For those who preferred more leisurely sports, there was table tennis, billiards, bowls, and picking out Miss Shapely Ankles – not every girl was prepared to exhibit herself in a swimsuit. At the Miss Radiolympia contest that summer, for which beauty, intelligence and charm were the criteria, one candidate walked out when she learned she was expected to parade in a bathing dress. 'I wouldn't expect to entertain in it,' she said. 'So why should I be judged in it?'

Another and more famous camp was the one founded in 1921 by the King when, as Duke of York, he had become convinced of the importance of breaking down the barriers between the social classes. At the annual Duke of York's Camps, boys from widely differing backgrounds spent a week together in an open-air setting as his guests, playing games, picnicking, and sitting round the bonfire at night for a sing-song, where they were frequently joined by the King.

At the first camp, the four hundred had met in the riding school in the Royal Mews at Buckingham Palace, where they sat down to lunch together. Though there was little mingling there, self-consciousness and embarrassment soon disappeared when they got to the camp site at New Romney in Kent, donned the camp uniform of shorts and shirt, and were split up into groups of twenty to compete against each other in games. Rugger and cricket were not included, as it was felt that here the public schoolboys would have an unfair advantage. By the end of the week the camp was declared a great success. From then on, these camps became a regular fixture and, for some of the poorer boys, the holiday of a lifetime. Their keynote was informality: nobody ever wore a tie and the camp handbook contained only one rule: the Kiplingesque 'Play the Game'.

The camp took place for the first time in 1939, at Abergeldie

Castle, near Balmoral, and the King himself was Camp Chief, spending a large part of every day with his two hundred guests. Among them were, as usual, miners' sons, public schoolboys, the children of small-businessmen, of railway clerks, Lancashire cotton workers and soldiers. Conversation broke out in a buzz from the moment when, on Friday 4 August, they climbed aboard the 10.55 p.m. from King's Cross to Edinburgh. Here they were divided up into the customary twenty-strong sections and, after breakfast and a morning seeing the sights, they made the six-hour journey to Ballater. From here coaches took them to Abergeldie, where the King was waiting to greet them.

Their sleeping quarters were in the castle stables ('very clean', commented one boy). Instead of a bell warning of supper, there was the Camp Piper, who also played during meals. On Sunday afternoon they walked the three miles to Balmoral Castle, where they had been asked to tea by the King and Queen. Lined up in single file in their sections, they were introduced individually by their section leaders; the King and Queen shook the hand of each one. Tea was served in the castle and afterwards the King and Queen showed them round the castle grounds.

During this last camp, there were fewer of the normal competitive games. Instead, there were expeditions and outings, which the King usually joined. Believing – like most of his countrymen – that war was imminent, he had wanted this last camp to have a more informal, personal flavour (the reason the normal quota of four hundred had been halved). On one occasion the King, the Queen and the princesses sang that national favourite, 'The Chestnut Tree', along with the boys, the King leading the chorus with the appropriate gestures. Few people could have ever seen the royal family so informally dressed: the King was in an open-necked shirt, the Queen was hatless and the two princesses wore simple blouses and skirts. Here is an account of the camp written by one boy, a railway clerk from Cadby:

'Monday we go by coaches to a place where we meet the King,

who takes us for a five-mile walk. During the morning we have the royal family at the camp, posing with us for photographers . . . then our sports, which consist of six items: throwing a tennis ball covered with French chalk at a target, putting-ball-in-bucket, hop-skip-and-jump, foot and hand netball, dribbling football round posts, and 100 yards relay race. The princesses watch us, and are excited at the close finish of the relay race.

'Nearly every day we ride in coaches to a spot where the King, or a guide, leads us for long walks. His Majesty is a very good walker; he talks and jokes with us on our long walks, and sits down and has lunch with us. We take our lunch from cartons in our haversacks – ¼lb chocolate, a tomato, cake, meat pastry. The food is excellent; for breakfast we have porridge, eggs and bacon . . . later a very nice tea, and hot dinner at night. Every night we attend the entertainment marquee for lectures, performances and films.'

The King spent all the time he could with the boys, leaving Balmoral for only one day, on 9 August, to inspect the Reserve Fleet. He was back again to dine at camp that evening, accompanied by the Queen and the princesses, while pipers played and entertainers amused the boys. After dinner he made a speech, the theme of which reverted to his idea of abolishing the barriers and misunderstandings between the classes through the friendships made at camp.

On Friday 11 August, the last night, the boys climbed into coaches at 10.00 p.m. and drove to Balmoral for the traditional bonfire. 'His Majesty leads us up a steep hill,' wrote the boy from Cadby. 'At the top are the King's pipers and a huge pile of wood and hay – which the King lights. The pipers play tunes while we all join hands and sing . . . a most wonderful sight to watch.' After the stirring Scottish airs, the evening concluded with 'Auld Lang Syne' and the national anthem.

'As we leave Balmoral for our last night in camp, the King stands in the road and waves us good-bye. We all cheer loudly. Saturday morning is most heartbreaking . . . the thought of leaving the best time of our lives behind us.' For the King, as well as the departing boys, an all too brief interlude was over.

All over England the rain went on pouring down. More than half an inch fell in one ten-minute storm at Seaton, in Devonshire, and many camps where Territorials and the newly conscripted militiamen were living under canvas were flooded. Some of the cooks walked out, for they had not bargained for such conditions. But in general morale was excellent and the Army Council issued an order for communication to all ranks recording its appreciation of the men's conduct in carrying out their tasks in these exceptionally trying circumstances.

The bucketing skies did not stop the annual pilgrimage north for the Glorious Twelfth (the opening day, 12 August, of the grouse-shooting season) when, as the *Evening Standard* noted, 'fewer dogs but the usual number of men left London for the North'. Over a thousand first class sleepers were booked from Kings Cross alone; earlier trains had taken up the motors of the more affluent to meet their owners at Fort William, Inverness, Arrochar and other Highland destinations. It was a good season, with grouse plentiful everywhere except on the moors of North Durham, Yorkshire and parts of Perthshire.

But though the continual rain spoilt tennis parties and damaged crops all over England, there was none, alas, where it would have been most welcome. The Prime Minister, taking his annual fishing holiday, wrote sadly from Lochmore Lairg on 13 August:

'The weather here could hardly have been worse from the fishing point of view. While the whole of the rest of the country was complaining of a never-ceasing flood of rain, it was bone dry here and the river was six inches below fishing level. I was therefore very fortunate in getting a salmon on Monday and another on Tuesday. But there my luck came to an end. The sea trout in the lock were very down and even Charles . . . who was an expert creek fisherman could not get a basket. The man on the next river pulled out 16 salmon.'

Mrs Chamberlain, meanwhile, was going for walks over the hills, and riding a Norwegian pony on the deer trails. For this she wore a divided skirt and commented, 'I am fast getting used to riding astride.'

Perhaps by contrast to the general gloom, the Paris collections of that August were more frivolous, lavish and extreme than for years. There were pale blue rabbit-fur coats, hooped or hobbled skirts with waists whittled to a maximum twenty-four inches by tight corselettes, enormous leg o'mutton sleeves, peplums, capes, the beginnings of the swagger coat, satin bloomers peeping out of side-slit skirts. Hats were like the bonnets worn by nursemaids but elaborately ruched and trimmed with nodding ostrich plumes, or shaped like small platters slapped against the side of the head; couturiers made strenuous attempts to encourage women to wear these confections during dinner.

Schiaparelli made an evening-dress of ermine, gloves of civet cat and introduced her famous shoe, of which the enormously high heel was joined to the sole, giving the effect of the tiny bound foot of a Chinese woman.

Though it was still quite easy to visit Europe – and indeed traffic between France and England had actually increased – by now it had become more difficult to travel further afield. From Wednesday 9 August, no more passenger bookings were accepted by Imperial Airways for any of their 22,000 miles of Empire routes, a ban caused at one remove by the threat of war. Because of the expansion of the Royal Air Force, the ex-RAF pilots who formed a large part of Imperial Airways' flying staff were being recalled to the Service, and serving officers were now no longer allowed to resign from the RAF to become civilian pilots.

Still it rained. It rained on Jewish refugees from Czechoslovakia who arrived starving and penniless, with no food left on the steamer that brought them; it had rained on the King when, on 9 August, down from the camp at Balmoral, he inspected the Reserve Fleet, manned by twelve thousand naval reservists recently recalled for duty. This, the greatest assembly of warships since 1914, consisted of 133 ships formed into fifteen lines of up to two nautical miles each. Through these the King, on the royal barge and escorted by a motor boat, threaded his way, and he was cheered as he passed by the crews lining the sides of the ships.

It was a rough passage. Spray broke over the bows of the royal barge, soaking the King as he approached the first ship, the aircraft carrier HMS *Courageous* (destined to be sunk two months later). So choppy were the waters of Weymouth Bay that he had to jump for the ladder leading to the quarterdeck. He lunched on board the *Victoria and Albert*, returning afterwards to the barge to continue his inspection. Several of the ships he inspected were familiar to him from his service with the navy during the 1914–18 war. One was the *Iron Duke* (now a training ship), formerly Admiral Jellicoe's flagship during the Battle of Jutland, the great naval engagement in which the King had fought as a junior officer in HMS *Collingwood*. Another was the cruiser *Cardiff* which had guided the German High Seas Fleet into the Firth of Forth when it had surrendered in November 1918. After the inspection, the Fleet dispersed for training and exercises.

The bad weather continued. It postponed the practice blackout planned for Thursday 10 August, at a cost of £74,000 – the low cloud base was so solid that no one in the spotter aircraft circling overhead could have told whether lights were showing or not. The previous night the same banks of cloud and thick mists had caused one or two casualties among the 1,300 aircraft taking part in a mock raid in which they flew without lights.

By Friday night, after a day of even worse weather, a squally wind finally blew the clouds apart and the first blackout took place over 25,000 square miles that included London and the home counties. With only the searchlights sweeping the dark skies as invisible aircraft droned overhead, it was a scene to be repeated times without number in the days ahead.

On this occasion, however, the blackout was not as successful as it might have been: far too many lights showed from London and at a height of four thousand feet the gleam of the river and the moving headlights of cars were clearly visible – so many that the Great North Road looked from above almost like a brilliant golden ribbon, said one observer. Mr Alec Clifton-Taylor suggested to the readers of *The Times* letters page that in any case the word 'blackout' was wrong and it really ought to be 'lightsout'; this was a 'good school expression which means what it says'.

Perhaps, though, there was hope in the fact that the bombers of the previous night's practice raid had been equally unsuccessful. 'Groping for targets' was how the official report put it – a prophetic phrase, for when Bomber Command fitted cameras to bombers early in the War, these disclosed that many pilots who had reported successfully bombing their targets in Germany were not getting within miles of them. Air Vice Marshal Sholto Douglas, in a speech to the cadets of the Public Schools Air Wing, had told them that the object of air defence was 'to cause so heavy a casualty rate to the enemy bombing forces that they will be compelled to restrict the scale of their attack on account of . . . the difficulty of replacing those casualties'. If the enemy lost ten per cent of their force every time they came over, and made a raid a day, they would, he said optimistically, 'be pretty well wiped out after ten days'.

Yet despite what was by now an almost universal expectation of war, and without any apparent objection from the authorities, *The Times* was still faithfully offering pages of the kind of information that must have been increasingly useful to the German High Command. Features called 'With the Army in the Field' described the training and organization of both the Regular and Territorial Army, and listed the battalions which formed the various brigades. The movements of liners and cargo vessels throughout the world were detailed; on 10 August, for example, there was a report of the arrival of the cruiser *Ajax* in Rio de Janeiro and the departure of the H Destroyer Flotilla from

Gibraltar. On 22 August, readers were informed of the arrival in Auckland of the *Achilles* (later, with *Ajax*, to play a major part in the sinking of the *Graf Spee*), the departure of *Repulse* from Scapa Flow and the arrival there of the H Flotilla. And on 21 August, the Cunard White Star Line announced that on 2 September the *Athenia* would be sailing from Glasgow to Quebec.

Thirteen days later, eight hours after war was declared, the *Athenia* was sunk by a U-boat 250 miles off the coast of Ireland. The rules of submarine warfare laid down clearly that 'no merchant ship may be sunk without warning, and that in any case no merchant ship is to be sunk until the safety of all passengers and crew is assured'. The shock at the blatant and immediate Nazi disregard of this agreement was so great, and the effect on American public opinion so adverse – 311 returning Americans were among the 1,400 on board the *Athenia* – that the German propaganda machine first issued an announcement that she had hit a mine, then that Churchill had ordered her sinking in order to damage German honour. More than all the immediate shock and rage at the loss of civilian life, though, the sinking of the *Athenia* signalled clearly the direction the war at sea would take.

Twenty-Eight

~

LAST DAYS

On 12 August the sun finally came out, to be followed by day after day of warm and brilliant weather, but in every other way, the sky was black with clouds: Britain was spending £1,300 a minute on rearmament and Hitler's eyes were fixed upon Danzig. There was still a last chance, however. The joint British and French military mission in Moscow was still hoping for a defensive pact and, if this alliance could be achieved, the prospect of a war on two fronts might deter Hitler.

Even the Prime Minister did not believe that war was absolutely certain. On 19 August he wrote from Scotland to his sister Ida, who was abroad. The letter, though pessimistic, did not suggest her immediate return:

'Alas, I have just had a telephone conversation with Downing Street from which it is clear that I can stay here no longer and I have arranged to return tomorrow, a day earlier than I had intended. That is not too bad. I must confess that I have never enjoyed a carefree mind the whole time I have been here and I have had a good deal of work sent up to me. Still, it has been something to get away from London and into the open air and I am sure that both of us will feel the benefit of it later. I have had one day in bed, last Monday, as the result of a liver chill [or perhaps a first gnawing of the cancer of the liver of which he died a year later?] brought on by too long exposure in a boat to rain and wind the preceding Friday. But the day's rest, combined with starvation, produced the desired effect and I got up on Tuesday, and caught three salmon between 11 and 12 o'clock. As for Annie, she took a day or two to get her mind settled down and she splendidly found herself able to mount a pony and enjoy it and since then she has steadily been getting better both physically and mentally. I am thankful for it, especially as we may have a difficult time ahead of us . . . I have put off my return to Scotland, which was provisionally arranged for Tuesday night but whether or when I come back must remain undecided till I see what awaits me in London. I know no reason why you should alter your plans but if at any time I think you ought to come back at once, I will wire you the words "I agree".

'Your affect. brother, Neville Chamberlain.'

The crisis was to intensify with terrifying rapidity. On 21 August came the bombshell that destroyed every last faint hope of peace. The news broke that Hitler had concluded a non-aggression pact with the Soviets even while the Franco–British delegation were in mid-negotiation with them. All hope of an alliance between Great Britain, France and Russia vanished, and with it the sole remaining obstacle to Hitler's plans. War, formerly an overwhelming likelihood, had become a certainty. From now on, it was only a question of days, although there were still those who refused to believe it.

The Times said that until the full terms of the pact were known, it was impossible to decide whether this was just another move in the war of nerves, designed at a critical moment to strike alarm and despondency into the minds of the Peace Front, or whether it would have 'far-reaching consequences'. For most people, a shocked refusal of the mind to comprehend the appalling prospect ahead, along with a conviction that it was inescapable, produced a combination of frenzied preparations and a curious denial of the reasons for it. Hitler was still 'Herr Hitler', and euphemisms such as 'should an emergency arise' were still used to avoid any mention of actual war.

And life, of course, had to go on. There were races to go to, football and cricket to watch – all to cease within a fortnight – and theatres to enjoy. The latter played to full houses: it was a particularly good season, with a sparkling production of *The Importance of Being Earnest* at the Globe, *The Desert Song* at the Garrick, *The Dancing Years* at Drury Lane, *Quiet Wedding* at the Comedy, *The Women* at the Lyric, Herbert Farjeon's *Little Revue* at the Little Theatre, Jack Hulbert and Cicely Courtneidge in *Under Your Hat* at the Palace, and *Twelfth Night* at the open-air theatre in Regent's Park.

The King had no illusions. On 23 August he received a letter from the Prime Minister, who had enclosed the minutes of the previous day's Cabinet meeting as the simplest way of imparting the urgency of the situation, and he left Balmoral immediately. Travelling overnight, he arrived at Euston station at eight o'clock the following morning; two and a half hours later he was holding a Privy Council at Buckingham Palace. The Queen followed him to London on Tuesday the 29th, leaving the princesses in Scotland.

All pretence had now vanished. Both Houses of Parliament rushed through the Emergency Powers (Defence) Act, giving the Government all the authority it needed to put the country on a war footing. Honourable members, though grave-faced, were noticeably more relaxed than during the Munich crisis of the previous year. Many looked bronzed and fit after their summer holidays abroad. Beside the tanned and healthy face of Captain Margesson, the Prime Minister's pallor was more noticeable than ever, underlining the painful sombreness of his tone when he rose to tell the House, 'The peril of war is imminent but I still go on hoping.'

Mr Arthur Greenwood, the acting Socialist leader, gave Labour's assurance that the House would stand united against aggression. When George Lansbury, the veteran pacifist, began to give voice to the pacifist viewpoint, many members left the Chamber. The House sat until late, finally adjourning until 31 August. Outside, patriotic crowds waited anxiously and silently for news; the Prime Minister, driving back to Downing Street, was cheered by the thousands who stretched down Whitehall and lined Downing Street six deep on each side. As he passed, they broke spontaneously into 'Rule, Britannia!'.

Each moment now saw a fresh aspect of a nation gearing itself for war. The Admiralty closed the Mediterranean to British ships and British merchant shipping was ordered to leave Baltic waters. All passages to New York and Canada were completely booked and the boat trains were so crowded that only passengers were allowed to travel on them; friends and relatives had to be content with saying their farewells at the railway station rather than at the ports. This was especially heart-rending for parents despatching their children to the New World for safety. The German liner *Europa*, en route from New York to Hamburg, ran for home instead of stopping at Southampton. The tender that went out with Hamburg-bound passengers had to return still loaded to the Southampton quayside, while the forty-odd luckless British and American passengers aboard the *Europa* were carried on to Germany.

By the following weekend the general rush for home or safety was fully under way, swelled by the thousands of Britons who lived abroad but who felt that their place was now in their own country. At Victoria station, boat trains were crowded with expatriate families returning home; their luggage – suitcases, bicycles, tennis rackets, golf clubs and as many other possessions as they could bring with them – crowding the platforms. Around them swirled a mêlée of porters, other passengers and relatives come to meet a returning child, student or friend. German families departing for the Fatherland passed returning British ones as they walked across Croydon airfield to their plane. Winston Churchill, who had been staying in the south of France with Mme Jacques Balsan (the former Consuelo, Duchess of Marlborough) had flown home on 23 August, immediately on hearing of the Nazi–Soviet pact, leaving his wife and youngest daughter Mary to follow the next day. On Saturday the 26th, the

British ambassador to Germany, Sir Nevile Henderson, was recalled from Berlin, and the Channel packets ran double shifts, shuttling back and forth, crowded to the rails with returning passengers perched on their luggage, before closing down their services one by one.

There was equal congestion on the roads. As everyone knew, the evacuation of three million people (mostly children) planned to begin the following Friday, would make virtually all other travel at the same time impossible, so roads leading out of London and other large cities were crowded. Many of the cars carrying families and their possessions to the safety of the countryside were driven by women, who had applied in thousands over the previous few days for provisional driving licences. Those leaving Coventry were no doubt speeded on their way by a further IRA outrage there: a bomb flung by a cyclist in the crowded Broadgate city centre killed five people, injured fifty, and wrecked cars and shops. This would prove to be a foretaste, though a mild one, of what that city was to suffer later.

In London, clerks spent their Sunday morning loading files and documents from their City offices on to vans which would take them to safety outside the capital. That night, the last inward ferry departed on the Harwich–Hook of Holland crossing, though there was an extra day's grace for those travelling from Zeebrugge. The telephone system, still comparatively new, almost ground to a standstill under the weight of calls, the overworked operators taking up to six hours to put through trunk calls from London to the major provincial cities. The Treasury withdrew its support of sterling and allowed it to fall against the dollar in order to conserve British stocks of gold; bus services were cut to save fuel.

War was very near. All over the country, people prayed for peace. Special services were held everywhere – the King and his brothers drove from Buckingham Palace to Westminster Abbey under the continuing brilliant sunshine. Churches remained open day and night, with men and women going to work, coming home, out shopping or simply passing by, slipping in for a few moments of prayer.

One of the cleverest minds in England still refused to believe that conflict was inevitable – indeed, took a diametrically opposite view. In a letter dated 25 August, George Bernard Shaw wrote to *The Times*:

'Sir, – A week ago, Dean Inge, writing in the *Evening Standard*, guessed that Herr Hitler had gone to Canossa. A few days later the joyful news came that the Dean was right and that Herr Hitler is under the powerful thumb of Stalin, whose interest in peace is overwhelming.

'And everyone except myself is frightened out of his or her wits.

'Why? Am I mad? If not, Why? Why? Why?

'G. Bernard Shaw.'

Even the Prime Minister did not seem finally and conclusively convinced, hinting that the Russo-German pact could rebound on those who made it:

'Phew! What a week. One or two more like this one would take years off my life. Whether this be a war of nerves only or just the preliminary stages of a real war, it takes strong nerves to stand it and retain one's sanity and courage. I feel like a man driving a clumsy coach over a narrow crooked road along the face of a precipice. You hardly dare look down lest you should turn giddy and then come times when your heart seems to stand still for minutes together and you somehow round the next corner and find yourself still on the track.

'Of course the place buzzes with rumours, and our own Secret Service continually reports information "derived from an abso-lutely reliable source" of the most alarming character. I don't know how many times we've been given the exact date and even hour when the Germans would march into Poland and the machinery started which must inevitably drag us into its cogs. Yet they haven't marched yet and, as always, I count every hour that passes without catastrophe as adding its mite to the slowly accumulating anti-war forces.

'Perhaps the worst trial came on Friday [25 August] when at 12.45 we learned that the Fuehrer had sent for Henderson at 1.30. What could we tell the ambassador to say, he wanted to know. We could only reply that, until he knew what he was sent for, we could not furnish him with a reply; if anything new transpired he must refer to his government. Thereafter ensured a most trying period of waiting. By bad fortune, my people could find me nothing to do and I sat with Annie in the drawing room, unable to read, unable to talk, just sitting with folded hands and a gnawing pain in the stomach. It seemed only too likely that Henderson would be presented with an ultimatum and given but a few hours to get out. Yet as hour after hour went by and nothing was heard, I began to cheer up a little. If it had been an ultimatum, surely Henderson would have been dismissed and come to the telephone before now? At last the F.O., tired of waiting, got on the telephone and learned that the ambassador had had one and a quarter hours with Hitler but he had received from him a proposal which we might think was an attempt to drive a wedge between us and Poland, and that finally Hitler had urged him to fly over next day with the text and offered to provide him with an aeroplane for the purpose. In the meantime, he was sending a record of his conversation in two long cypher telegrams.

'I got the first telegram at dinner that night and found it unilluminating, but as they told me the second would not be deciphered until after midnight I refused to sit up for it and went to bed, and to sleep! Next morning it was on the breakfast table but I had my breakfast and read the papers before opening the box. At last I got to it and during the whole of yesterday I was studying it and trying with Halifax and our respective officials to concoct a reply. Henderson didn't arrive till nearly lunchtime and at about a moment's notice Annie prepared luncheon for six, opened up the rooms, and then absented herself while we discussed the situation. I had a Cabinet in the late afternoon and then sat up again until long after midnight drafting our reply . . . Today has been quieter and in response to certain indications we have detained our ambassador till tomorrow. The fact that there has been no explosion is in itself a good omen, for every postponement of the crisis serves to enable world opinion to show itself and to isolate the man or the nation that would disturb the peace.

'I believe myself that the statement we issued after the Cabinet, showing our determination to fulfil our obligations in spite of Russian treachery, was an important, perhaps a decisive, factor in the development of the situation. The hope that this bombshell would destroy the peace front was disappointed and as time goes on I believe this coup, which occasioned such joy in Berlin, will be found to have been a boomerang. Ciano asked our ambassador in Rome with some malice what he thought of it. To which the ambassador replied with admirable spirit that it had given him the first hearty laugh he had had for weeks. Ciano was startled at such an unexpected reply and, quite disconcerted with Loraine, said he would come back in six months and ask him what he thought of his partner's brilliant stroke.

'I think we may be fairly certain that thanks to the policy we have pursued, Italy will not come in if Hitler goes to war over Poland. And Japan has been so deeply shocked that we may find our anxieties in that quarter greatly relieved if not removed. I am expecting to see a change of government there which will be to our advantage. Spain, too, has had a shock and we may expect to find a lessening of Franco's difficulties. As to Hitler's proposals, they do not, as put about in Berlin, constitute an offer of a peaceful solution to the Polish difficulty. On the contrary, they brush Poland aside as a matter to be settled by Germany and, after *that* (i.e. if we leave Germany alone), Hitler will make us a splendid offer which in effect will be an Anglo–German alliance. The mentality of that extraordinary man would be incredible to anyone who had not seen and talked with him. I believe that in his excitement over the prospect of this Anglo–German alliance, the possibility of which has come upon him with a new force, after the ease with which he brought off the Russian agreement, he has almost forgotten Poland. But we can't forget it. And so, for the moment, we are no further advanced.

'We are not through the jungle; on the contrary the issue is still doubtful. But on Friday, the motto on my calendar was "Remember that the tide turns at the low as well as at the high level"!'

Three days later the British ambassador flew back to Germany, taking with him Britain's reply to the various statements made by Hitler. At this tense and desperate moment the Duke of Windsor, describing himself as 'a citizen of the world', decided to send a telegram to Hitler urging him to refrain from plunging Europe into war. This rather futile gesture was reminiscent of his broadcast from the battlefield of Verdun in May, which the BBC had refused to broadcast (although it was widely reported in America, causing a minor embarrassment during the King and Queen's State Visit there). On the same day, 29 August, the Duke also sent a similar telegram to King Victor Emanuel of Italy, asking him to 'use your influence to prevent the catastrophe which now seems imminent', and signing it 'David'. But perhaps it was more to relieve his own feelings than anything else, for all anyone could do now was wait.

As the countdown to war continued, in the playgrounds of Europe the toys of the rich were put away. In Monte Carlo the Sporting Club and the Summer Casino shut, all over the Riviera hotels dismissed staff. In Paris, stations were seething with soldiers, and shops and restaurants were besieged by those seeking a last taste of the pleasures of peace.

In England, the annual September yearling sales at Doncaster were postponed indefinitely and the social-sporting events of the autumn cancelled. 'Lord and Lady Gage were invited to go and shoot duck by King Carol of Rumania in September but it is feared the engagement will not now be kept,' mourned the *Tatler*. There was a sudden spurt of business in beauty and hairdressing salons, as women stocked up with their favourite face-creams, or invested in the perms they hoped would keep their hair tidy above the collar of a Wren or Fany uniform, or in remote country villages where many would be marooned during petrol-less months ahead. Boarding schools in the heart of the country opened so that parents could send their children there for safety. In the personal columns of *The Times*, advertisements beginning 'In the Event of War . . .', or 'A.R.P.', offered flats or houses to let in safe areas ('Lady would receive Two Friends') or requested refuges for animals: 'Wanted: Country home for three pedigree corgis . . .' The Blue Cross launched an appeal for horse ambulances and 'convalescent fields' for horses in France; and a dachshund-owner wrote to plead that these sporting little animals should not be made the butt of jokes or, worse, persecution as they had been in the 1914–18 war.

Those outside the age of conscription or with reserved occupations flocked to join up. 'There is a symbolic difference between fighting as a soldier and serving as a civilian, even if the civilian is more valuable,' wrote Evelyn Waugh in his diary. Without any of the elation or the sheer excitement that had preceded the outbreak of the previous two wars they had fought, the British people prepared themselves for a future divested of all except survival and defence. Civil aircraft flights over the eastern half of England and Scotland were now prohibited, various underground stations shut down and services cut, kerbs painted white to help traffic in the coming blackout, trains fitted with dim blue lights insufficient for reading but giving just enough illumination for a game of cards. Trenches had been dug round houses on London estates, basements converted to shelters, and on beaches holidaymakers, clad in bathing dresses to enjoy the warm sunshine, were filling sandbags – many stored from the Munich crisis – whose price had doubled to 5d since June. The Civil Defence authorities were asking for volunteers for stretcher parties, firefighting and for the harvest which, owing to earlier delay by the rain, now had to be gathered quickly. The calling up of reservists for all three services was almost complete.

On Wednesday 30 August, there was a momentary quiver of hope. Hitler's message, which had arrived during the night, read: 'The German Government, though sceptical as to the outcome, are nevertheless prepared to accept the English proposal [taken over by the British ambassador] and enter into direct negotiations.'

But it was a mirage. On 1 September, Hitler struck, his troops invading Poland at dawn. (While the Luftwaffe was bombing Warsaw the Duke of Windsor was woken by the postman bringing Hitler's reply to his telegram; it simply said that if war broke out it would be England's fault.) Immediately, Britain and France instructed their ambassadors in Berlin to inform the German government that unless Germany withdrew, their respective governments would be forced to fulfil their obligations to Poland. The country was put under blackout order, the Navy, Army and Air Force mobilized, and it was announced that all men between the ages of eighteen and forty-one were liable for call-up.

In the German embassy, luggage stood ready in the corridor as documents were burned; the fragments of charred paper blew out into the street through the windows kept open on that scorching day. In Berlin, listening to foreign wireless stations was made an offence punishable by penal servitude or, in the case of persistent offenders, death. The King drove to Downing Street – the first time a monarch had ever paid a visit there that was not purely social – as the Prime Minister felt he could not leave the telephone. The Admiralty took control of all British merchant shipping (two-thirds, 1,545 vessels, were at sea); the stock exchange closed; first class cricket, due to continue for a few days more, shut down abruptly; and most racing was cancelled – in any case, there were no trains on which jobbers, brokers, spectators or racegoers could travel as the great evacuation had begun.

This was an unparalleled upheaval. In the course of one weekend, over three million people, mainly mothers and children, were uprooted from their homes and taken to surroundings which to some of them were completely alien. First to leave were the children, those under five years old travelling in parties of fifty under the supervision of teachers (twenty-two thousand, all told) and voluntary helpers; so great were the crowds that mothers were not allowed into stations to say goodbye to them. The suggested list of what these small deportees had to take with them included a far grander wardrobe than many had ever known: strong walking shoes, light indoor shoes, night clothes, spare socks, spare vest, pants or knickers, handkerchief, toothbrush, comb, towel, soap and mackintosh. 'Sunday clothes can be sent later. If the children have to remain in the country,' advised the *Daily Mail*, 'don't wrap clothes in newspaper but give the child an old pillowcase or cushion cover. If the child is travelling on Saturday you will have time to make a rucksack out of cheap hessian.' The main body of children were followed by the rest of the evacuees: expectant mothers and those accompanied by small children, the blind and patients from London hospitals, for whom Green Line buses had been converted into ambulances.

On 2 September, for the fifth day running, the temperature was over 70°F but the beaches and golf links of a week ago were forgotten. The House sat all day, waiting tensely for some reply from Germany. None came; and in the evening, the Government despatched its ultimatum. A telegram was sent to the British ambassador in Berlin requesting him to inform the German government that, unless satisfactory assurances were given by eleven o'clock the next morning that the German government had ceased all aggressive action against Poland and was prepared to withdraw its forces immediately, a state of war would be deemed to exist between Britain and Germany.

In Downing Street a silent crowd waited through the night, watching as ministers arrived for a Cabinet meeting at 11.30 p.m., and talking quietly among themselves as they waited for news. It did not come until next day. Early on the morning of

Sunday 3 September, the BBC asked all listeners to stand by for an important announcement. At 11.15 a.m., speaking from Downing Street, the Prime Minister told the nation: 'This country is now at war with Germany.'

There were few who did not hear those words – or, later, remember what they had been doing at that precise moment. Entire households were clustered round the family wireless, others heard the news during the morning service at church, even as last-minute prayers for peace were being offered. Queen Mary was one of these: at matins in the church of St Mary Magdalene in Sandringham, where the rector had installed his wireless in the nave, she learned that the country over which her son reigned was now at war with the land where her cousins lived.

At six o'clock that evening the King broadcast to the nation:

'For the second time in the lives of most of us we are at war. Over and over again we have tried to find a peaceful way out of the differences between ourselves and those who are now our enemies. But it has been in vain. We have been forced into a conflict. For we are called, with our allies, to meet the challenge of a principle which, if it were to prevail, would be fatal to any civilized order in the world.

'. . . It is to this high purpose that I now call my people at home and my peoples across the seas, who will make our cause their own. I ask them to stand calm and firm and united in this time of trial. The task will be hard. There may be dark days ahead, and war can no longer be confined to the battlefield. But we can only do the right as we see the right, and reverently commit our cause to God. If one and all we keep resolutely faithful to it, ready for whatever service or sacrifice it may demand, then, with God's help, we shall prevail. May He bless us and keep us all.'

In his diary that night the King wrote:

'At the outbreak of war at midnight of August 4th–5th 1914, I was a midshipman, keeping the middle watch on the bridge of

H.M.S. Collingwood at sea, somewhere in the North Sea. I was 18 years of age.

'In the Grand Fleet everyone was pleased that it had come at last. We had been trained in the belief that war between Germany and this country had to come one day, and when it did come we thought we were prepared for it. We were not prepared for what we found a modern war really was, and those of us who had been through the Great War never wanted another.

'Today we are at war again, and I am no longer a midshipman in the Royal Navy.'

SELECT BIBLIOGRAPHY

Alexandra, Queen of Yugoslavia, *Prince Philip, A Family Portrait*, London, 1960

Arch, Nigel, and Joanna Marschner, *Splendour at Court*, London, 1987

Argyll, Margaret Campbell, Duchess of, *Forget Not*, London, 1975

Benson, James, and C. E. T. Warren, *'The Admiralty Regrets . . .'*, London, 1958

Bloch, Michael, *The Duke of Windsor's War*, London, 1982

Blythe, Ronald, *The Age of Illusion*, Oxford, 1983

Bradbrook, M. C., *'That Infidel Place'*, London, 1969

Buckley, V. C., *Good Times: At Home and Abroad Between the Wars*, London, 1979

Butler, Mollie, *August and Rab*, London, 1987

Caffrey, Kate, *Last Look Round*, London, 1978

Calder, Angus, and Dorothy Sheridan (eds.), *Speak For Yourself, a Mass Observation anthology 1937–49*, London, 1984

Clive, Lady Mary, *Brought Up and Brought Out*, London, 1938

Cooper, Lady Diana, *The Light of Common Day*, London, 1959

Crewe, Quentin, *The Frontiers of Privilege*, London, 1961

Davie, Michael (ed.), *The Diaries of Evelyn Waugh*, London, 1976

Donaldson, Frances, *Edward VIII*, London, 1977

Ellacott, S. E., *A History of Everyday Things in England*, Vol. V, London, 1968

Fergusson, Bernard, *Eton Portrait*, London, 1937

Fitzgibbon, Theodora, *With Love*, London, 1982

Gielgud, John, *An Actor in His Time*, London, 1979

Goodwin, Doris Kearns, *The Fitzgeralds and the Kennedys*, London, 1987

Graves, Robert, and Alan Hodge, *The Long Weekend*, London, 1940

Gray, Edwin, *Few Survived*, London, 1986

Hill, B. J. W., *Eton Medley*, London, 1948

SELECT BIBLIOGRAPHY

Kee, Robert, *The World We Left Behind*, London, 1984

King, Stella, *Princess Marina: Her Life and Tiems*, London, 1969

Lejeune, Anthony, *The Gentleman's Clubs of London*, London, 1979

Lewis, Lesley, *The Private Life of a Country House*, Newton Abbot, 1980

Lowndes, Susan (ed.), *Diaries and Letters of Marie Belloc Lowndes*, London, 1971

Minney, R. J., *No 10 Downing Street*, London, 1963

Muggeridge, Malcolm, *The Infernal Grove*, London, 1975

Pye, Michael, *The King Over the Water*, London, 1981

Rhodes James, Robert (ed.), *'Chips': The Diaries of Sir Henry Channon*, Harmondsworth, 1970

Sitwell, Sir Osbert, *Laughter in the Next Room*, London, 1949

Vickers, Hugo, *Gladys, Duchess of Marlborough*, London, 1979

Walker-Smith, Derek, *Neville Chamberlain, Man of Peace*, London, 1940

Wentworth Day, James, *H.R.H. Princess Marina, Duchess of Kent*, London, 1962

Westminster, Loelia, Duchess of, *Grace and Favour*, London, 1962

Wheeler-Bennett, Sir John, *King George VI*, London, 1958

SOURCES OF ILLUSTRATIONS

INDEX